DATE DUE		

Conversations with Eugene O'Neill

Literary Conversations Series

Peggy Whitman Prenshaw
General Editor

Conversations with Eugene O'Neill

Edited by
Mark W. Estrin

University Press of Mississippi
Jackson and London

Copyright © 1990 by the University Press of Mississippi
All rights requested
Manufactured in the United States of America
93 92 91 90   4 3 2 1
The paper in this book meets the guidelines for permanence and durability
of the Committee on Production Guidelines for Book Longevity of the Council
on Library Resources.

Library of Congress Cataloging-in-Publication Data

Conversations with Eugene O'Neill / edited by Mark W. Estrin.
    p. cm. — (Literary conversations series)
    Includes index.
    ISBN 0-87805-446-4 (cloth). — ISBN 0-87805-447-2 (paper)
    1. O'Neill, Eugene, 1888-1953—Interviews.   2. Dramatists,
American—20th century—Interviews.   I. O'Neill, Eugene,
1888-1953.   II. Estrin, Mark W.   III. Series.
PS3529.N5Z626   1990
812'.52—dc20   90-38144
                                              CIP

British Library Cataloguing-in-Publication data available

Books by Eugene O'Neill

Thirst and Other One Act Plays [*The Web, Warnings, Fog, Recklessness*]. Boston: Gorham Press, 1914.

Before Breakfast. New York: Frank Shay, 1916.

The Moon of the Caribbees and Six Other Plays of the Sea [*Bound East for Cardiff, The Long Voyage Home, In the Zone, Ile, Where the Cross Is Made, The Rope*]. New York: Boni & Liveright, 1919.

Beyond the Horizon, New York: Boni & Liveright, 1920.

The Emperor Jones, Diff'rent, The Straw. New York: Boni & Liveright, 1921.

Gold. New York: Boni & Liveright, 1921.

The Hairy Ape, Anna Christie, The First Man. New York: Boni & Liveright, 1922.

All God's Chillun Got Wings and Welded. New York: Boni & Liveright, 1924.

The Complete Works of Eugene O'Neill. 2 vols. New York: Boni & Liveright, 1924. Includes first printing of *Desire Under the Elms*; reprints all previously published plays except those in *Thirst and Other One Act Plays*.

Desire Under the Elms. New York: Boni & Liveright, 1925.

The Works of Eugene O'Neill. 4 vols. New York: Boni & Liveright, 1925. Reprints *The Complete Works*, excluding *The Moon of the Caribbees and Six Other Plays of the Sea*.

The Great God Brown, The Fountain, The Moon of the Caribbees, and Other Plays [the "six other plays of the sea" previously published with *Moon of the Caribbees*]. New York: Boni & Liveright, 1926.

Marco Millions. New York: Boni & Liveright, 1927.

Lazarus Laughed. New York: Boni & Liveright, 1927.

Strange Interlude. New York: Boni & Liveright, 1928.

Dynamo. New York: Horace Liveright, 1929.

Mourning Becomes Electra: A Trilogy. New York: Horace Liveright, 1931.

Nine Plays by Eugene O'Neill [*The Emperor Jones, The Hairy Ape, All God's Chillun Got Wings, Desire Under the Elms, Marco Millions, The Great God Brown, Lazarus Laughed, Strange Interlude, Mourning Becomes Electra*]. New York: Horace Liveright, 1932. Reissued by Random House as the "Nobel Prize Edition," 1936, and as a Modern Library Giant Edition, 1941.

Ah, Wilderness! New York: Random House, 1933.

Days Without End. New York: Random House, 1934.

The Plays of Eugene O'Neill. 12 vols. Wilderness Edition. New York: Scribner's, 1934–35. Limited edition; includes plays O'Neill identified as comprising his official canon to 1934.

The Plays of Eugene O'Neill. 3 vols. New York: Random House, 1941. Based on the Wilderness Edition. Reissued with the addition of *The Iceman Cometh*, 1951.

The Iceman Cometh. New York: Random House, 1946.

Lost Plays of Eugene O'Neill [*Abortion, The Movie Man, The Sniper, Servitude, A Wife for a Life*]. New York: New Fathoms, 1950. Unauthorized edition of early plays.

A Moon for the Misbegotten. New York: Random House, 1952.

Long Day's Journey into Night. New Haven: Yale University Press, 1956.

A Touch of the Poet. New Haven: Yale University Press, 1957.

Hughie. New Haven: Yale University Press, 1959.

More Stately Mansions. Ed. Donald Gallup. New Haven: Yale University Press, 1964. A shortened and restructured version of the play, based on the acting edition prepared by Karl Ragnar Gierow for production at the Royal Dramatic Theatre, in Stockholm, Sweden.

Ten "Lost" Plays of Eugene O'Neill. New York: Random House, 1964. Reprints texts of *Thirst and Other One Act Plays*, 1914, and *Lost Plays of Eugene O'Neill*, 1950.

The Later Plays of Eugene O'Neill [*Ah, Wilderness!, A Touch of the Poet, Hughie, A Moon for the Misbegotten*]. Ed. Travis Bogard. New York: Random House, 1967. Modern Library edition.

"Children of the Sea" and Three Other Unpublished Plays by Eugene O'Neill [an early draft of *Bound East for Cardiff, Bread and Butter, Now I Ask You, Shell Shock*]. Ed. Jennifer McCabe Atkinson. Washington, D.C.: NCR Microcard Editions, 1972.

Poems: 1912–1944. Ed. Donald Gallup. New Haven: Ticknor & Fields, 1980.

Chris Christopherson. New York: Random House, 1982. Early version of *Anna Christie*.

The Plays of Eugene O'Neill. 3 vols. New York: Random House, 1982. Modern Library edition containing 30 plays.

More Stately Mansions: The Unexpurgated Edition. Ed. Martha Gilman Bower. New York: Oxford University Press, 1988.

The Unfinished Plays: Notes for the Visit of Malatesta, The Last Conquest, Blind Alley Guy. Ed. Virginia Floyd. New York: Continuum, 1988.

The Unknown O'Neill: Unknown or Unfamiliar Writings of Eugene O'Neill. Ed. Travis Bogard. New Haven: Yale University Press, 1988. Miscellaneous drama, fiction, and essays.

Eugene O'Neill: Complete Plays. 3 vols. Ed. Travis Bogard. New York: Library of America, 1988. The most comprehensive single edition of O'Neill's plays.

Long Day's Journey into Night. New Haven: Yale University Press, 1989. Restores and corrects dialogue missing or in error in earlier printings.

Contents

Introduction   xi

Chronology   xxv

Behind the Scenes   *Philip Mindil*   3

Playwright Finds His Inspiration on Lonely Sand Dunes
by the Sea   *Olin Downes*   6

Making Plays with a Tragic End: An Intimate Interview with Eugene
O'Neill, Who Tells Why He Does It   *Malcolm Mollan*   13

The Artist of the Theatre: A Colloquy between Eugene O'Neill
and Oliver M. Sayler   *Shadowland*   21

The Extraordinary Story of Eugene O'Neill   *Mary B. Mullett*   26

Eugene O'Neill, World-Famous Dramatist, and Family Live
in Abandoned Coast Guard Station on Cape Cod
Charles A. Merrill   38

O'Neill Defends His Play of Negro   *Louis Kantor*   44

Eugene O'Neill—The Inner Man   *Carol Bird*   50

Back to the Source of Plays   *Charles P. Sweeney*   56

Eugene O'Neill Talks of His Own and the Plays of Others
New York Herald Tribune   60

O'Neill Lifts Curtain on His Early Days   *Louis Kalonyme*
[*Louis Kantor*]   64

Fierce Oaths and Blushing Complexes Find No Place in Eugene
O'Neill's Talk   *Flora Merrill*   70

Eugene O'Neill: Writer of Synthetic Drama   *Malcolm Cowley*   75

A Eugene O'Neill Miscellany   *New York Sun*   81

Realism Doomed, O'Neill Believes   *Richard Watts, Jr.*   84

O'Neill as the Stage Never Sees Him
   Montiville Morris Hansford   88

Out of Provincetown: A Memoir of Eugene O'Neill
   Harry Kemp   95

The Boulevards After Dark   *Ward Morehouse*   103

Exile Made Him Appreciate U.S., O'Neill Admits
   Ernest K. Lindley   108

O'Neill Picks America as His Future Workshop
   Richard Watts, Jr.   113

O'Neill Plots a Course for the Drama   *S. J. Woolf*   116

Eugene O'Neill   *George Jean Nathan*   121

O'Neill Is Eager to See Cohan in *Ah, Wilderness!*
   Richard Watts, Jr.   134

The Recluse of Sea Island   *George Jean Nathan*   137

Eugene O'Neill Undramatic over Honor of Nobel Prize
   Seattle Daily Times   145

O'Neill: An Impression   *Theresa Helburn*   148

O'Neill Turns West to New Horizons   *Richard L. Neuberger*   152

Eugene O'Neill Lets Us in on Why *The Iceman Cometh*
   Earl Wilson   158

Eugene O'Neill Discourses on Dramatic Art
   George Jean Nathan   161

O'Neill on the World and *The Iceman*   *John S. Wilson*   164

Eugene O'Neill Returns after Twelve Years   *S. J. Woolf*   167

Eugene O'Neill after Twelve Years   *George Jean Nathan*   174

Contents

The Ordeal of Eugene O'Neill   *James Agee*   180

Mr. O'Neill and the Iceman   *Kyle Crichton*   188

The Black Irishman   *Croswell Bowen*   203

Profiles: The Tragic Sense   *Hamilton Basso*   224

Index   237

Introduction

The conversations with Eugene O'Neill recorded in this volume
convey a striking collective portrait of a man so reticent and
uncomfortable with oral discourse that they habitually stammer into
silences with Eugene O'Neill, recurringly forcing the hapless interviewer to transcribe the playwright's words in the more developed
voice of his or her own—not O'Neill's—persona. Attempts to capture
the essence of those silences through descriptions of O'Neill's piercing
eyes, angular physique, mannerisms or imagined thought processes,
coupled with an ornate twenties and early-thirties journalistic style
that usually rejects verbatim question-and-answer accounts, blur
distinctions among the terms "interview," "conversation," "reminiscence," and (most accurately in O'Neill's case) "profile." As a result,
an especially vivid composite picture emerges of the process by
which Eugene O'Neill came to be mythologized in both the popular
and the more "literary" press, a process intriguingly complicated by a
current reader's post-*Long Day's Journey into Night* hindsight, which
punctuates these pieces as ongoing subtext.

In a very real sense, it is miraculous that so many of the conversations took place at all. "Interviewing Eugene O'Neill," writes
Carol Bird in one of many attempts to describe the difficulty of
putting the man into print, "is like extracting testimony from a
reluctant witness. In fact, to use the word 'interview' in conjunction
with him is to employ almost a misnomer. An interview presupposes
a colloquy. A flow of words between two persons. Nothing more
erroneous could be circulated about [him]. . . . Silence. Silence.
More questions, probings, attempts to secure opinions, statements,
anything but monosyllables. Futility! Suddenly, I am overcome with a
sense of the ridiculous. Here are two people whose very careers
oppose this sort of conduct. A playwright who deals in words. A
writer who juggles them daily. Sitting across from each other in

silence, apparently overcome with shyness" (*Theatre Magazine,* 1924).

Kyle Crichton, commenting on his sessions with O'Neill at the other end of the playwright's career, makes it clear in a piece based on a 1946 interview that the speech pattern so frustrating to interviewers was in fact life-long: "There was no difficulty in getting him to talk; the trouble was in knowing when he had stopped. I would launch him with a question, and he would start off in his quiet, hesitant way and gradually seem to disappear into a haze. Words would come out of the mist, to be followed by long periods of silence. If I broke in with another question, I invariably found that the silence was merely a pause and O'Neill had taken up the narrative again. . . . If I *didn't* break in, that was the time O'Neill had definitely finished, and I found myself sitting there like a dummy" ("Mr. O'Neill and the Iceman," 1946).

Interviewers (including Bird) often remark in error that O'Neill has never been interviewed before, thereby implying that they have been made privy to an occurrence which, while in fact infrequent, is not quite as rare an occasion as they would like to suppose. Others, like Charles P. Sweeney, prefer to perpetuate the image of O'Neill as reluctant conversationalist, then to shatter the notion with liberal citations of splendid O'Neill commentary which, they subtly imply, has been extracted through their skills as interviewers—self congratulation that is often appropriate.

Thus Mr. Sweeney: "John D. Rockefeller and Eugene O'Neill have been supposed to be the most difficult American characters to interview. You can't get to Rockefeller, and O'Neill, they say, won't talk. So much for the credit for having managed to be the audience of one to whom the shyest man in show business directed thirty minutes' conversation about his plays, his point of view on numerous problems of the theatre and himself, following a rehearsal of *Desire Under the Elms*" (*New York World,* 1924). For, like so many others represented in this collection, Sweeney's interview discloses an O'Neill who, despite his legendary shyness, is anything but reticent.

On the one hand, then, these conversations reveal an anomaly: the most verbose American dramatist, one who even in his personal writing penned vast numbers of letters (*three thousand* of which survive) and with little prompting issued written manifestos on the state of the drama in general and the meaning of his individual plays in particular, is pictured in ordinary small talk (in the words of Mary B. Mullett) as a "good imitation of a sphinx" (*American Magazine*, 1922). Even in O'Neill's most forthcoming conversations, there are more pauses than in a Pinter play.

On the other hand, it should not be surprising to discover that this collection corroborates, in his frequent willingness to respond candidly to the probing of the dreaded press, another side to O'Neill. He had much to say and the motives to say it—about his life *and* about his plays—and (though we now know how much more he did *not* say) he shared a great deal with the writers represented in this volume, in voices by turns plaintive ("Sure, I'll write about happiness, if I ever happen to meet up with that luxury," 1922); epigrammatic ("A work of art is always happy; all else is unhappy," 1922); ironic ("There's been a lot of romantic nonsense built up about that t.b. of mine. Keats died of it and people like Stevenson had it, so if you want to do the right thing in a literary way, you get it," 1946); embittered ("This American Dream stuff gives me a pain. Telling the world about our American Dream! I don't know what they mean. If it exists, as we tell the whole world, why don't we make it work in one small hamlet in the United States?" 1946).

Virtually born in a trunk to a theatre family, he was steeped through tours with his actor-father's company in the very *idea* of theatre, its pleasures and, vitally for O'Neill, its romantic, nineteenth-century excesses, which he fought in his plays to transform. Concomitantly, he grew into the most aware and pragmatic of playwrights, a man concerned with all details of casting, the values of stage production and theatre economics, and, through voracious reading throughout his life, the implementation and manipulation of dramaturgical devices (masks, soliloquies, asides, heightened language) in the manner of Shakespeare and the Greek dramatists to his own contemporary ends.

That pragmatic sense extended centrally to his relationships with drama critics and the general press. His earnest private solicitation of evaluation of his plays from such critics as George Jean Nathan, Joseph Wood Krutch, and Brooks Atkinson was surely not as entirely ingenuous as it initially appeared. And he learned early on the double-edged value of publicity regarding his plays, whose daring

subject matter (miscegenation in *All God's Chillun Got Wings;*
Freudian sexuality in *Desire Under the Elms, Strange Interlude,* and
Mourning Becomes Electra) and strong language (in his sea plays
and numerous others) seemed to demand that he speak out when
attempts at censorship erupted into controversy reported in the press.
That controversy frequently helped to sell tickets (and, as in the case
of *Strange Interlude,* to turn his published work into best sellers) but
small-minded failure to grasp his larger dramatic intent severely
distressed him. (From a letter to drama scholar Arthur Hobson
Quinn, dated 3 April 1925: "But where I feel myself most neglected is
where I set most store by myself—as a bit of a poet who has labored
with the spoken word to evolve original rhythms of beauty where
beauty apparently isn't—*Jones, Ape, God's Chillun, Desire* etc.—
and to see the transfiguring nobility of tragedy, in as near the Greek
sense as one can grasp it, in seemingly the most ignoble, debased
lives.") O'Neill had strong reasons to struggle with his innate social
reticence.

Even his interviews thus confirm the repeated marks of dual
personality observed in O'Neill in other contexts by his later critics
and biographers, those irreconcilable character conflicts expressed in
such key works as *The Great God Brown* (a play he consistently tells
interviewers is a personal favorite), *The Hairy Ape,* and *Strange
Interlude.*

O'Neill was that rare American writer who, by the relatively tender
age of thirty-one, when these interviews begin, already made extraordinarily good copy. His imposing appearance and adventurous,
hell-raising youth flew in the face of the stereotypical writer's persona.
As the son of actor James O'Neill he carried with him certain
glamorous associations, despite inherent national suspicion regarding
the mores of theatre people. By rejecting the respectability, the hard-
won middle class values to which his family aspired, he compounded
his lure to the press and, as publicity came his way, appears to have
nurtured assiduously the image conveyed by stories of his youthful
prodigality. The biographical background repeated in one interview
after another—the famous father, expulsion from Princeton, travel to
exotic shores as a seaman, early marriage and divorce—took him
through legitimate claims of redemption-by-disease and the new-
found gospel of hard work as playwright discovered in the

"san"[atorium], all of which made him sound as if he were a happily reclaimed embodiment of the profligate Ejlert Lovborg in Ibsen's *Hedda Gabler*. By 1924, the rapid succession of prize-winning plays had already released the American theatre into territory heretofore unimagined. And as these conversations illustrate, the power of O'Neill's talent was recognized very early, as were his maddening demands on critics and audiences alike in his plays' length, complexity, and more than occasional inflated pretentiousness. As the interviews progress, most elements of the O'Neill persona remain intact, though certain myths—including the claim that he threw a beer bottle through Princeton President Woodrow Wilson's home— O'Neill later tries to correct.

The experimental risk-taking in both the apparatus and subject matter of the plays seemed to match the rebellious biography of the creator. O'Neill thus is often cast in these pieces in the mold of the English Romantic poets—having had tuberculosis did not hurt in this regard—or the Irish dramatists Synge and O'Casey (whom O'Neill very much admired), or the Heathcliffean heroes of British fiction. Interviewer Olin Downes compares him in one of this collection's earliest essays to another Eugene: Marchbanks from Shaw's *Candida* (*Boston Sunday Post*, 1920). Contributing further to the image were O'Neill's attachment to the sea, a central subject in his early plays, and, especially, his preoccupation with a tragic tone so alien to American dramatic literature. ("Are you our foremost apostle of woe?" asks Malcolm Mollan, thereby triggering one of O'Neill's most eloquent explanations of the function of tragedy. *Philadelphia Public Ledger Sunday Magazine*, 1922.) The personal quality of brooding isolation identified early by interviewers was, for them, a logical transference from the plays to the man. It was also a partially correct apprehension of his in-person demeanor, but a mistaken attribution of sullenness for his genuine shyness.

The gradual development of the O'Neill persona as it is displayed to the American public is, then, a thread of particular interest running through these essays. The romantic image occasionally leads some writers to their own stylistic excesses as they describe their encounters with O'Neill. Inflated rhetoric is especially evident in certain pieces of the twenties and early thirties, when a turgid (and occasionally infuriating) reportorial style dominated feature-writing. Present read-

ers also will be startled to discover openly expressed examples of
journalistic racism and sexism. (See, for example, O'Neill's curiously
oblique response to Louis Kantor's insistence on the racial superiority
of whites over blacks [*New York Times,* 11 May 1924]; or John S.
Wilson's reference to the "little blonde" reporter too frightened to ask
O'Neill a question [*PM,* 3 September 1946].)

The image etched as early as 1920 remained essentially intact
throughout O'Neill's lifetime. While waxing rhapsodic on O'Neill's
wanderlust, Olin Downes, for example, first employs the notion of a
"curse" in the playwright's makeup, a term that would be more
explicitly developed late in O'Neill's life and in major critical and
biographical studies well after his death, as the autobiographical
nature of his work came more fully to light following the production
and publication of *Long Day's Journey into Night* in 1956.

Despite the florid prose of such writers as Montiville Morris
Hansford, whose style represents not only the fashion of his day but
an attempt to compensate for the scarcity of direct quotation from the
tight-lipped O'Neill, astute insights into the dramatist's work and
personality are achieved throughout these portraits, often when the
reader least expects them. Hansford, a Bermuda friend of O'Neill
from 1924 to 1927, attributes, for example, the dramatist's "helplessness in a rapid conversational bout" to an "unusual ability to
concentrate," which he "possesses . . . to a high degree." Any
interruptions, especially in the guise of small talk, "leave him
stranded," primarily Hansford implies, because O'Neill prefers to
express himself in the "dreams of his puppets," the characters on the
page. "He is entirely wrapped up in his work. . . . I believe that the
man never feels quite at home with anybody, and certainly nobody
ever feels at home with him" (*Boston Evening Transcript,* 1930). For
all his hyperbole, Hansford identifies that element of isolation in
O'Neill's character worked out (as we now know) in such characters
as Dion Anthony and Edmund Tyrone.

Hansford's essay, written with a detachment gained by his three-
year absence from O'Neill, is in the strictest sense not an interview
but a profile and reminiscence based on informal conversations
recorded, without direct quotation, sometime after the fact. Numerous factors combine in the case of O'Neill to limit severely the extent

of direct question-and-answer conversations which would subsequently become the style in later twentieth-century journalism.

The elaborate writing style of choice in this pre-mini-recorder era of journalism generally mitigated against the colloquy form, especially in newspapers, which provided the primary venues for O'Neill interviews. Moreover, O'Neill's natural taciturnity intensified into outright suspicion and hostility toward the press following a period of marital crisis in the late twenties, when he felt (justly) hounded by reporters, and limited the nature of his subsequent encounters and, apparently, the number of direct statements he gave for attribution.

Richard Watts, Jr., who interviewed O'Neill for the *New York Herald Tribune,* confronts the matter pointedly in his report of a conversation shortly before the opening of *Mourning Becomes Electra*. Though he never so states it directly, Watts is almost certainly reflecting O'Neill's explicit refusal to be taken down verbatim, a desire Watts seems determined to honor in order to ensure future access. "It strikes me," Watts writes, "that this report of Mr. O'Neill has, in its refusal to quote from its subject directly, something of the quality to be found in accounts of a vague and mysterious White House Spokesman. It should be noted, therefore, that this is not intended as an 'interview' with the First Playwright. It is merely intended as an effort to express, in a rather free-handed way, a number of the ideas expressed by Mr. O'Neill in an utterly informal conversation which had about it nothing, I fear, of the air of a prosecutor grilling a suspect" (*New York Herald Tribune,* 27 September 1931).

In other words, the notion of "interview" is denied to give an appearance of "utterly informal conversation," a ruse somehow intended to protect O'Neill from uncontrollable demands for future "interviews." Such semantic games illustrate further why so many of these pieces reflect that curious amalgam of interview sub-genres— suggesting once again that in O'Neill's case considerably more than a particular period's journalistic style is behind it. Even the longest, most comprehensive interview-profiles reprinted in this volume, based on sessions granted by O'Neill, combine career overview, play analysis, paraphrase, and direct citation, though in several of these pieces O'Neill is quoted at much greater length than in others. (See, for example, this volume's final four essays by James Agee, Kyle

Crichton, Croswell Bowen, and Hamilton Basso—all of them inspired by conversations with O'Neill between 1946 and 1948, all of them functioning as a coda to the twenty-eight year collective portrait revealed here.)

Despite the innate shyness and stratagems just described, from the time he won his first Pulitzer Prize for *Beyond the Horizon* in 1920 until about 1928, when *Strange Interlude* opened, O'Neill expressed his views on a wide variety of subjects in conversations for the public record, usually on the eve or just after the opening of a new play. The interviews of the years to 1926 reflect the enormous rush of excitement bound up in the overall public response to the major new voice in the American theatre and to O'Neill's high-minded idealism captured in the experimental successes of the Provincetown Players on Cape Cod and in New York; in the producing "triumvirate" he formed with critic Kenneth Macgowan and designer Robert Edmond Jones; in the notion, above all, that American dramatic literature—through O'Neill—could at last be judged as seriously as the nation's poetry or fiction.

The fact that his plays outgrew the production and management capacities of the Provincetown Playhouse is significant as a further factor in the appearance of press interviews designed to aid his transfer to Broadway. In 1927 O'Neill linked arms with the prestigious Theatre Guild, producers of the most important and intellectually-oriented playwrights in the American theatre. Between 9 January 1928 and 11 February 1929, the Guild produced three O'Neill plays (*Marco Millions, Strange Interlude,* and *Dynamo*) and would produce the four subsequent Broadway productions in his lifetime (*Mourning Becomes Electra,* 1931; *Ah, Wilderness!,* 1933; *Days Without End,* 1934; and *The Iceman Cometh,* 1946). Guild management would also oversee his major interviews.

In 1926, after eight years of marriage to writer Agnes Boulton, by whom he had two children, O'Neill began a relationship with actress Carlotta Monterey. An embittered Agnes refused to give him a divorce and O'Neill left the United States with Carlotta for a three-year period, primarily spent in France, to escape the scandal-hungry press. He married Carlotta three weeks after Agnes finally granted the divorce, but he remained skittish with the press, despite the fact that he had nurtured friendships among major drama writers of the

period, including the acerbic and highly regarded George Jean
Nathan (four of whose profiles are reprinted here). Relieved by the
settlement of his marriage woes and encouraged by his swift progress
on the trilogy Mourning Becomes Electra, written between 1929 and
1931 at the chateau he and Carlotta rented in France, O'Neill
permitted an occasional interviewer to visit him there, though he
remained coy about the new play. (See Ward Morehouse, New York
Sun, 14 May 1930.)

Upon his return to New York in the spring of 1931, in preparation
for the fall Broadway production of Mourning Becomes Electra,
O'Neill agreed to his first "mass" press interview, arranged by the
Guild and held in its offices, with the expectation that such a pro-
cedure would minimize his discomfort. No full transcript of this—or
the 1946—mass interview was recorded and one must depend upon
individual stories written by various reporters in attendance. O'Neill
stipulated in advance that only one writer—in this instance, John
Chapman of the New York Daily News—would be permitted to ask
the questions, a notable sign in retrospect of O'Neill's intensified
distrust of such public occasions after the unhappy personal period
now seemingly ended. He insisted that questions be restricted to
matters concerning the new play, fearful of any prying into his
relationship with Carlotta and, particularly, into the suicide of Ralph
Barton, Carlotta's former husband, soon after the O'Neills' arrival in
New York and just two days prior to the scheduled interview. Barton's
brother had suggested in the press that the suicide's timing was not
coincidental, that the O'Neills had visited Barton shortly before the
act (a visit they maintained had never taken place), and that his
suicide note proclaimed Barton's undying love for his "lost angel,"
Carlotta. Such was the context of O'Neill's first interview upon his
return to American shores.

Questions were apparently tactful, restricted to Electra, but near
interview's end unauthorized questions regarding Carlotta's where-
abouts prompted Guild representatives to curtail the proceedings. In
an effort to avoid reporters who, it was feared, might follow him to
the secluded Carlotta, O'Neill accepted a Guild press agent's suggestion that he exit via the roof, cross to an adjacent building, and leave
from another connecting street. It is no wonder that O'Neill was to
remain wary of the press for the rest of his life.

Ironically, the fullest depiction of the Guild interview was written
not by John Chapman but by Ernest K. Lindley—for the *New York
Herald Tribune,* 22 May 1931, reprinted in this collection. On that
date, Chapman's *New York Daily News* buried a brief, unsigned
report of the interview on its theatre page, but featured on page three
a banner-headlined account ("O'NEILL SENDS BARTON'S 'LOST
ANGEL' INTO HIDING") of the suicide aftermath. The story, by
Grace Robinson, incorporated references to O'Neill's anger at the
intrusion of personal questions during the Guild interview and to his
premature retreat from the session. Lindley restricted his account of
the interview exclusively to theatre matters.

The remaining interviews of the 1930s surround the October 1931
opening of *Electra;* the arrival two years later of—*mirabile dictu!*—an
O'Neill *comedy* starring George M. Cohan, *Ah, Wilderness!;* the
opening of *Days Without End* which, in 1934, would prove to be his
last Broadway play for twelve years; and, notably, his winning of the
Nobel Prize for Literature in 1936, the first and only time an American dramatist has won the award.

In his twelve years on the West Coast, O'Neill remained in general
seclusion from the press, aside from occasional pieces celebrating the
Nobel laureate. (See Richard L. Neuberger, *New York Times
Magazine,* 22 November 1936.) In that seclusion, despite enormous
pain and frustration from illness and an intensifying tremor of the
hands, he wrote an astonishing array of plays which, for most O'Neill
scholars, comprises his greatest legacy to the American drama:
numerous drafts of a planned eleven-play cycle (see chronology);
*Long Day's Journey into Night; The Iceman Cometh; A Moon for the
Misbegotten;* and *Hughie.*

In 1946, twelve years after the critical failure of *Days Without End,*
he returned to New York for the Guild's mounting of *The Iceman
Cometh,* which would be his last play to reach Broadway in his
lifetime. A mass interview was again arranged by the Guild in its
offices, attended by a reverential, post-Nobel press, awed by his
reputation and shocked by how much beyond his fifty-eight years he
appeared to have aged. This time, questions were open to the
general group, though many remained silent, and *Variety's* account of
the session attacked some reporters for their "sophomoric and silly"
questions. Reprinted here are the most comprehensive reports of that

interview, including James Agee's then anonymous cover story for *Time.*

No doubt at the behest of the Guild, in an affort to increase publicity for his first Broadway foray in such a long period, and amid fears that he had lost his talent, O'Neill also granted a number of private interviews, both before and after the mass interview of 2 September 1946, all relating primarily to *Iceman's* opening on 9 October. (See especially George Jean Nathan, *New York Journal-American,* 26 August 1946, and *American Mercury,* 63 [October 1946]; and S. J. Woolf, *New York Times Magazine,* 15 September 1946.)

With the disappointing response to *Iceman* and the out-of-town failure of *A Moon for the Misbegotten* during its pre-Broadway tour, O'Neill was perceived increasingly as a writer whose best time had long passed. The extraordinary story of the revitalization of his critical reputation demands, however, that the collective portrait etched by these conversations effectively conclude not with Hamilton Basso's *New Yorker* profile (13 March 1948), based on the last interview O'Neill ever granted, but with the reader's retrospective awareness of *Long Day's Journey's* impact on his entire dramatic canon—and the knowledge of Carlotta's pivotal role in extricating the play from her husband's legal restrictions. In his lifetime the object of his eternal love and frequent wrath, a mother-wife locked with him in a marriage that mocked the plots of Strindbergian drama, Carlotta after his death became the reviver and sentinel of O'Neill's reputation. Her deceptively innocuous appearance in so many of the interviews recorded in this volume assumes a particular level of ironic poignancy.

These interviews combine, then, to reveal multiple pleasures. The stylistic excesses of occasional early pieces require the reader to ferret for O'Neill's insights but the effort is rewarded. Perhaps the most surprising element to emerge from these conversations is the fact that so much of the O'Neill mythology and mystique has been borne out by subsequent detailed study of the man and his plays. A serious American drama begins—and, to many, still ends—with O'Neill. It is in his comments on American drama and society in general, and O'Neillian drama in particular, that this collection yields its richest insights.

Consistent with policies established for the Literary Conversations series, all interviews are published in their entirety, with minimal, silent editorial changes when warranted for clarity or correction of identifiable error. Certain spellings have been regularized, and newspaper subheads deleted. Titles of O'Neill's plays and other published works have been italicized as appropriate. Some information, particularly relating to O'Neill's unusual biographical background, is repeated in various pieces, in part because writers often relied on earlier interviews as their own source material to flesh out contexts for O'Neill's responses to their questions. Thus, occasional hyperbolic details would tend to have been accepted as truth even when fallacious, unless at some later stage O'Neill sought to correct them. It is clear, however, (as can be inferred from several of these interviews) that O'Neill himself contributed to certain notions exaggerated in the press early in his career. Such repetition and occasional correction implicitly contribute to the persona's cumulative presentation, as do certain questions repeated by interviewers and sometimes answered by O'Neill with the subtlest variation (most evident in the 1946 series of *Iceman Cometh* conversations). I have especially sought to bring together difficult-to-find, scattered O'Neill conversations originally printed in newspapers and periodicals.

Several pieces considered for inclusion have been omitted from the volume when they appear to rely excessively on material expressed more eloquently elsewhere in the collection, or when the writer's direct confrontation with O'Neill seems minimal and the playwright's voice is overwhelmed by the reporter's repetition of the biography or commentary on the plays. Omissions in the former category include Harold Stark's "Young Boswell Interviews Eugene O'Neill" (*New York Tribune,* 24 May 1923, sec. 1, 13); Karl Schriftgiesser's "*The Iceman Cometh*" (*New York Times,* 6 October 1946, sec. 2, 1, 3), one of the numerous pre-*Iceman* interviews, which adds little new material to O'Neill's other utterances of the period save the literal remark that the play is "about pipe dreams"; and Muriel Band's "O'Neill is Back" (*Mayfair,* 3 [October 1946], 66–67, 71–72).

Deletions in the second category include David Karsner's "Eugene O'Neill at Close Range in Maine" (in Karsner's *Sixteen Authors to One,* 1928; rpt. Freeport, N.Y.: Books for Libraries Press, 1968, pp. 101–22); Elizabeth Shepley Sergeant's well-written "O'Neill: The Man with a Mask" (*New Republic,* 16 March 1927, 91–95); and Fred Pasley's often cited, but apparently rarely checked, superficial life

story serialized in the *New York Daily News* ("Odyssey of Eugene
O'Neill—the Ulysses of the Drama," 24 January 1932, 3, 32–33; 25
January 1932, 3, 12; 26 January 1932, 3, 18; 27 January 1932, 3,
16; 28 January 1932, 20; 29 January 1932, 18; 30 January 1932,
10).

I would like to thank the people who made significant contribu-
tions in bringing this collection into print: Natalie DeRissio rearranged
her schedule to prepare major portions of the manuscript with her
incomparable intelligence and proficiency; Robin Estrin meticulously
transcribed interviews unintelligible in their original form; Doreen
DeLuca and Beata Grysakowska provided reliable research assistance; Linda Green accepted inter-library loan challenges above
and beyond the call of duty, and invariably prevailed on this volume's
behalf; and Barbara Estrin amiably responded to my requests with
superb editorial advice at all stages of the volume's preparation.

My thanks also go to members of the reference staff of Adams
Library at Rhode Island College, especially to Tish Brennan and
Rachel Carpenter; to the college's Faculty Research Committee; to
Patricia Willis and Lori Misura of Yale's Beinecke Rare Book and
Manuscript Library, where the O'Neill collection is housed; to
Jackson R. Bryer, Tess and Charles Hoffmann, Joseph Plut, Arlene
Robertson, and Meg Wallace; and to numerous unknown persons at
the Library of Congress, the New York Public Library, and the British
and Westminster Libraries, London. I also extend thanks to holders
of copyrights for permission to reprint, noted as appropriate within
the volume, and—especially—to Seetha Srinivasan of University
Press of Mississippi.

This book is for Barbara in eager anticipation of the next twenty-
five years of exquisite conversation.

MWE
August 1989

Several works have eased the burden of this venture by aiding in the identification of material
appropriate for inclusion and in the daunting navigation of the maze of detail charting O'Neill's
life in the theatre: Louis Sheaffer, *O'Neill, Son and Playwright* (Boston: Little, Brown, 1968),
and *O'Neill, Son and Artist* (Boston: Little, Brown, 1973); Arthur and Barbara Gelb, *O'Neill*
(New York: Harper & Row, 1973); Ulrich Halfmann, *Eugene O'Neill: Comments on the Drama
and the Theater: A Source Book* (Tubingen: Gunter Narr, 1987); Travis Bogard, *Contour in
Time: The Plays of Eugene O'Neill*, rev. ed. (New York: Oxford University Press, 1988); Travis

Bogard and Jackson R. Bryer, eds., *Selected Letters of Eugene O'Neill* (New Haven: Yale University Press, 1988); Virginia Floyd, *The Plays of Eugene O'Neill: A New Assessment* (New York: Ungar, 1987). For verification of matters pertaining directly to the plays, I have relied upon Travis Bogard's edition of *Eugene O'Neill: Complete Plays*, 3 vols. (New York: Library of America, 1988).

Chronology

Parenthetical dates following titles of O'Neill's plays cite premiere performances, all in New York City unless otherwise specified.

1888   Eugene Gladstone O'Neill born 16 October in a room at Barrett House, a New York City hotel, to Mary Ellen (Ella) Quinlan O'Neill and actor James O'Neill. [Oldest brother James, Jr. (Jamie) born 1878; second brother Edmund born 1883, dies of measles 1885. Prescriptions following Edmund's birth result in Ella's addiction to morphine.]

1888–95   Early years spent traveling with family on father's theatre road tours and summering at Monte Cristo cottage, the house in New London, Connecticut, named for James O'Neill's most famous role, where the family resides when not living in hotels

1895–   Saint Aloysius boarding school, at the Academy of Mount
1900   St. Vincent, Riverdale, New York, run by Catholic nuns

1900–02   De La Salle Institute, New York City, a Catholic boarding school run by the Christian Brothers

1902–06   Attends Betts Academy, a nonsectarian private boarding school in Stamford, Connecticut. By the age of fifteen, EO'N is drinking heavily. During this period of his life he learns of his mother's drug addiction. Also a key formative period of intellectual development through early exposure to iconoclastic literary and political writings of (among others) Shaw, Ibsen, Baudelaire, Emma Goldman.

1906–07   Enters Princeton University, September 1906; dismissed
           for "poor scholastic standing," June 1907. Despite
           EO'N's later claim that "Princeton was all play and no
           work," while there he maintains a self-directed program
           of voracious reading—Wilde, Dostoevsky, Tolstoy, Gorki,
           and, especially, Nietzsche.

1907–08   Works in New York City as secretary in a supply company
           in which James O'Neill holds stock

1909   Marries Kathleen Jenkins, pregnant with his child, on 2
           October. Departs two weeks later for Spanish Honduras
           on a gold prospecting voyage arranged by his father.

1910   Returns to New York with a case of malaria. Son Eugene
           Gladstone, Jr., born 5 May to Kathleen Jenkins. Tours
           with father's company in production of *The White Sister*.
           Sails for Buenos Aires, where he works at a variety of
           briefly held jobs, followed by a period of near destitution.

1911   Returns to New York on the *Ikala,* a British tramp steamer
           in April. Lives in New York City at Jimmy the Priest's, a
           waterfront saloon-rooming house. Sails as ordinary sea-
           man for Southampton, England, aboard the luxury
           passenger liner *New York,* returning one month later as
           able-bodied seaman aboard the *Philadelphia.* Attends
           every New York production of Dublin's Abbey Players
           during the company's American tour late in the year;
           particularly impressed by Synge's *Riders to the Sea*.

1912   Attempts suicide at Jimmy the Priest's. Tours briefly with
           father's company in *The Count of Monte Cristo*. Divorced
           by Kathleen Jenkins in July. Obtains employment as
           reporter for the *New London Telegraph,* which also
           publishes some of his poetry; lives at Monte Cristo
           cottage. Hospitalized for tuberculosis, briefly at state
           sanatorium in Shelton, Connecticut, then—from Christ-

mas Eve 1912 until June 1913—at Gaylord Farm
Sanatorium, Wallingford, Connecticut.

1913–14   During Gaylord Farm confinement EO'N reads exten-
           sively in dramatic literature of all periods, paying
           particular attention to Greek and Elizabethan classics and
           to Strindberg. Returns to New London for final recupera-
           tion in June 1913, determined to become a playwright. In
           this period he writes obsessively, focusing on the one-act
           form, and completes *Thirst, The Web, Recklessness,
           Warnings,* and *Fog* (published in 1914, with his father's
           financial support, as *Thirst and Other One-Act Plays*);
           Bound East for Cardiff; Abortion; The Movie Man; and
           two longer plays, *Bread and Butter* and *Servitude.* In
           Spring 1914, Ella O'Neill enters a convent in a successful
           attempt to overcome her drug dependency permanently.

1914–15   Admitted to Professor George Pierce Baker's English 47
           drama workshop at Harvard, where he spends the
           academic year and writes *The Sniper* and *The Personal
           Equation.* After summering in New London, goes to
           Greenwich Village in the fall, where he meets an array of
           politically active intellectuals and frequents such bars as
           the Hell Hole, his favorite.

1916   Joins writer George Cram ("Jig") Cook, his wife—
           playwright Susan Glaspell, John Reed, Louise Bryant,
           Saxe Commins, Robert Edmond Jones, and others in
           their Cape Cod summer theatre venture at the Wharf
           Theatre, Provincetown, Massachusetts. The company,
           known as the Provincetown Players, stages *Bound East
           for Cardiff* (28 July, with EO'N cast in the one-line role of
           the second mate) and *Thirst* (uncertain date in August,
           with O'Neill as the mulatto sailor) in Provincetown. The
           group opens The Playwright's Theatre—a name sug-
           gested by EO'N—in Greenwich Village that fall, where it
           again produces *Bound East for Cardiff* (3 November, with
           EO'N in the same role) and *Before Breakfast* (1 Decem-

ber, with EO'N playing the unseen husband, Alfred).
Before Breakfast is directed by EO'N, "assisted by James
O'Neill."

1917   Short story "Tomorrow" published in *The Seven Arts*
        magazine (June), the only story EO'N ever sees pub-
        lished. At their New York theatre, the Provincetown
        Players produces *Fog* (5 January), *The Sniper* (16 Febru-
        ary), *The Long Voyage Home* (2 November), and *Ile* (30
        November). *In the Zone* is produced by rival company,
        the Washington Square Players, at the Comedy Theatre
        (31 October). *The Long Voyage Home* is published in
        The Smart Set (October).

1918   Marries writer Agnes Boulton in Provincetown, 12 April.
        In New York, the Provincetown Players produces *The
        Rope* (26 April), *Where the Cross Is Made* (22 Novem-
        ber), and *The Moon of the Caribbees* (20 December).
        Publishes *Ile* and *The Moon of the Caribbees* in *The
        Smart Set*. The Playwright's Theatre, New York, is
        renamed the Provincetown Playhouse.

1919   Buys isolated former Coast Guard station at Peaked Hill
        Bar, in Provincetown. Son Shane is born 30 October.
        Publishes *The Moon of the Caribbees and Six Other
        Plays of the Sea*. *The Dreamy Kid* is produced at the
        Provincetown Playhouse (31 October).

1920   Plays produced: *Beyond the Horizon* (by Broadway
        producer John D. Williams, Morosco Theatre, 3 Febru-
        ary); *Chris Christopherson* (by Broadway producer
        George C. Tyler, in Atlantic City, N.J., 9 March; produc-
        tion fails); *Exorcism* (Provincetown Playhouse, 26 March;
        later destroyed); *The Emperor Jones* (Provincetown
        Playhouse, 1 November); *Diff'rent* (Provincetown Play-
        house, 27 December). Wins Pulitzer Prize for *Beyond the
        Horizon*. Father James O'Neill dies 10 August. Now
        recognized by the press as a significant American drama-

tist, EO'N responds to pleas for interviews. *Emperor Jones* emerges as major success for the Provincetown Players, although, as *Beyond the Horizon*'s Broadway production illustrates, EO'N is surpassing the limits of the Provincetown's production capabilities.

1921 Plays produced: *Gold* (John D. Williams, producer, at the Frazee Theatre, 1 June); *Anna Christie* (final revised version of *Chris Christopherson*, Arthur Hopkins producer and director, at the Vanderbilt Theatre, 2 November); *The Straw* (produced by George C. Tyler at the Greenwich Village Theatre, 10 November).

1922 Mother Ella O'Neill dies 28 February in Los Angeles; brother Jamie accompanies body back east on train which arrives in New York on the night *The Hairy Ape* opens (Provincetown Playhouse, 9 March). EO'N plans to meet train, instead of attending opening, but is emotionally unable to do either. *The First Man* is also produced (Neighborhood Playhouse, 4 March). Wins second Pulitzer Prize for *Anna Christie*. Original Provincetown Players disband. Buys Brook Farm, winter home at Ridgefield, Connecticut.

1923 Elected to the National Institute of Arts and Letters and awarded its gold medal for drama. Brother Jamie dies 8 November in a New Jersey sanatorium of complications from alcoholism. *Anna Christie* opens to acclaim in London, his first important overseas production and the first of many to follow in Europe, though the run is disappointing. With critic Kenneth Macgowan and designer Robert Edmond Jones EO'N forms the Experimental Theatre, a production "triumvirate" dedicated to dramatic innovation at the Provincetown Playhouse and the Greenwich Village Theatre. Silent film version of *Anna Christie* released.

1924 The triumvirate produces *Welded* (the first production of a new O'Neill play in two years, at the Thirty-ninth Street

Theatre, 17 March); and, at the Provincetown Playhouse,
The Ancient Mariner (6 April) and *All God's Chillun Got
Wings* (15 May 1924). *All God's Chillun,* already pub-
lished in *American Mercury* magazine, encounters consid-
erable pre- and post-production controversy because of
its interracial aspects. The triumvirate produces *Desire
Under the Elms* at the Greenwich Village Theatre (11
November). EO'N moves to Bermuda in November and
lives there periodically until 1927. Publication of *The
Complete Works of Eugene O'Neill,* 2 vols. (Boni and
Liveright).

1925   Daughter Oona born 14 May. The triumvirate produces
The Fountain (Greenwich Village Theatre, 10 December).
Publication of *The Works of Eugene O'Neill,* 4 vols. (Boni
and Liveright).

1926   Triumvirate produces *The Great God Brown* (Greenwich
Village Theatre, 23 January). Undergoes psychotherapy
in New York; with rare future lapses, stops drinking
permanently. Receives honorary Litt.D. from Yale, 13
June, the only honorary degree he will accept in his
lifetime. Summers with family at Loon Lodge, Belgrade
Lakes, Maine, where he meets and begins relationship
with actress Carlotta Monterey, who had played Mildred
in *The Hairy Ape* following its Broadway transfer from
the Provincetown Playhouse. The Macgowan, Jones,
O'Neill production group dissolves. Buys home,
Spithead, in Hamilton, Bermuda.

1927   Meets with Lawrence Langner, managing director of the
Theatre Guild in Bermuda. Guild accepts *Marco Millions*
and *Strange Interlude* for Broadway and produces all
subsequent EO'N plays staged there in his lifetime. Writes
screenplays for *The Hairy Ape* and *Desire Under the
Elms,* continuing periodic forays into screenwriting begun
as early as 1913. None of his own screenplays is ever
produced, although seven films are made from EO'N

plays during his lifetime, adapted, and in his judgment usually botched, by others.

1928   Theatre Guild produces *Marco Millions* (Guild Theatre, 9 January) and *Strange Interlude* (30 January). *Strange Interlude* is biggest success of career and brings EO'N his third Pulitzer Prize for drama. When published (Liveright), *SI* becomes first drama to reach best-seller lists. On 10 February, begins a three-year absence from the United States, traveling with Carlotta to England and France. Still married to Agnes, he seeks desperately to escape a scandal-hungry press until he and Carlotta marry the following year. Rents villa in Guéthary, near Biarritz, and tours Spain. Travels with Carlotta on tempestuous three-month journey (which includes temporary resumption of drinking) to the Far East, with Ceylon, Singapore, Saigon, Shanghai and Manila among ports of call. *Lazarus Laughed* is produced as huge spectacle by the Pasadena Playhouse, Pasadena, California (9 April), but is never produced on Broadway.

1929   Settles in France with Carlotta where they remain until 1931. In that period works on *Mourning Becomes Electra*. Agnes Boulton finally agrees to a divorce, granted on 1 July. EO'N marries Carlotta on 22 July. Theatre Guild produces *Dynamo* (Martin Beck Theatre, 11 February), which runs for only fifty performances. Enraged by expense and renewed notoriety resulting from a plagiarism suit against *Strange Interlude,* which is eventually rejected by the presiding judge as "wholly preposterous." Sound version of *Anna Christie* is released.

1930   Tours Italy, Spain and Morocco. Sees Moscow's Kamerny Theatre productions of *Desire Under the Elms* and *All God's Chillun Got Wings* in Paris.

1931   Returns with Carlotta to United States 17 May. Grants a number of interviews including a mass interview arranged

by the Theatre Guild in anticipation of the Broadway
opening of his trilogy *Mourning Becomes Electra* (Guild
Theatre, 26 October), which is a huge success. Lives on
Long Island, then Park Avenue. Builds house, christened
Casa Genotta as a symbol of couple's mutual devotion,
on Sea Island, Georgia.

1932   Moves to Casa Genotta. Coedits *American Spectator*
            magazine (with James Branch Cabell, Theodore Dreiser,
            and George Jean Nathan). Publication of *Nine Plays by
            Eugene O'Neill* (Liveright; rptd. Random House, 1936;
            Modern Library, 1941). Film version of *Strange Interlude*
            is released.

1933   *Ah, Wilderness!* (Guild Theatre, 2 October) surprises New
            York audiences as rare specimen—an O'Neill *comedy,*
            starring George M. Cohan—and becomes EO'N's second
            (next to *Strange Interlude*) biggest success. Elected to the
            American Academy of Arts and Letters. Diary notes and
            drafts of *Days Without End* reflect strong preoccupation
            with his lapsed Catholicism. Film version of *The Emperor
            Jones* is released.

1934–35   Theatre Guild opens *Days Without End* (Henry Miller
            Theatre, 8 January 1934) to largely unfavorable reviews.
            Though buoyed by a request from William Butler Yeats
            for permission to stage *Days* at the Abbey Theatre later in
            the year, EO'N is deeply distressed by responses to the
            play, particularly to the play's Catholic strains. On the
            brink of nervous exhaustion, he is advised by his doctor
            to take extended rest. *Days Without End* is his last
            Broadway play for twelve years. Publication of the
            Wilderness edition of *The Plays of Eugene O'Neill,* 12
            vols. (Scribner's). Conceives idea for what eventually
            develops into an eleven-play cycle, *A Tale of Possessors
            Self-Dispossessed,* detailing the stories of two American
            families from the early years of the Republic to the 1930s.

1936   Significant health problems mount. Decides to sell Casa
              Genotta and leaves for Seattle 30 October. Notified 12
              November that he has won the Nobel Prize for Literature.
              State of health and lifelong aversion to publicity dissuade
              him from going to Stockholm to collect the award.
              Hospitalized in Oakland, California, from late December
              to early March 1937 for serious complications from
              appendicitis.

1937–45   Builds and moves with Carlotta into Tao House, Danville,
              California, December 1937, which they occupy until
              1944, when ill health and wartime constraints force them
              to sell and move to San Francisco. Despite increasing
              physical affliction, including a frequently uncontrollable
              tremor that severely impedes writing, EO'N completes in
              the years at Tao House: drafts of the cycle; *The Iceman
              Cometh; Long Day's Journey Into Night; A Moon for the
              Misbegotten;* and *Hughie.* Only *Iceman* and *Moon* will be
              produced in his lifetime. (He forbids production of *Long
              Day's Journey* until twenty-five years following his death.)
              Of the cycle, drafts of which he destroys as early as 1943,
              only *A Touch of the Poet* and *More Stately Mansions*
              survive. *The Long Voyage Home* (film based on
              S.S.Glencairn plays) is released in 1940. In 1943 daughter
              Oona, now seventeen, marries screen star Charlie Chap-
              lin, a man just one year younger (54) than her father;
              EO'N cuts her off permanently. Film version of *The Hairy
              Ape* is released in 1944. Returns with Carlotta to New
              York in October 1945 in preparation for Guild's produc-
              tion of *The Iceman Cometh* the following year.

1946   In anticipation of *Iceman's* opening, EO'N grants his first
              real interviews in a decade, including a mass press
              interview arranged by the Theatre Guild. The much
              heralded *Iceman* premieres (Martin Beck Theatre, 9
              October) to mixed, if guardedly reverential, reviews which
              fail to grasp the play's complexity. The last EO'N play to
              be produced on Broadway in his lifetime, *Iceman* is

dwarfed by its inadequacies of casting and production, particularly in the key role of Hickey, and contributes to EO'N's continuing decline in critical reputation. Grandson Eugene O'Neill III, son of drug and alcohol-addicted Shane, dies in crib at one year of age.

1947   Produced by the Theatre Guild, *A Moon for the Misbegotten* (Hartman Theatre, Columbus, Ohio, 20 February) closes in its pre-Broadway tour. Guild's plans to recast for postponed Broadway opening are thwarted by EO'N who comes to "loathe" the play. Does allow it to be published shortly before his death but play's failure to open in New York heightens public perception that his artistic decline is permanent. Film version of *Mourning Becomes Electra* is released.

1948–52 EO'N and Carlotta buy home in Marblehead, Massachusetts, once again facing the sea, where they live from 1948 to 1951. Their always stormy relationship reaches new intensity, exacerbated by the serious health problems, physical and psychological, of both, resulting in EO'N's sporadic renewed drinking and alternating periods of separation and temporary reconciliation, reported in the press. Son Eugene, Jr., commits suicide, 25 September 1950, one of greatest blows of EO'N's life. Publication in 1951 of *The Plays of Eugene O'Neill*, 3 vols. (Random House, rpnt. of 1941 edition, with inclusion of *Iceman*). That year the pair moves to the Shelton Hotel, Boston, where he is isolated by Carlotta and ravages of illness. EO'N destroys scenarios and drafts of the cycle and other material to ensure that incomplete work will not be reshaped after his death.

1953   EO'N dies at the Shelton Hotel, Boston, 27 November. Buried at Forest Hill Cemetery, Boston, "in exact accordance with his wishes and instructions to the very end" (H. L. Kozol, his physician), and with only Carlotta, Kozol, and EO'N's nurse in attendance.

1956   Despite EO'N's edict that *Long Day's Journey into Night* be withheld for twenty-five years after his death, Carlotta gives permission for publication (Yale University Press) and for production by the Royal Dramatic Theatre of Stockholm (10 February). The production is greeted with excitement and the text becomes a best seller. *The Iceman Cometh* is given a landmark reinterpretation at the Circle in the Square Theatre in Greenwich Village, directed by José Quintero and starring Jason Robards as Hickey (8 May). Carlotta selects Quintero to direct *Long Day's Journey* on Broadway, where it opens (Helen Hayes Theatre, 7 November) with a remarkable cast (Fredric March, Florence Eldridge, Robards, and Bradford Dillman) as the four haunted Tyrones. The play wins a posthumous Pulitzer Prize, O'Neill's fourth.

Conversations with Eugene O'Neill

Behind the Scenes

Philip Mindil/1920

Reprinted from the *New York Tribune*, 22 February 1920, sec. 3, 1.

The son of that sturdy old veteran of the stage, James O'Neill, bears an uncommon resemblance to his father, despite the difference in physique and in temperament. He is just recovering from an attack of "flu" after a long siege with grippe, and the terrifying thought of talking about himself was almost too much. However, under a gentle but insistent incising of the probe the causes of the great effect, *Beyond the Horizon*, were located and finally revealed to view.

First and most important revelation is that young Eugene O'Neill—the playwright is thirty-one—is the father of a son of three months with the unmistakably Irish Christian name of Shane. The father has written one act of a new play and must hurry back to Provincetown as soon as he is fit to travel, lock himself up and write the rest of it.

Two more plays from his pen are about to be produced by George C. Tyler, the first in three weeks and the other soon after. The first is *Chris,* a drama, offering a character study of an old Swedish deep-sea sailor dating back to the old clipper ship days whom the playwright knew when he lived in a rough boarding house for seafaring men in Fulton Street, near West, some years ago. The title role will be played by Emmett Corrigan.

The second is *Straw,* described by the author as "a tragedy of human hope." It is a play of tuberculosis, and all the action takes place in a sanatorium. At the same time, he says, it is not sad or in any sense pathological.

"My whole idea," said Mr. O'Neill, "is to show the power of spiritual help, even when a case is hopeless. Human hope is the greatest power in life and the only thing that defeats death. I saw it at close quarters, for I was myself an inmate of a tuberculosis sanatorium and through hope and spiritual help beat it."

"Where did you get your sea atmosphere?"

"I shipped as an ordinary seaman when I was twenty-one on the

3

Charles Racine, a Norwegian bark, from Boston to Buenos Aires. I had been assistant manager of *The White Sister,* in which George Tyler was presenting Viola Allen. My father was in the company."

"John Williams told me last week he was so glad when he found you were not a laboratory made playwright and not a college man. Where did you learn how to write plays?"

"Well," and the ghost of a smile flitted across Mr. O'Neill's serious face, "I am a sort of a college man. I went to Princeton for a year, and, as for the laboratory, well—I studied for a year under George Pierce Baker at Harvard."

"Was it your idea to be a playwright or a writer of stories? What was your early ambition?"

"I didn't have any idea. My ambition, if you call it that, was to keep moving and do as many things as I could. I just drifted along till I was twenty-four and then I got a jolt and sat up and took notice. Retribution overtook me and I went down with t.b. It gave me time to think about myself and what I was doing—or rather, wasn't doing— and I got busy writing one-act plays."

"How long did you stay in Buenos Aires?"

"About two years. I just free lanced along. I had to do something to live, and I wanted to live. I did manual work for the Swift Packing people, drafting for the Westinghouse Electric Company and office work for the Singer Sewing Machine Company. I wasn't doing much choosing. I was grabbing whatever came along. I shipped as an ordinary seaman on a British tramp steamer for Durban, South Africa. I've forgotten the name of the ship. She was loaded with mules."

"Did you stay in South Africa at all?"

"No, you must have $100 before you can be admitted to South Africa.

"I went back to Buenos Aires," he continued, "and shipped on another tramp for New York, where I became an able seaman on the American line ships. When in New York I lived in a little waterfront dive and finally went to New Orleans to join my father, who was playing a condensed *Monte Cristo* in vaudeville. I played the juvenile very, very badly, but I had a good time and when we got back home I did a little newspaper work on the *New London Telegraph* six months.

"Then came the old t.b., and after I had beaten it I started to write one-act plays. The best seven are in my book, *The Moon of the Caribbees*. They were presented by the Provincetown Players, the Washington Square Players and the Greenwich Villagers. I played in some of them. I have been a member of the Provincetown Players ever since they were organized, four or five years ago. A lot of that time I was writing for the stage, but the stage never knew it.

"*Beyond the Horizon* is my first long play. I felt sure when I saw the woebegone faces of the audience on the opening day that it was a rank failure and no one was more surprised than was I when I saw the morning papers and came to the conclusion that the sad expressions on the playgoers' faces were caused by their feeling the tragedy I had written."

Playwright Finds His Inspiration
on Lonely Sand Dunes by the Sea
Olin Downes/1920

Reprinted from the *Boston Sunday Post*, 29 August 1920, 40.

New York's playwright find of the year lives obscurely in a clean little cottage, miles from nowhere on Cape Cod.

He doesn't care for money.

He laughs at fame.

The story of Eugene O'Neill, son of James O'Neill, the veteran actor, who died only the other day, is a tale such as Jack London might have written.

O'Neill virtually ran away from college. He has been an ordinary seaman, a prospector for gold, a newspaper man and an actor.

Olin Downes discovered him on the sand dunes the past week, visited his home and learned many things of the man whom critics proclaim a rising genius.

Two of us, tramping about Cape Cod the other day, came on a life-saving station. The man up in the tower, peering through the fog, said that in a storm you could see nothing for the whirling sand, that the captain of a wrecked barge, a strong swimmer, had nearly made land on a winter night, when a comber, fathoms high, broke over him, and snapped his neck like a twig.

This man, showing us his lights and gears, was humbly grateful even for a few minutes' conversation. He leaned over the rail of his cupola as long as he could see us down the stairs.

"Come again! Come again!"

He was so darned lonely, out there in the dunes, off Provincetown.

His only neighbor, so far as the eye could see, and farther, is Eugene O'Neill, son of James O'Neill, the recently deceased actor, and writer of plays which have made him famous. He lives about a quarter of a mile from the watch-tower, in a place which only those kin of the sea, and wary of the crowd, would inhabit.

He is there, in a house held together not only by bolts and bars, but by cables to keep the wind from tearing it apart, with his wife, formerly Agnes Boulton, also a writer, and his year-old son, who has the beautiful name—perhaps there is a queer Celtic spelling of it— which sounds like "Shane."

Eugene O'Neill reminded me in some ways of another Eugene: Eugene Marchbanks, and if you don't see what I mean, refresh your memory with *Candida*. Marchbanks, though, was almost feminine in his sensibilities and his physical tremors and fears. This O'Neill is fully a man's man, an adventurer born, reasonably close-cropped spare, fit-looking and very brown, loathing roiled shirts, and regretting the passage of the 18th amendment.

"Any wrecks hereabouts?" I called as we bore down on him in the fog.

"Not lately," he said, "or I might have a bottle with a label on it to offer you."

"We are newspaper men. Will you talk?" as two ships would hail each other passing in the west.

"I'll try anything once," he shouted. "Come on in and sit down."

We went into a rather Washington-Square-like study, with an open fireplace and practicable fire in it. We sat around while friend wife brewed tea. The wind hummed in the timbers, and I should not have been the least surprised if I had seen, sailing through the foggy sky, the body and the spars of the bark of the Flying Dutchman.

He told me about his beginnings as a dramatist, and the story had an odd twist to it. He went to school, and went to college—"tried to get as much fun and as little work out of it as possible," he remarked. But that wasn't the beginning. No! The real beginning was when Eugene O'Neill, his head ringing with Jack London and Josef Conrad, shipped, at Mystic wharf, Boston, as ordinary seaman before the mast, on a Norwegian brigantine, bound out of Buenos Ayres, 69 days in the going, out of sight of land, sailing the incomparable sea.

"You're musical," he said. "Well, let me ask you: did you ever hear chanties sung on the sea? You never did? It's not surprising. There are even fewer sailing vessels now than there were 10 short years ago when I pulled out for the open. They don't have to sing as they haul the ropes. They don't humor a privileged devil who has a fine voice and h-ll inside of him, as he chants that wonderful stuff and they pull to the rhythm of the song and the waves. Ah, but I wish you might hear that, and feel the roll of the ship, and I wish you might listen to an accordion going in the forecastle, through the soughing of winds and the wash of the sea."

He broke off for a moment and his eyes were "fey." And I felt homesick, not for the house and lot, but for the fuss and singing of shadowy waters.

"It happened quite naturally," he said—"that voyage—as a consequence of what was really inside of me—what I really wanted, I suppose. I struck up one day by the wharf in Boston with a bunch of sailors, mostly Norwegians and Swedes. I wanted to ship with somebody and they took me that afternoon to the captain. Signed up, and the next thing we were off. They were fine fellows. I've never forgotten them, nor, I hope, they me. Indeed, I look on a sailor man as my particular brother, and next to the passing of the 18th amendment, perhaps, you can put down my regret that the 'hang-out' of many of my old pals, Jimmy the Priest's, down by Fulton street, in New York has gone the way of many good things, nevermore to be seen."

He fell in later with a man who wanted him to go prospecting for gold in the Spanish Honduras. "Of course I went along," he said. "My friend had acquired more or less tangible prospects of gold along the course of a 21 mile river, which he bought from the government. A lot of land, you say? Oh, they give land away for nothing down there if you'll only agree to pay the taxes. Why not? With thousands of miles of it still unknown, marked on the map, 'inexplorada.'

"It's a fine country, and the people, like most of the people in the southern part of South America, a fine lot, whom I got along with first rate. True, there are insects. I never knew there could be such a variety of creeping, crawling, flying, stinging things—some of them rank poison—in the world. (Although I'll tell you, that contrary to what some people write, very few die of tarantula bite.)

"Great hunting and fishing, and now and then a jaguar up on the hillside yowling you to sleep.

"Gold? Oh, yes, we got a little. But what I got principally was the favorite fever of the locality. Laid me up for eight months. Wherefore

I quit the job. The other fellow was getting along fairly well, I heard, when his dam broke on him.

"Where he finished up I don't know. But I quit that job, right there. Had to. Up in Buenos Ayres again, I worked in several extremely inferior positions for the Singer Sewing Machine, the Swift packing people, and as draftsman for the Westinghouse Electric Company. That job was probably my most dignified and best. And then I hadn't any job at all, and was down on the beach—'down,' if not precisely 'out.'

"I sailed on a big tramp to South Africa, but just touched there, and we came back. My last sea trip was as able seaman—that means you can box the compass and do several other things which the ordinary seaman cannot, on a line which ran from South America to Cherbourg. An ugly, tedious job, and no place for a man who wanted to call his soul his own. I did not love it. This was a steamer, you know, and what we did mainly was to swab decks and shift baggage and mail. Those South American Germans—they used to send the folks home souvenirs and Christmas presents which included stuffed beasts, ore, anything in the world, provided, as it seemed to me, that it would break your back for you.

"At last I was back in the States. My father got me a job as an actor in his *Monte Cristo* troupe that was going along the Orpheum circuit in the West. In four days, on the train from New Orleans to a place in Utah, I memorized the part of Albert, son of Mercedes. I was scared stiff on the stage, and was a very poor actor. I'd never [have] been able to keep the job as long as I did if it had not been for my father. The audiences were great fun, though, and I suppose the experience of the stage was some help to me later on."

Then terror stalked him. He spent six months in a sanitarium as a "lunger." Oh, yes, all these things go into the making of art and artists.

"But caught it in time and headed it off," he said. "Then, I became a newspaper man, a reporter of the common or garden variety on the *New London Telegraph,* and also contributor to a column of poetry and general nonsense which we published on our editorial page. It was about then that I commenced to write plays, and produced five or six in as many months, not very good, but I sent them to Professor Baker at Harvard and got into his classes for a year.

"I don't think any real dramatic stuff is created," he went on, "to use an excellent expression of Professor Baker, 'out of the top of your head.' That is, the roots of a drama have to be in life, however fine and delicate or symbolic or fanciful the development. I am perhaps excusing myself for the way I loafed and fooled and got as much fun and as little work as I could out of my one year at Princeton, but I think that I felt there, instinctively, that we were not in touch with life or on the trail of the real things, and that was one consideration that drove me out. Or perhaps I was merely lazy. Who knows just what is going on inside of him? Anyhow, my real start as a dramatist was when I got out of an academy and among men, on the sea."

"Has reading affected your work very much?"

"Oh, yes, very much indeed, from the beginning. And with reading, as with my college studies, it was not until I had to shift, mentally as well as physically, for myself, that my awakenings came. Thus, in college, a work which made an indelible impression on me was Wilde's *Dorian Gray*. Meanwhile I was studying Shakespeare in classes, and this study made me afraid of him. I've only recently explored Shakespeare with profit and pleasure untold. In college, Wilde, London, Conrad were much nearer me than him. And so, later, was Ibsen."

"Ibsen, hey?"

"Are you surprised?"

"The populace think of Ibsen as very dreadful and deep. He's deep, all right, and sometimes dreadful, like life itself, but he's also intensely human and understandable. I needed no professor to tell me that Ibsen as dramatist knew whereof he spoke. I found him for myself outside college grounds and hours. If I had met him inside I might still be a stranger to Ibsen.

("Why can't our education," he suddenly asked, "respond logically to our needs? If it did we'd grab for these things and hold on to them at the right time; viz., when we've grown to them and know we need them.)

"Then there were the Russians. Certain novels of Dostoievsky and Tolstoi's *War and Peace* have become parts of my life."

For O'Neill, Provincetown is very much of home. The talk turned on the production of his plays. It was the Provincetown Players, one of those minor, uncommercial, sincere and artistic dramatic efforts which are popping up today in different places in America, and which are doing what none of the big theatres or theatrical concerns are doing for the development of a real dramatic art, who gave the first production of his *Thirst* soon after they had been established at Provincetown. The same players, succeeding beyond their own expectations, produced *Bound East for Cardiff* as their opening performance in New York in the autumn of 1916. The Washington Square Players, before they evolved the desire to emulate Broadway, opened in 1917 with *In the Zone,* the action of which passes in the forecastle of a tramp steamer in the submarine zone during the war. *The Moon of the Caribbees,* inspired by an evening on-ship off Trinidad, when the moon shone and the strange songs of the natives coming over the waters mingled with the sounds aboard, was given in 1918.

"As I've said," O'Neill remarked, "I have never written anything which did not come directly or indirectly from some event or impression of my own, but these things often develop very differently from what you expect. For example, I intended, at first, in *Beyond the Horizon*, to portray, in a series of disconnected scenes, the life of a dreamer who pursues his vision over the world, apparently without success, or a completed deed in his life. At the same time, it was my intention to show at last a real accretion from his wandering and dreaming, a thing intangible but real and precious beyond compare, which he had successfully made his own. But the technical difficulty of the task proved enormous, and I was led to a grimmer thing: the tragedy of the man who looks over the horizon, who longs with his whole soul to depart on the quest, but whom destiny confines to a place and a task that are not his."

I've read *Beyond the Horizon.* It is intensely and pitiably human, harsh, bleak in its realism, spiritual and infernal in the merciless logic of the final scene. It won, last year, the Pulitzer Prize, offered for the best American drama. One is naturally suspicious of prize dramas, but this one won its spurs at the hands of the merciless press of New York City, which welcomed the great, young talent into its own.

I think that Eugene O'Neill might have been the hero of that drama if he had stayed on in fatness and commonplace security; if he had not a kindred spirit in his wife; if they had not, even now, the project of traveling up the Amazon next year, providing mother could be induced to take care of the baby!

I never saw a man whose life, personality and work seemed more of a piece. I suppose I may see him some night, all dolled up in a theatre, bowing to applause, but I shall always remember him in his old duds, in the sea. Why is it, anyhow, that we read Irish plays of Yeats or Synge, marvelling at their sea-scapes, and the sense of nature, brooding and strange, which permeates every line of the story, and then leave it to a wandering poet to discover the same wonderful things "inexplorada"—in odd corners of places lying ready to hand, such as, for instance, Cape Cod?

There are men, you know—witness O'Neill—whose home is as regards in particular nowhere. For them, home is where it is most free. His adventures will never come to an end, not while he lives, nor, if he has his way, after he dies. On him is the stamp, the curse, if you like—of "the beauty of the far off and unknown . . . the secret which is hidden just over there, beyond the horizon"—and now I'm quoting from his play.

Making Plays with a Tragic End: An Intimate Interview with Eugene O'Neill, Who Tells Why He Does It

Malcolm Mollan/1922

Reprinted from the *Philadelphia Public Ledger Sunday Maga-zine*, 22 January 1922, 3.

Time was when interviewing Eugene G. O'Neill was part of my daily routine. I used to bawl out, "O'Neill!" and O'Neill would come to my desk and say, "Yes, sir."

"This is a lovely story about that Bradley street cutting!" I would say. "The smell of the rooms is made convincing; the amount of blood on the floor is precisely measured; you have drawn a nice picture of the squalor and stupidity and degradation of that household. But would you mind finding out the name of the gentleman who carved the lady and whether the lady is his wife or daughter or who? And phone the hospital for a hint as to whether she is dead or discharged or what. Then put the facts into a hundred and fifty words and send this literary batik to the picture framer's!"

I can see the abashed, puzzled look of the boy as he carried away his beautifully written sketch and pulled his hair about his eyes while he tried to do a conventional, phlegmatic news item in newspaper style.

Young as he was, O'Neill had been around much of the world and had witnessed many things. Facts, ordinary, obvious facts, standing by themselves, as such could not surprise him and so didn't interest him much. It was what they signified, what led to them and what they in turn led to, their proportionate values in the great canvas of life, that intrigued his rapt attention. What difference did it make whether this particular brother of the ox, who had graven the proof of his upbringing on a woman's body, was called Stan Pujak or Jo Wojnik? What difference whether the knife found a vital or missed it by a hair? What O'Neill saw in the affair was just one more exhibit in the case of Humanity vs. the State of Things, another dab of evidence of

13

the puzzling perversion of mankind, with its needless conflicts and distorted passions. He saw equally squalid bestiality usurping normal humanism in human beings. What he saw he wrote, that others might see. He had to.

I interviewed O'Neill again the other day. There is in this connection a side-light which unhappily cannot be quite fully appreciated by those outside the newspaper craft. There have been many better city editors than I was, but never one who more faithfully lived up to the tradition that such a creature must cut the hearts of his subordinates to ribbons with malignant criticism. Yet when I sought to interview O'Neill, who is far from an easy man to get at for that purpose, I was greeted like a long-lost uncle. If O'Neill had been in the very least the morose, pessimistic gloomster that some of the critics have been making him out, he would have received me with a demoniac shriek and booted me from the door of his Provincetown home far into the wintry sea—for old times' sake.

Instead of which he gripped my hand with a grip that his own slim fingers learned on shipboard. And presently he was saying things that he hadn't said to any interviewer before.

"Are you our foremost apostle of woe?" I asked him right off the bat. "Many say you are."

He grinned. Grin is the word. Anybody can smile. Any old musty hypo, any melancholiac, any self-centered poseur can organize some sort of smirk on occasion. Nobody can grin who hasn't red corpuscles and a throbbing heart inside him. O'Neill used to grin, often, at his trying to be a reporter. He grins yet, at funny things.

"Oh, I don't know," he drawled, "there's Volstead."

"But the critics demand that you shake yourself, come out of your grouch, take off the blue spectacles and put on pink ones, and write some plays just as powerful and just as true and just as compelling as *Emperor Jones* and *Anna Christie* and *The Straw,* only—well, happier, you know."

O'Neill's eyes are very big and very dark and he can do things with them. He made them look preternaturally solemn as he answered:

"Far be it from me to carp at the critics. Ingratitude is a base sin, and, taking them by and large, they have been more than fair to me."

I knew that look of old; so I merely remarked, "Huh!" and took another tack. "I came down here," said I, "principally to ask you one question—the thing everybody wants to know. Have you any present purpose, or expectation, of writing a play with an out-and-out happy ending? You'll grant, I suppose, that there are interesting situations in life, even dramatic situations, out of which genuine happiness sometimes issues?"

"Apropos of that," volunteered the dramatist, "nearly all the critics accused me of dragging in a happy ending in *Anna Christie*. Where they got the idea that the ending is happy I don't know, unless it be that there is a kiss and a mention of marriage in the last act.

"As a matter of fact, there is no ending at all to *Anna Christie,* either happy or unhappy. The final curtain falls just as a new play is beginning. At least that is what I meant by it. A naturalistic play is life. Life doesn't end. One experience is but the birth of another. And even death—"

O'Neill doesn't shrug his shoulders; he uses his eyebrows.

"Sure," he said, coming back to my question; "I'll write about happiness, if I ever happen to meet up with that luxury, and find it sufficiently dramatic and in harmony with any deep rhythm of life. But happiness is a word. What does it mean? Exaltation: an intensi-fied feeling of the significant worth of man's being and becoming? Well, if it means that—and not a mere smirking contentment with one's lot—I know there is more of it in one real tragedy than in all the happy-ending plays ever written.

"See here," demanded O'Neill, turning the tables for at least half a dozen of those old-time city editorial scowls, "it's a sheer present-day judgment to think of tragedy as unhappy! The Greeks and the Elizabethans knew better. They felt the tremendous lift to it. It roused them spiritually to a deeper understanding of life. Through it they found release from the petty considerations of everyday existence. They saw their lives ennobled by it."

O'Neill is no epigrammatist, but he pulled himself up and summarized. "A work of art is always happy; all else is unhappy," said he.

"One critic," he went on, "an eminent one, and justly so, has said tragedy is not native to our soil, has no reason for being as American drama. I take most strenuous exceptions to this claim. If it were true, it would be the most damning commentary on our spiritual barrenness. Perhaps it was true a decade ago, but America is now in the throes of a spiritual awakening. The signs are on all sides, for even the maddest joy rider to read.

"A soul is being born; and when a soul enters, tragedy enters with it. Suppose some day we should suddenly see with the clear eye of a soul the true valuation of all our triumphant brass band materialism; should see the cost—and the result in terms of eternal verities! What a colossal, ironic, 100 per cent American tragedy that would be—what?

"Tragedy not native to our soil? Why, we *are* tragedy—the most appalling yet written or unwritten!"

I came pretty near quitting at this. This one-time cub of mine was getting me into deeper water than I was prepared to swim in. But it's a long way to Provincetown from most anywhere, and there were certain other matters.

"What," I asked him, "shall I say for you to those persons who picture you as a sort of melancholic, shaking dice with himself after each piece of work to see whether he'll begin another one, to be built out of still thicker slabs of gloom, or take a long hop into the Atlantic by way of getting out of such a rotten world?"

"If there are any who picture me thusly—and I hate to believe it—then you can tell them I've guessed their secret," replied the dramatist gaily. "They are romanticists, and all is romance to their eyes, especially queer people like authors. I'll expect to hear next that I'm an inveterate home-brew hound, an opium smoker or a hashish eater. Authors, particularly the 'gloomy' ones, ought to go in for that sort of thing you know. However, I'll succumb to all the vices in their fairy tales if they'll go to see my plays. As for the dive into the Atlantic, may I do it often. I find it sometimes bitter cold, but never to a suicidal degree—quite the contrary; most invigorating."

"Now, I've asked you a couple of questions," said I, "as a sort of envoy of the public. Here's one on my own hook. Has there come to you, since your work received recognition, any new sense of warmth or cordiality toward life—toward the world—which you yourself suspect may be likely to temper your future writings? I mean, of course, in contrast with the depressing influence of years of unappreciated struggling."

The playwright thought this over for a moment. I didn't get a categorical answer—I wasn't his boss any more. But an answer I did get; a complete one, it seems to me.

"I love life," he said. "I always have. If, to the superficial, I have appeared not to, it is only because they cannot understand diffident folk who do not wear their hearts on their sleeves. But I don't love life because it is pretty. Prettiness is only clothes-deep. I am a truer lover than that. I love it naked. There is beauty to me even in its ugliness. In fact, I deny the ugliness entirely, for its vices are often nobler than its virtues, and nearly always closer to a revelation.

"I love human beings as individuals (as any kind of a crowd from a club to a nation they are detestable), but whether I like them or not, I can always understand and not judge them. I have tried to keep my work free from all moral attitudinizing. To me there are no good people or bad people, just people. The same with deeds. 'Good' and 'evil' are stupidities, as misleading and out-worn fetishes as Brutus Jones' silver bullet.

"But what ho! How I do go on! Let's call it a day's work and tea up a bit. No? What else? Oh, yes. Is the nature of my work likely to change? In form, yes—in content, again yes. Wait till you see *The Fountain,* a play quite unlike any I have written before.

"I intend to use whatever I can make my own, to write about anything under the sun in any manner that fits or can be invented to fit the subject. And I shall never be influenced by any consideration but one: Is it the truth as I know it—or better still, feel it? If so, shoot, and let the splinters fly where they may. If not, not.

"This sounds brave and bold—but it isn't. It simply means that I want to do what gives me pleasure and worth in my own eyes, and don't care to do what doesn't. I don't deserve any credit for this 'noble' stand because there is no temptation for me to compromise. My 'unhappy' plays have done very well, considering—quite well enough for a person to whom Rolls-Royce and similar titillations mean less than nothing, and who desires no greater extravagance than food, and lots of it. Which reminds me: Let's go and see when do we eat!"

Now you might interview Eugene O'Neill from this day to kingdom come and there are things about him, bearing on the peculiar quality of his dramatic composition, that you wouldn't and couldn't get out of him, because of an excessive personal modesty that prevents him from telling them even to himself. But out of an intimate acquaintance of many years, covering the entire period of his development as a writer, I can perhaps make it clearer than he himself can why O'Neill deals so largely with the dark side of life.

"I am a dramatist," said O'Neill to me; "that is the answer. What I see everywhere in life is drama—human beings in conflict with other human beings, with themselves, with fate. All else is a side issue. I just set down what I feel in terms of life and let the facts speak whatever language they may to my audience. It is just life that interests me as a thing in itself. The why and wherefore I haven't attempted to touch on yet."

Perfectly candid, perfectly true, but not quite sufficient. As a matter of fact, the man is as sensitive as a seismograph. There is no point of contact with human existence at which his fine-spun nature does not detect and suffer from the discords and maladjustments of human affairs. It is quite impossible for his mind to dwell on a group of happily placed characters, for example, without reaching further out and discovering that inevitable underlying submerged group that has contributed to the happy placement. If he were to think of a fine, self-sacrificing individual devoting himself to the alleviation of suffering, O'Neill's thoughts, instead of becoming absorbed in the nobility of this character, would leap straightway to the fundamental unnecessity of the suffering itself, and his admiration for the sacrificant would become lost in resentment against the blundering and ignorance and selfishness that begat the need of the sacrifice.

In other words, though he declares and sincerely believes that he "hasn't attempted to touch on the why and wherefore" of so much tragedy and misery in the world, O'Neill is really, before everything else, a crusader. His work is a continual outcry against poverty, ignorance, human degradation and the vices and miseries that grow out of them. Propounding no theories of reform, with native strategic genius he has sensed the need that first of all the more intellectual and consequently more powerful minority be pricked and stabbed and slashed into acute consciousness of the state of the majority.

O'Neill is slapping the world in the face with truth. It is his message that millions are living in neglect, in one aspect or another; that men and women have no right to be smugly content in their own happiness when most of humanity suffers and sorrows. He voices his protest with an abandon that recks little of what the world thinks of him if he can only command its attention to its own problems of civilization. His part is to strike society's sores and convince it of its illness. Then, when it is frightened into realization, let it go to the doctors to be cured.

When you understand this to be O'Neill's job in the world the futility of asking him to amend his work to conform to his auditor's pleasure is obvious. It is like asking that the alarm of fire be sounded on a dulcimer. Those critics who are in effect demanding just that have missed the keynote of the playwright's character.

"The life of the waterfront and the barges that O'Neill pictures in his play (*Anna Christie*) is of the lowest sort," says one. "The atmosphere that envelops his characters is gloomy and stifling. But the characters, though ignoble and repellent, live, and in living they exert a strange fascination. You get to know them as real human beings, not as puppets in a show. You feel for them, not because you sympathize with them, but for the reason that you are persuaded that they suffer. Yet when all is said and done not an edifying thought to repay your interest has emerged from the play."

In that paragraph is crystallized about all the furore over O'Neill's "morbidness." They simply want O'Neill without O'Neill. They want impact with bruising truth without the bruises. They want the thrill and suspense of rapier plays—with pudding bags on the swords' points.

There is no edification to be had from *Anna Christie* for the tremendously good reason that there is no edification to be had from contemplation of the phase of existence which it pictures—only transcendent drama. O'Neill would have had to write his play out of the head of some other man altogether—and swap his living characters for puppets indeed—if his purpose had been to send his audience home full of mental sugarplums.

The critics applaud the creator of impressive tragedies—and in the next breath complain because he doesn't equip his scripts with shock absorbers. As well ask the author of *Emperor Jones* to get up the next show for Al Jolson.

Eugene O'Neill's plays stand out from among those of all other American playwrights because of no trick of stagecraft, but because of their author's scorn of compromise with the truth. They are, though

O'Neill himself would never think of so describing them, magnificent propaganda for war against human degradation in every form—and their power comes from the bottom of their creator's aching heart. If O'Neill were ever to listen to the voice of expediency and undertake to write plays for the full approval of conventionalized critics, no doubt he would do them technically well. But the structure of his genius would come crashing to the ground, undermined by the destruction of its foundation purpose.

Years ago, when O'Neill began writing, he used to show me his stuff. Fatuously I used to rail at him just what the critics are preaching now. It had as much effect as, I am convinced, their appeals will have. He had to write what he saw then. He has to write what he sees now. We should be profoundly grateful that he can.

The Artist of the Theatre: A Colloquy between Eugene O'Neill and Oliver M. Sayler
Shadowland/1922

Reprinted from *Shadowland*, 49 (April 1922), 49, 66, 77; republished in *Theatre Arts*, 41 (June 1957), 23–24, 86.

Scene—*Peaked Hill Bar, Provincetown, Mass.*
Time—*Midsummer, 1921*

The Critic: I wonder whether you have ever faced the responsibility of the artist *in* the theatre, the responsibility of becoming, if possible, what Gordon Craig has defined as the artist *of* the theatre. Take a look at yourself. More than any of our playwrights, you are perfecting your mastery of the craft of the dramatic author. But what do you know of the other crafts of your profession? What are you doing to equip yourself to carry through to their full realization—on a stage before an audience—the dreams that you dream?

Craig, you know, insists that the artist *of* the theatre, when he comes, must be "capable of inventing and rehearsing a play: of writing any necessary music: capable of designing and superintending the construction of both scenery and costume; and of inventing such machinery as is needed and the lighting that is to be used."

Now, it seems to me that as a playwright, you are in a position very like that of the scenic designer. As those who follow the affairs of the theatre may recall, Robert Edmond Jones recently expressed his doubts on this point in these words: "What are the designers of scenery who have caught the spirit of the new theatre going to do? Must we quit for a while and sit back and wait for the producers to catch up with us?" And my answer was: "No. That's no solution. You yourselves will simply have to learn to produce." To produce, my dear O'Neill, in the broadest sense of the word—to devise the dramatic action and then with intelligence won through experience to direct, if not actually to carry out, all the interweaving processes by which that action comes to life in a theatre.

The Playwright: The superman of the theatre? Like Nietzsche's, a too-rigorous ideal for the finite potentiality of the present, working under infinite handicaps. The artist, until he grows many planes beyond and above his present power of concentration, will only achieve—at best—a harmonious mediocrity by the attempt to become protean creator. Jack-of-all-trades, he will lose his mastership of the one—like Gordon Craig himself. In a quaking, hectic age it is difficult enough for the artist to conserve his soul and hew to his own line.

The Critic: But what else are you achieving now except a rather superior mediocrity? I grant you may, with fortune, approximate your dream with the assistance of Arthur Hopkins as producer and Robert Jones as designer and Ben-Ami or John Barrymore as interpreting actor. But you will only approximate it. Just as Hopkins and Jones and the rest will approximate theirs. Each one of you will have to study more closely the craft of the others before you can fully achieve. Perhaps even then you will work together as you do now— in much the same relationship. But you will understand each other better, to the advantage of the unity of your art. And one of you—it doesn't matter much which—will have the guiding hand in each particular work of art you produce.

The Playwright: Speaking from a playwright's angle, though, I cannot imagine myself writing a play and at the same time seeing it— creating it—from the standpoint of the scenic artist, the director, etc. Yet if I were creative in all these crafts, I would be bedeviled by each and all at every moment of creation. The necessary compromises within myself at this point might result in an unprecedented unity in the production—i.e., the produced play—but I am sure the inner spiritual and psychological unity of the written play as a thing in itself would be destroyed. Would I not be tempted to write my play, partly at least, for an end outside itself—for *my* theatre instead of any theatre, the dream theatre, no theatre at all? After all, is not the written play a thing? Is not *Hamlet*, seen in the dream theatre of the imagination as one reads, a greater play than *Hamlet* interpreted even by a perfect production? The latter would lack the unity of the first. If Shakespeare could have played the part of Hamlet, he could never have written it. The "not to be" in the soliloquy would never have occurred to him.

The Critic: Don't you think you're roaming rather far afield? You're questioning the whole position of the theatre as an art inferior to literature. And that's wide of the point. Besides, I don't believe you really think it is inferior, or you wouldn't be working in it. Besides, too, why *shouldn't* you write for *your* theatre if it were a better theatre than any other?

The Playwright: Yes, I suppose I am shooting beside the mark. Your superman, of course, would be a perfect unity within himself of the artist *of* the theatre and have no trouble with himself. What I am driving at, though, is that you hold out an ideal many generations beyond the horizon of an age noted for its paradoxical japery in being short on concentration but long on specialization. Let your God first become man if he would save us. Shooting at stars is an amiable dreamer's pastime but here we must needs *prove* our marksmanship by some target—oh, way far off but still within range of our farsighted strongest.

The Critic: But isn't Craig's target within sight? Surely he has made it concrete and definite enough. Your artist *of* the theatre has simply to conceive of the theatre as a single, unified art, instead of a patchwork of several arts, and prepare himself to understand and control all its elements, no matter which he chooses to carry out with his own hands.

The Playwright: Let us peer at the gospel according to Nietzsche and we will find what I mean. What is the step to the Superman? The Higher Man. Yes, I can almost hear the birth cry of the Higher Man in the theatre. There is a goal, blessedly difficult of attainment. And what will he be? Well, remember I speak with a playwright's bias— not so much from egotism as from a desire to make my case clear by stating in terms I understand the best. Well, the Higher Man of the theatre will be a playwright, say. He will have his own theatre for his own plays, as Strindberg had his Intimate Theatre in Stockholm. He will have grouped around him as fellow workers in that theatre the most imaginative of all the artists in the different crafts. In no sense will he be their master, except his imagination of his work will be the director of their imaginations. He will tell them the inner meaning and spiritual significance of his play as revealed to him. He will explain the truth—the unity—underlying his conception. And then all will work together to express that unity. The playwright will not interfere except where he sees the harmony of his imaginative whole is threatened. Rather, he will learn from his associates, help them to set their imaginations free as they help to find in the actual theatre a medium ever-broadening in which even his seventh last solitude may hope to speak and be interpreted. And soon all of these would be Higher Men of the theatre.

The Critic: That all sounds very well. And it is more than I hoped you would admit when you began.

The Playwright: But first the Higher Playwright is needed, he with the seventh last solitude to express. Alas, he is of next year; and we others of today—or at best tomorrow—deserve no theatres of our own but get little worse than we deserve when we pry our way into the segregated district of Broadway.

The Critic: That kind of frank humility and unsentimental refusal to bewail your lot is quite in keeping with the ruthless way in which you strip to their souls the characters in your plays. And the courage to face truth, just like the fear of the Lord, is the beginning of wisdom. You admit that a certain unity in the art of the theatre is possible, which we do not possess today.

The Playwright: Yes, but with the centralized imagination right at the heart of the play itself.

The Critic: I'm afraid you don't fully grasp one of the fundamental facts of the new theatre. The strategically central position of the play, as we have known it in the past, is fast losing its grip. In the recent past, and even yet, except in the minds of certain theorists who have seldom put their ideas into practice, the written play is the starting point for any activity inside a theatre. But it was not always so, and I don't believe it will always continue so. There is on the one hand the possibility of a return to the fluid impromptu dramas of the *commedia dell'arte*. But more important in extending the range of the theatre as an art are the various groping efforts to find drama in mere movement without the use of words—bodily movement made abstract and significant in form rather than after the representative fashion of the old pantomime, and, even further afield, the movement of colored shapes and lights without the aid, not only of words, but of the human figure in any capacity. Manifestly, the men who develop these dramas will not be such as yourself—writers of words. But if they will take the pains to comprehend, if not fully to master your craft, they will achieve the more effectively. They must learn and forget the old theatre before they can attain the new. And ultimately you must master or at least comprehend what they are trying to do, for after they have had their day with their new toys, the elder traditions will reassert themselves, not with a full return to power, oblivious of what has happened in the meantime, but drawing new life therefrom and by an eclectic process achieving a more perfect and all-embracing unity of expression.

The Playwright: A return to the fluid, impromptu drama of the *commedia dell'arte?* On that day we might also just as well resume our old ancestral impromptu gesture of scratching for fleas. "Groping efforts to find drama in mere movement without the use of words"? Why do you use the word "groping"? Does the Russian Ballet grope? And hasn't it achieved just what you demand, while still retaining its integrity as the Dance, a separate and self-sufficient art? What excuse has the Drama for intruding its ungainliness here? And to go on to your human-figureless play of shapes and lights, that presupposes the existence of a new race for audience, or else an esoteric cult to whom such abstractions will not have to be translated. In calling such experiments toys, you used the right word—toys for the few; but the Drama is and always must be the art of the many. As such it may attain true grandeur; as anything else it is bastardized into piffle. Furthermore—

After all, we agree in the main point: The theatre of the present must be destroyed. Let us then first—oh sweet and lovely thought!— poison all the actors, then guillotine the managers, hang the playwrights—with one omission—feed the critics to the lions (except you, of course), and as a final act of purification, call upon a good God to send a second flood to wipe out the audience, root and branch. Being a just God, and a Great Producer, he will no doubt spare the two of us; and we can then rehearse this dialog on Mount Ararat as a first step toward the Theatre of the Future.

The Extraordinary Story of Eugene O'Neill

Mary B. Mullett/1922

Reprinted from *American Magazine*, 94 (November 1922), 34, 112, 114, 116, 118, 120.

Three years ago, Eugene O'Neill was practically unknown, except to a small group of people in New York. A few of his one-act plays had been produced by the Provincetown Players in a makeshift theatre down in the Greenwich Village part of the city; but to up-town Broadway, and to the great world outside, he was not even a name. Yet to-day he is the most talked-of playwright in America.

It is less than three years since *Beyond the Horizon*—which was the first of O'Neill's long plays to get a production—made the general public realize that here was a man who not only had something interesting to say but could say it in a new way. All New York began to talk about Eugene O'Neill.

Then, two years ago, the Provincetown Players put on *The Emperor Jones* in their little theatre made out of an old stable. It crowded the wooden benches; turned people away; was taken to an uptown theatre and became the sensation of the dramatic season. It was on tour last year and will be taken to London.

Twice O'Neill had scored and he had done it with plays which the average theatrical manager would have sworn the public would not accept.

Then came last season, with another brace of O'Neill plays: *Anna Christie* and *The Hairy Ape*. Grim pictures of grim life, a rough slap in the face to people accustomed to the conventions of society and the traditions of the theatre. Yet crowds of these people went to see both plays—and applauded enthusiastically when their faces were metaphorically slapped.

It wasn't the slap itself that got this reaction. It was the thing, the force itself, the meaning behind the blow. As O'Neill said to me:

"The audiences sat there and listened to ideas absolutely opposed to their ordinary habits of thought—and applauded these ideas."

"Why?" I asked.

"Because they had been appealed to through their emotions," he said, "and our emotions are a better guide than our thoughts. Our emotions are instinctive. They are the result not only of our individual experiences but of the experiences of the whole human race, back through all the ages. They are the deep undercurrent, whereas our thoughts are often only the small individual surface reactions. Truth usually goes deep. So it reaches you through your emotions."

The inference is that O'Neill thinks he gives us the truth in his plays. Certainly he tries to give us the truth as he sees it. He has courage and sincerity. But he does not use it to preach a hidebound creed. He does not tell us flatly what we "ought" to do. He shows us human beings, living in an environment that is absolutely strange to the average person: a negro, crazed by superstitious terror; a girl, drinking in a waterfront dive; a stoker, shoveling coal in the furnace-room of an ocean steamer—"queer" people with whom we might think we could have nothing in common.

O'Neill puts these "queer" people before us, and shows them groping their way through the very same spiritual problems we know to be our own. He wants to accomplish two things: He wants to give us a better understanding of ourselves and a better understanding of one another.

He gained his own understanding of human beings through his extraordinary experiences as a young man. He is only thirty-four years old now. But the experiences I refer to began when he was nineteen and continued through the next five or six years.

His father was James O'Neill, famous as an actor a generation ago, especially in the rôle of "Monte Cristo." The boy traveled around with his father and mother until he was seven years old. Then he was put into a convent school. Later he went to preparatory school and, at eighteen, entered Princeton. In all those years, he had almost no home life at all. The nearest approach to it was when, occasionally in the summer, the O'Neill family stayed at New London, Connecticut, where they had a house. But nine-tenths of the boy's time was spent in hotels and schools. Perhaps this helps to account for the things he did later.

As I said before, he entered Princeton at eighteen. He lasted there just one year. Some of his escapades were more than the college authorities could stand and he was suspended for a year. He might come back then, if he would promise to be good and to attend to his studies.

But nineteen-year-old Eugene O'Neill did not *want* to be "good." As for studies, the only one that interested him was the one known as "the proper study of mankind," which, of course, is man himself. He had no ambitions, not even any dreams, for his future. All he cared about was to live! And his idea of living was to have a wild time.

His father owned an interest in a small mail-order business; and this fact was what got the young man his first job. He was made secretary of the company. His chief duty was to handle the correspondence; but the stenographer knew more about it than he did, so she did most of the work.

After a year of this sort of thing, the business was more than willing to let him go—and for once he was more than willing to agree with his employers! A friend of his was going down to Honduras to prospect for gold; an enterprise which appealed to O'Neill's craving for adventure. So he went along.

Six months he stayed down there; six months of heat and tropic storms, of natives that wouldn't work and of insects that worked unceasingly. Then he got the fever and was sent home. He had found neither gold nor glamour. At that time, James O'Neill was playing with Viola Allen in *The White Sister.* He made his son assistant manager; and for six months Eugene traveled with the company. But he hated that sort of life far more than he had hated Honduras.

In spite of his lack of interest in his studies at college, he was even then a voracious reader; especially of books on philosophy and sociology. He used to haunt the bookshop of the anarchist Tucker. He read Nietzsche and Karl Marx, and Kropotkin—books which encouraged his own instinctive rebellion against conventional people and conventional ideas.

Also, he read books about the sea, especially Conrad's wonderful stories. They stirred his imagination as nothing else had. They promised real adventure, escape from people who seemed to him mere shadows cast by the rigid customs and ideas of society. That was what he wanted: to live his own life among men who were brutally themselves. So when his father's season closed, at Boston, Eugene O'Neill shipped aboard a Norwegian bark, and went to sea.

Let me describe the man as he is to-day. It will help you to

appreciate the strangeness of the life he led during his early twenties.
He is tall and dark and thin. Everything about him (except his hair
and eyes!) seems to be long and thin. I believe his hands, for
instance, are the longest and the most slender I ever have seen. They
are the type of hands that go with the dreamer temperament.

His eyes are very dark, very intense. His hair is dark; but, young as
he is, it is already showing a little gray at the temples. He is quiet and
slow of speech with strangers. When it comes to ordinary "small talk"
he is a good imitation of a sphinx. Even when he is interested, there
are long pauses, when, unless you know his ways, you think he isn't
going to say anything more. Then, unexpectedly, he begins again;
and he is likely to say something so interesting that you soon learn
not to break in on these pauses.

I went to see him recently at his summer home, though he
sometimes stays there as late as November. The house, until a few
years ago, was the Peaked Hill Bars Coast Guard station, on the
dunes a few miles from Provincetown, Massachusetts. From it, not
another house is to be seen. The only human habitations are the new
station, a quarter of a mile away, and a small shack. But these are
hidden by the hills of sand.

It is a desolation of sand and sea; but very beautiful—also very
remote! Few persons could plow through the soft sand to reach it,
fewer still *would* do so. An automobile would be "mired" in sand
within a few feet. Only a horse can make the trip.

From June until late in the autumn, O'Neill lives and works there.
The household consists of himself, his wife, their three-year-old son, a
housekeeper, and the child's nurse.

And here is an interesting fact: O'Neill has a *regular habit* of work.
The craving for freedom, for the indulgence of his own desires, which
controlled him in his early manhood, is subordinated now to the
good of his work. He, who used to be a rebel against a routine,
voluntarily follows a routine now, in this one direction. Like the rest of
us, he has found that he *must* follow a regular habit of work if he is to
accomplish anything.

Well, this is the man who, at twenty, shipped as a common sailor
on a voyage that lasted sixty-five days, all of the time out of sight of
land. The food was chiefly dried codfish, sea biscuit, sweet soup, and
"something they called coffee, and something they called tea."

His quarters below deck were in the forecastle—the "fo'c'sle"—

shared by all the seamen of the crew. Practically without ventilation, it reeked of tobacco smoke, wet clothing, and unkempt human beings.

The voyage ended at Buenos Aires; and here again the young man tried his hand at the sort of work which would appeal to most men of his breeding and education. One after another, he got jobs with the Westinghouse Company, the Swift Packing Company, and the Singer Sewing Machine Company. But in each case he either was fired, or else gave it up in disgust.

"The Singer people," he explained, "made about five hundred and seventy-five different types of sewing machines at that time, and I was supposed to learn every detail of every one of them. I got about as far as Number Ten, I guess, before they gave me up as hopeless.

"I had spent a good deal of my time down on the waterfront when I should have been studying bobbins and needles. Now I went there again, like a boy let out of school; and when my money was gone I shipped on a British vessel bound for Portuguese South Africa. I made the voyage over there and back, then shipped on another British vessel for New York.

"In New York, I lived at 'Jimmy the Priest's'; a waterfront dive, with a back room where you could sleep with your head on the table if you bought a schooner of beer. 'Jimmy the Priest's' place is the original of the saloon in *Anna Christie*. And an old sailor whom I knew there is the original of 'Chris,' the father in the play.

"Again I hung around the waterfront for a while. There, as at Buenos Aires, I picked up an occasional job aboard a vessel that was loading or unloading. The work was mostly cleaning ship; painting, washing the decks, and so on.

"After a few weeks, or months, I shipped on the American Liner 'New York,' as an able seaman. I made the voyage to Southampton; and as the 'New York' was disabled, I came back on the 'Philadelphia.' But there was about as much 'sea glamour' in working aboard a passenger steamship as there would have been in working in a summer hotel! I washed enough deck area to cover a good-sized town.

"It was on these two voyages that I got to know the stokers, although it did not really begin aboard ship. There is class distinction even among the groups that make up the crew of an ocean liner. But in this case, one group does not regard another as superior to it. Each has a healthy contempt for the others.

"I shouldn't have known the stokers if I hadn't happened to scrape an acquaintance with one of our own furnace-room gang at Jimmy the Priest's. His name was Driscoll, and he was a Liverpool Irishman. It seems that years ago some Irish families settled in Liverpool. Most of them followed the sea, and they were a hard lot. To sailors all over the world, a 'Liverpool Irishman' is the synonym for a tough customer. It was through Driscoll that I got to know other stokers. Driscoll himself came to a strange end. He committed suicide by jumping overboard in mid-ocean."

"Why?" I asked.

"That's it," said O'Neill thoughtfully. "That's what I asked *myself.* 'Why?' It was the *why* of Driscoll's suicide that gave me the germ of the idea for my play, *The Hairy Ape.*"

He went on to talk about this; and I will tell later some of the things he said about how he writes his plays and the meaning he puts into them. But first let us get through with his personal story.

Two voyages on an ocean liner sickened him of being an "able seaman" who wielded a mop as a chief implement of his seamanship, so he again hung around the New York waterfront for a few weeks. Then, one morning he woke up to find himself on board a train, with a ticket for New Orleans. He didn't recall having bought it.

By chance, father and son arrived there at about the same time. James O'Neill was then playing a tabloid version of *Monte Cristo* in vaudeville. Eugene saw the advertisement, went to call on his father, and the latter persuaded him to take one of the minor rôles in the play. He was with the company until the season ended—hated the whole thing, and, according to his own account, was a hopelessly bad actor. When the season was over he went to New London with his father and mother, and got a job there as a reporter on a local newspaper.

But now he found that you can't dance, without sooner or later having to pay the fiddler. For about five years he had been dancing to the tune of his desire for a wild life. He had taken what he wanted. Now the bill was presented for payment. His right lung "went bad," and the doctors, with solemn head-shaking pronounced their verdict: "Tuberculosis! You must go to a sanatorium."

He went, and for six months he had to lead a sane and simple and absolutely quiet existence. It was the first time, in his whole life, that he had taken time to think what he was going to make out of that life.

He had known only the wish to crowd it with sensations, experiences—the wish to "live." And in gratifying this wish he had almost lost life itself. Moreover, he was twenty-five years old. In the months of enforced bodily quiet, at the sanatorium, he began really to use his mind.

"Before that time," he said to me, "I had written some poetry. Everybody does that when he is young. And while I was on the New London paper, a man who ran a daily column used to let me write things for it. At the sanatorium I wrote some more poetry. I began to think about my future, too; and before I left there I had made up my mind that I would rather write than do anything else.

"I came out with my health very much improved. Still, I would have to be careful for a long time. So I went back to New London, to my family. When my father's season began and the house was closed, I stayed with some English people who had a place overlooking Long Island Sound. There was a porch facing the water; and I used to sit there and work almost every day. During that first year, I wrote eleven one-act plays and two long plays. Some of them have been produced and many of them have been published.

"I had known the theatre pretty intimately, because of my father's connection with it. But, with me, to know it had not been to love it! I had always been repelled by its artificiality, its slavish clinging to old traditions. Yet, when I began to write, it was for the theatre. And my knowledge of it helped me, because I knew what I wanted to avoid doing.

"However, I needed to study the technique of play-writing. So, after my year of working by myself, I spent a year in Professor Baker's famous class at Harvard. There, too, I learned some things that were useful to me—particularly what not to do. Not to take ten lines, for instance, to say something that can be said in one line."

"When did you begin to get your plays accepted?" I asked. "There seems to have been quite an interval between your writing of them and their production."

"There was!" he agreed, smiling. "But that wasn't my fault. I sent two of the plays to a well-known New York manager. After two years, having heard nothing from them, I wrote, asking for their return. They came back to me in the original package in which I had sent them. They hadn't even been read.

"Another time, I asked my father, who was a personal friend of George Tyler, to send two of my plays to him. I thought a little influence might at least get them read. Mr. Tyler's firm failed a year or two later, but it wasn't due to my plays. For when the affairs of the firm were settled up the 'scripts were returned to me; and again they were unread.

"Tyler told me afterward that when they came to him, with a letter from my father, he said to himself, 'Oh! So Jim O'Neill's son has been writing some plays. Well, they can't be any good, because plays by actor's sons *are* never good!' And he put them away in a drawer and didn't even look at them.

"The first recognition of any kind that I received was from *The Smart Set*. I sent three of my one-act plays to Mencken, the editor. They were all three 'fo'c'sle' plays, not at all the kind of thing *The Smart Set* prints. I wrote Mencken that I knew this, but that I merely wanted his opinion of them. I had a fine letter from him, saying that he liked them and was sending them to George Jean Nathan, the dramatic critic. I received a letter from Nathan also, and to my surprise the three plays were published in *The Smart Set!* That was my first ray of recognition.

"Then, one summer I came to Provincetown, and here I met the group that had organized under the name of the Provincetown Players. They had a little theatre in an old building on one of the wharves. It's rather a curious coincidence that my first production should have been on a wharf in a sea town. The piece itself was *Bound East for Cardiff.* The scene was laid on shipboard; and while it was being acted you could hear the waves washing in and out under the wharf."

It is only a trifle over fifteen years since harum-scarum Eugene O'Neill was sent away from Princeton. They have been fifteen of the most extraordinary years on which any man of thirty-four can look back. Some of the things he did seem inexplicable when one sees him now. Once, when he was talking about the men who were his friends along the waterfront and in the fo'c'sle, I said to him, "Why did you do it? Why did you want to be with men of that type?"

"I guess," he said in his slow way, "it was because I liked them better than I did men of my own kind. They were sincere, loyal, generous. You have heard people use the expression: 'He would give away his shirt.' I've known men who actually did give away their shirts. I've seen them give their own clothes to stowaways.

"I hated a life ruled by the conventions and traditions of society. Sailors' lives, too, were ruled by conventions and traditions; but they were of a sort I liked and that had a meaning which appealed to me.

"You might think, for instance, that I would have rebelled at the discipline aboard ship. But 'discipline' on a sailing vessel was not a thing that was imposed on the crew by superior authority. It was essentially voluntary. The motive behind it was loyalty to the ship! Among seamen, at that time, this love of the ship was what really controlled them.

"Suppose, just as an example, that one of the yards was loose, hanging by a thread, so to speak. Suppose a gale was blowing and the captain or the mate ordered two men to go aloft to secure this loose spar. This might be a dangerous proceeding. The men could refuse to do it. And they would be entirely within their rights, because if any complaint was made of them, or any punishment imposed, they could go before their consul at the next port and justify their refusal to obey.

"Now the motive of the captain, or of the mate, in giving the order, might be simply a wish to save a spar which, if lost, would add an item of expense to the owners of the vessel. But the men who risked injury, or even death, by carrying out the order, would be impelled solely by their love of the ship. They wouldn't care about saving the owners a few dollars, nor about saving the captain's face. They would go simply because of their feeling that they owed the service to the ship itself.

"This feeling, by the way, does not exist so strongly now. Labor leaders have organized the seamen and have got them to thinking more about what is due *them* than what is due *from* them to the vessel. The new type of sailor wants his contract, all down in black and white; such and such work, so many hours, for so many dollars.

"Probably some abuses have been corrected by this new order of things. But under it there has been lost the old spirit. It was more like the spirit of medieval guilds than anything that survives in this mechanistic age—the spirit of craftsmanship, of giving one's heart as well as one's hands to one's work, of doing it for the inner satisfaction of carrying out one's own ideals, not merely as obedience of orders. So far as I can see, the gain is overbalanced by the loss."

"That probably will surprise a good many people who know your plays about life at sea," I said. "They undoubtedly think you are trying to arouse pity for the sailor."

"Yes, I know," said O'Neill. "Take the fo'c'sle scenes in *The Hairy Ape*, for instance. People think I am giving an exact picture of the reality. They don't understand that the whole play is expressionistic.

"Yank is really yourself, and myself. He is *every* human being. But, apparently, very few people seem to get this. They have written, picking out one thing or another in the plays and saying 'how true' it is. But no one has said: 'I am Yank! Yank is my own self!'

"Yet that was what I meant him to be. His struggle to 'belong,' to find the thread that will make him a part of the fabric of Life—we are all struggling to do just that. One idea I had in writing the play was to show that the missing thread, literally 'the tie that binds,' is understanding of one another.

"In the scene where the bell rings for the stokers to go on duty, you remember that they all stand up, come to attention, then go out in a lockstep file. Some people think even that is an actual custom aboard ship! But it is only symbolic of the regimentation of men who are the slaves of machinery. In a larger sense, it applies to all of us, because we all are more or less the slaves of convention, or of discipline, or of a rigid formula of some sort.

"The whole play is expressionistic. The coal shoveling in the furnace-room, for instance. Stokers do not really shovel coal that way. But it is done in the play in order to contribute to the rhythm. For rhythm is a powerful factor in making anything expressive. People do not know how sensitive they are to rhythm. You can actually produce and control emotions by that means alone.

"In *Beyond the Horizon*, there are three acts of two scenes each. One scene is out of doors, showing the horizon, suggesting the man's desire and dream. The other is indoors, the horizon gone, suggesting what has come between him and his dream. In that way I tried to get rhythm, the alteration of longing and of loss.

"Probably very few people who saw the play knew that this was definitely planned to produce the effect. But I am sure they all

unconsciously *get* the effect. It is often easier to express an idea
through such means than through words or mere copies of real
actions. Sometimes I try to do it in the one way, sometimes in the
other. If I thought there was *only* one way," he said with a smile, "I
should be following the mechanistic creed, which is the very thing I
condemn."

"Just how do you get, and work out, an idea for a play?" I asked.

"Oh, the idea usually begins in a small way," he said, "I may have
it sort of hanging around in my mind for a long time before it grows
into anything definite enough to work on. The idea for *The Emperor
Jones* was in my mind for two years before I wrote the play. I never
try to force an idea. I think about it, off and on. If nothing seems to
come of it, I put it away and forget it. But apparently my subconscious mind keeps working on it, for, all of a sudden, some day, it
comes back to my conscious mind as a pretty well-formed scheme.

"When I finally get to work I write the whole play out in long hand.
Then I go over it, and rewrite it in long hand. Then I type it, making a
good many changes as I go along. After that, I like to put it away for
a few months, if possible; then take it out and go over it again. There
wasn't any difficulty in doing this until recently," he said with a laugh.
"When I began writing, I would have put my plays away for a few
years, without anyone knowing or caring. It is getting to be different
now."

"Is that one of the dangers of success?" I asked.

"I hardly think I am in much danger," he said. "A man's work is in
danger of deteriorating when he thinks he has found the *one best
formula* for doing it. If he thinks that, he is likely to feel that all he
needs is merely to go on repeating himself. I certainly haven't any
such delusion. And so long as a person is searching for better ways of
doing his work he is fairly safe."

It seems a strange transformation—this change from the Eugene
O'Neill, who used to hang around dives like Jimmy the Priest's, to
this man who is already placed in the front rank of American
dramatists. "The most significant playwright in America," as one
English critic called him. No one can do the kind of work he is doing
without having some sort of a fundamental scheme of life: a creed, a
philosophy—call it whatever you want to. I asked him once what it
was.

"Well," he said, "I suppose it is the idea I try to put into all of my plays. People talk of the 'tragedy' in them, and call it 'sordid,' 'depressing,' 'pessimistic'—the words usually applied to anything of a tragic nature. But tragedy, I think, has the meaning the Greeks gave it. To them it brought exaltation, an urge toward life and ever more life. It roused them to deeper spiritual understandings and released them from the petty greeds of everyday existence. When they saw a tragedy on the stage they felt their own hopeless hopes ennobled in art."

"Hopeless hopes?" I echoed.

"Yes," said O'Neill, "because any victory we *may* win is never the one we dreamed of winning. The point is that life in itself is nothing. It is the *dream* that keeps us fighting, willing—living! Achievement, in the narrow sense of possession, is a stale finale. The dreams that can be completely realized are not worth dreaming. The higher the dream, the more impossible it is to realize it fully. But you would not say, since this is true, that we should dream only of easily attained ideals. A man wills his own defeat when he pursues the unattainable. But his *struggle* is his success! He is an example of the spiritual significance which life attains when it aims high enough, when the individual fights all the hostile forces within and without himself to achieve a future of nobler values.

"Such a figure is necessarily tragic. But to me he is not depressing; he is exhilarating! He may be a failure in our materialstic sense. His treasures are in other kingdoms. Yet isn't he the most inspiring of all successes?

"If a person is to get the meaning of life he must 'learn to like' the facts about himself—ugly as they may seem to his sentimental vanity—before he can lay hold on the truth *behind* the facts; and that truth is never ugly!"

Eugene O'Neill, World-Famous Dramatist, and Family Live in Abandoned Coast Guard Station on Cape Cod

Charles A. Merrill/1923

Reprinted from the *Boston Sunday Globe*, 8 July 1923, Editorial and News Feature Section, 1, courtesy of The Boston Globe.

PROVINCETOWN, July 7—Eugene O'Neill is back on Cape Cod, polishing up a couple of new plays, shoveling away a fresh sand dune which a Cape Cod Winter piled up at the front door of his Summer home, way out on Peaked Hill Bar and dreaming a wonderful dream.

He is dreaming of that romantic, mystical island where once the O'Neills were kinds [*sic*] and where his actor-father, the late James O'Neill of *Monte Cristo* fame, was born.

When the first raw Autumn winds sweep across the Atlantic, whipping the rain and sand against the window panes of the abandoned Coast Guard Station, now the warm-weather abode of the O'Neills, the most gifted of American dramatists plans to turn the key in the side door, pack his family and luggage in an old-fashioned buggy (for Peaked Hill Bar is inaccessible to flivvers) and drive off across the desolate sand dunes toward Provincetown on the first leg of a long pilgrimage—a pilgrimage to Ireland, the land of his ancestors.

While Mr. O'Neill is over there, he will probably have the privilege of seeing one of his own plays performed on the stage of that made-over undertaker's shop in Dublin, the Abbey Theatre, famous as the home of the Irish Players.

Eugene O'Neill's creative genius has won world recognition abroad as well as in America. In the Fall, London, Paris, Berlin and Stockholm will pay tribute to the art of this young American, in his 30s, who only a few years ago was roughing it over the world, sailing the seven seas as an ordinary seaman, sorting hides in Buenos Aires, tending cattle en route to South Africa, sharing the rough adventures of the under-dog and learning by painful experience what it means to travel about without a nickel in one's jeans.

The latest O'Neill drama, *Anna Christie,* is now being played in London, and *The Hairy Ape* will go there in the Fall. At the same time Kathe Deutsch, "Germany's Sarah Bernhardt," will be playing a leading role in *The Hairy Ape* at Berlin. Paris will see the French version of *The Emperor Jones* at the Odion, the Government-endowed theatre, in September, and about the same time *The Emperor Jones* and *The Hairy Ape* will be billed in Stockholm.

But it is doubtful if all these European productions will mean as much to Eugene O'Neill as the experience of having Lennox Robinson produce his Yankee play *Diff'rent,* conceived and written in Provincetown, on the boards of the little Abbey Theatre in Dublin. *Diff'rent* is a Cape Cod play.

Mr. O'Neill chuckles when he thinks about it.

"You know," he said, "everybody in it is a hard-bitten New Englander. Think of putting that piece on in Ireland."

Eugene O'Neill is proud of his Irish ancestry. No wonder. His daddy, who thrilled thousands of American theatre audiences, hailed from Kilkenny.

The second American in this branch of the O'Neill family wants to cross the sea to bask in the atmosphere of the Gaelic Renaissance, to sit at the fireside of "A.E.," the Irish philosopher, and to taste the flavor of the literary revival which went back for its inspiration to Ireland's cultural beginnings and produced such interpreters as Yeats and Synge, Lady Gregory and James Joyce. Indirectly, Eugene O'Neill drank from the same fountain.

"I'm all Irish," he said in his interview for the *Globe.* "I have always wanted to go to Ireland. My father, of course, knew the old Irish legends and folklore. I started to study Gaelic, but it was too difficult, and I had to give it up.

"You will understand why I want to go to Ireland if I tell you that I first saw the possibilities for dramatic realism when I witnessed a performance of the Irish Players in New York.

"My early experience with the theatre through my father really made me revolt against it. As a boy I saw so much of the old, ranting, artificial, romantic stage stuff that I always had a sort of contempt for the theatre.

"It was seeing the Irish Players for the first time that gave me a glimpse of my opportunity. The first year that they came over here I went to see everything they did. I thought then and I still think that they demonstrated the possibilities of naturalistic acting better than any other company.

"In my opinion the Moscow Art Players could not hold a candle to the original Abbey Theatre Company, which toured America."

If you have any further doubts about Eugene O'Neill's flair for Ireland and things Irish, they are dissipated when you learn the names he has bestowed upon the newer members of his household.

His handsome little 3-year-old son is named Sean [sic] Rudriaghe, and there is a 3-months-old Irish wolfhound, who so far has achieved a length of something over six feet, called Finn.

The O'Neills have a housekeeper, a Filipino cook and a maid to look after their material wants, but they lead a simple, informal life in their picturesque home on the sand-dunes.

When a detachment from the Globe came plodding up from the beach, the dramatist, clad only in a pair of swimming trunks and a skin tanned almost as dark as that of the leading character in The Emperor Jones, was exercising his back muscles shoveling sand.

Mrs. O'Neill, an attractive, smiling little woman, served tea in the living room, where the Peaked Hill Coast Guard crew, now installed in a fine, new Government home a few hundred yards up the beach, used to keep its life boat. By a former marriage, Mr. O'Neill has another son, Eugene, Jr., 13 years old, who comes every Summer to be with his daddy here, but Eugene, Jr., hasn't arrived yet on his annual visit.

The present Mrs. O'Neill was born in London. The O'Neills met in New York and were married in Provincetown. There are two writers in the family. Mrs. O'Neill writes under her maiden name, Agnes Boulton, and is now at work on a novel, her first venture beyond the depths of the short story.

The long, cool living room of the O'Neill bungalow is an oasis in a scorching desert. To reach it, unless you are equipped with a horse and carriage, you have to plod ankle deep in sand from Province-town. After passing through a thin grove of pines the path to Peaked Hill Bar is a carriage trail winding up and down hills of glistening sand and across the parched and dreary desert, which stretches away as smooth as a ballroom floor to the place where it drifts against the skyline.

The old life-saving station inhabited by the O'Neills is sheltered by a sand dune and faces the sea, toward the northwest. All day long the ocean churns up soap suds for little Sean on the beach, right in his own front yard, and at night the measured roar of the breakers sings the O'Neills to sleep.

The bungalow is plainly furnished. There are comfortable wicker chairs and cool blue vases filled with wild roses on the mantle over the fireplace, but no paintings adorn the wooden walls of the living room. None are needed, for Nature is perpetually painting with her own gorgeous colors outside. On every fair night she fills the Western sky with them, as the sun sinks below the floor of the ocean and throws a dazzling sheen across the sea straight at the O'Neill dwelling.

After the head of the household had pulled on flannel trousers and a sweater, he came out and chatted of his contemplated journey to Ireland and of other things, including his past—dark, somber years, when he saw the seamy side of life.

A childhood of travel with his actor-father; a brief year at Princeton ended by request of the college authorities; a trial as secretary of a mail order house in New York; a quest for fortune as a gold prospector in the Spanish Honduras which was terminated by malaria; hoboing back to the States; a short inglorious career as an actor on the Pacific Coast with his father in a boiled-down version of *Monte Cristo*; a year as manager of a theatrical company which closed in Boston and gave the young adventurer a chance to ship from the Mystic docks for Buenos Aires; two lean, hard years in South America; a voyage to South Africa as a cattle tender; numerous voyages as a sailor; then repatriation, a reporter's job on a New London paper, a chance to think in a sanatorium in Wallingford, Conn., and the beginning of an amazing career as a writer of dramatic fiction in Prof. Baker's "Workshop 47" at Harvard.

There you have a synopsis of Eugene O'Neill's life story.

There are probably rough characters in the odd and sundry corners of the world who, if they could look in on the slow, deliberate, easy-going man with the black mustache and black hair, fringed gray around the ears, now living at Peaked Hill Bar, would recognize the mannerisms of an old crony. Mr. O'Neill says he got his hankering for the sea and a roving life from the yarns of Joseph Conrad and Jack London.

"When I was 24 years old," said the dramatist, "I had no idea what I was going to do. Now, that I look back on it, I realize that I couldn't have done better for myself if I had deliberately charted out my life.

"It was when I joined the staff of the *New London Telegraph* that I found I wanted to write for a living. My health finally broke down, and I had to go to a sanatorium. I was there for six months. It gave me the chance to mull over the experiences I had had in life. Ideas began to formulate in my head, and I wrote some one-act plays.

"Clayton Hamilton, the critic, came up one day, and looked over some of my stuff. He advised me to go to Harvard and take Prof. Baker's course. So I did.

"My first plays went into the manager's pigeon holes, and a few found their way out later. The first one produced was a one-act sea play, *Bound East For Cardiff.* I had written it before I entered Prof. Baker's course.

"It was first produced by the Provincetown Players on the old wharf in Provincetown, where this branch of the little theatre movement had its origin. Later the Provincetown Players opened their theatre in New York, and seven years ago I played a part there in *Bound East for Cardiff.* It was the late Jack Reed who first brought me to Provincetown.

"No, I never expected to make a lot of money from play writing. I had little hope that my plays would go at all. I wrote them because I wanted to write them. Of course, all the time I felt the urge to do what I could to have them accepted. I felt sure there would be enough people who would like them to make money for the managers, for the actors and for myself. But money was never the major motive. I got just as much satisfaction writing plays when I didn't have a nickel in my pocket as I do today.

"I think my experience ought to be encouraging to those who are trying to write something besides commercial plays. As a matter of fact, there are a great many persons who are trying to write for money, people who have no other motive, and very few who are getting money. There are fewer writers who are following their own creative instincts, and their chances of making money are much better for that very reason.

"In my case I found the public more courageous than the managers. The public is always about 10 years ahead of the managers, very likely because the latter have to put up about $20,000 to take a chance on something new. In my case, the greatest pleasure is the satisfaction of being able to do the thing I want to do in life. I don't think there is any special virtue in the playwright who prefers realism to sentimentalism. He is doing what he can do best. The so-called commercial playwrights who are making money are making it, no doubt, because they are doing very well the work they want to do."

Anyway, Eugene O'Neill has proved that there is a wider market for the kind of plays he writes than for the so-called bedroom farces. The latter find a barrier erected on the American Coast. Few of them cross the ocean.

Mr. O'Neill has had many rough experiences in many lands, but one of the weirdest happened down here on Cape Cod, when he was poor and no such distinguished figure in Provincetown as he is today.

"It was just before we entered the war," said the dramatist. "I was the victim of war hysteria. I had come here in November with Harold DePolo, the short story writer. We used to walk over these sand dunes, and I guess we carried notepaper and jotted down impressions.

"Somebody over at the wireless station watched us, and decided we were German spies. We were having dinner in a hotel in town one evening, when some Secret Service men pounced on us at the point of a revolver and carried us to the lockup in the basement of the town hall.

"The technical charge upon which we were arrested was vagrancy, but the Secret Service men were sure they had nabbed a couple of German spies. We were held incommunicado for 24 hours. They wouldn't even let us see a lawyer."

Eugene O'Neill has a regular routine now. He works every morning from about 9 until 1 p.m. and sometimes longer. It has become a habit, he says, and is no longer difficult.

He is finishing a play called *Welded,* a study of love and marriage. He describes it as an attempted interpretation of realism and naturalism. Another new play, *The Fountain,* is finished and will probably be produced in the Fall.

O'Neill Defends His Play of Negro

Louis Kantor/1924

Reprinted from the *New York Times*, 11 May 1924, sec. 9, 5.
Copyright © 1924 by The New York Times Company. Reprinted
by permission.

Once more is Eugene O'Neill the centre of a dramatic storm. This
time it is about a play not yet produced—*All God's Chillun Got
Wings*—which deals with the marriage of a white woman to a
negro. This is not the first time O'Neill has stirred up a tempest. His
Emperor Jones and his *Hairy Ape* brought about long and heated
debate.

What sort of person is this playwright who, like Shaw, has this
extraordinary faculty for provoking controversy? What is his conception of the theatre? The answers to these questions I sought
recently from him at his home in Ridgefield, Conn.

O'Neill is popularly regarded as America's poet laureate of gloom,
and the belief is held that he is a sick man (in the romantic Robert
Louis Stevenson tradition); a hermit, an advocate of revolution, a
misanthrope, a pessimist—a man, in fine, probably unable to smile.

Well, it's all nonsense. He's not sick nor a conscious advocate of
anything. He's just interested in the progress of "humanity toward
Humanity." (The distinction is in the sizes of the "h.") Spiritually, of
course, he's a hermit, as is any man of spirit; but he loves life with a
Dionysian madness. Any one who has seen him drive his frail white
and red kyak (a canoe especially built for him after the Eskimo
original) out to sea, singing exultingly, while coast guards trembled
for his safety; literally climbing over tall green waves; darting, lithe
and slender hipped, down a golden stretch of strand fronting his
home in Provincetown, Mass. ("The House Where the Wind Blows"
four-year-old Shane O'Neill, calls it), knows that Eugene O'Neill loves
life and is constantly affirming it.

He likes and is interested in people, and people like him; his
friends—bootleggers, bums, literary persons, society folk, prize
fighters, even actors—love "Gene." But he just isn't a social being.

44

He prefers quiet, needs it for his work. He works intensively, eight or ten hours a day, for months at a stretch—and when he is free of the pencil and typewriter no hobo could criticize him for breaking the rules of laziness. O'Neill doesn't pretend to be a business man, but he likes to earn money and feels that his work is as important to the community as turning out Fords. He likes to dance, and doesn't so badly. He smiles at least once a day, and I have even seen him eat candy.

The key to O'Neill is found in his belief that the theatre should be used for the presentation of the struggle for existence—man's elations, conquests, sorrows, defeats, joys, doubts—and that his job as dramatist is to express his vision of that struggle, without compromise to any prejudice, using all the means at his disposal in the theatre.

This conception is made clear in his discussion of the new play. Hardly had it been announced for presentation at the Provincetown Playhouse—an experimental theatre—when the storm broke. These were the objections set down against it: that in it O'Neill advocates, or at least encourages, inter-marriage; that in casting Paul Robeson, a negro actor, for the part of Jim Harris so that Ella, his white wife, has to kiss his hand, O'Neill has not considered the deep-rooted prejudice the public has against such a situation; that he is encouraging negroes to aspire above their station in life.

"I don't admit," O'Neill said, "that there is a genuine prejudice against my play. Judging by the criticism it is easy to see that the attacks are almost entirely based on ignorance of *God's Chillun.* I admit that there is prejudice against the intermarriage of whites and blacks, but what has that to do with my play? I don't advocate intermarriage in it. I am never the advocate of anything in any play— except humanity toward Humanity."

It was pointed out to Mr. O'Neill that the objections to *God's Chillun,* ignorant or not, indicated it was felt that some things might not be done in the theatre; that the dramatist had at least to consider, if not accept, the community's social code, that if the community didn't like the notion of a black man and a white woman married on the stage the dramatist should not present such a play.

His reply was that he didn't think the whole discussion would have arisen had he chosen a white actor for the part of Jim Harris; in any event, the dramatist was governed by his vision, and not the community's social code; and what the objectors seemed to forget was that the play wasn't being offered for public consumption, but to a special public, subscribers of the Provincetown Theatre, not one of whom had objected either to the play or to the casting of a negro.

"The prejudice," he thought, "is primarily economic and social. It is the fresh result of the same resentment which a Paris audience would have against a play in which a German and a Frenchwoman were married; or the resentment in many parts of the world against intermarriage of Jews and Gentiles. Then consider the resentment against intermarriage in our own Far West between Chinese or Japanese and whites; or in India the anger aroused by the marriage of a Britisher to a Hindu."

"But, don't you think there is a difference? Isn't the white race superior to the black?"

"Spiritually," he replied—"spiritually speaking, there is no superiority between races, any race. We're just a little ahead mentally as a race, though not as individuals.

"But," Mr. O'Neill continued, "I've no desire to play the exhorter in any racial no-man's land. I am a dramatist. To me every human being is a special case, with his or her own special set of values. True, often those values are just a variant of values shared in common by a great group of people. But it is the manner in which those values have acted on the individual and his reactions to them which make of him a special case.

"The persons who have attacked my play have given the impression that I make Jim Harris a symbolical representative of his race and Ella of the white race—that by uniting them I urge intermarriage. Now Jim and Ella are special cases and represent no one but themselves.

"Of course, the struggle between them is primarily the result of the difference in their racial heritage. It is their characters, the gap between them and their struggle to bridge it which interests me as a dramatist, nothing else. I didn't create the gap, this cleavage—it exists. And members of both races do struggle to bridge it with love. Whether they should or not isn't in my play."

Mr. O'Neill went on to speak of how bored he had become with

praise for things he had not done or said and of being attacked for
things he did not believe.

"Why," he demanded, "was I made an apostle of revolution by the
I. W. W. and proper timber for the Republican Party by conservatives
as a mocker of the I. W. W. when my Hairy Ape was produced?

"What bearing had such comment on my function as dramatist?
The only point involved in that play was did I or didn't I realize the
stoker 'Yank'—make this inarticulate human being and his world
articulate; did I convey, make visual, his struggle to affirm himself, to
'belong,' to make his 'I' mean something?"

And that, he insisted, was the only test for God's Chillun; for any
play, in fact. The artist, he said, expresses his vision. Criticism tries to
judge whether it is inspired or uninspired.

Breakfast finished, Mr. O'Neill proposed a walk on his estate, acres
of fields, woods, streams, a small lake, one rooster (private property
of Shane O'Neill), two dogs, an Irish terrier named Mat Burke after
the swaggering hero of Anna Christie, and Finn, a huge wolfhound.

"I chose Robeson," he said, "because I thought he could play Jim
Harris better than any one else. And what's been said about having a
white actor for the part is beside the point. I don't believe it follows
that a white actor could play the part of Jim any better than Mr.
Robeson just because he is a white actor, any more than a black actor
couldn't do Othello just because he isn't white.

"Isn't it a commonplace to say that the artist must be a breaker
down of barriers? Isn't Mary Garden's offer to sit next to Charles
Gilpin, the negro actor, who appeared in my Emperor Jones, because
he was a fellow-artist, the only acceptable attitude? In England no
one protested when Mr. Robeson played the King to Mrs. Patrick
Campbell's Queen in the play Voodoo. She is white.

"What is the theatre for if not to show man's struggle, whether he is
black, green, orange or white, to conquer life; his effort to give it
meaning? Doesn't that struggle, that endless effort to conquer life,
show that man loves life." It may conquer him, but it never beats
him, else he would have stopped struggling 10,000 years ago."

And the function of the dramatist as O'Neill sees it is to use all the
facilities of the theatre to make his poetry visual.

"The dramatist does not present life, but interprets it within the limitations of his vision," he said. "Else he's no better than a camera, plus a dictograph. The dramatist works just as Beethoven did, employing every sound in existence, molding tones, giving them color, new meaning, thus creating music. Well, when a dramatist interprets the world, and thus creates his own world, he uses the human soul, all life if you like, as a keyboard. He is the creator of this world and like all creators absolute boss. If he isn't a sound creative architect his structure crumbles."

"You don't believe in naturalism then, do you?"

"Naturalism is too easy," said O'Neill. "It would, for instance, be a perfect cinch to go on writing Anna Christies all my life. I could always be sure of the rent then."

"Was it very successful?" I asked.

"Well, it ran for more than a season in New York, a year on the road and for more than a hundred performances in London. It is enormously successful as a moving picture. It goes all over in stock. But I don't choose to write naturalistic Anna Christies all my life. I consider it the least worthy of my plays with one possible exception—though, I think the last act, which was so criticized as conventional, was the most courageous and original act of the play. However, the point I wish to make is that I'm not writing any more Anna Christies because the purely naturalistic play doesn't interest me any more, never did interest me much."

"Why?"

"Because you can say practically nothing at all of our lives since 1914 through that form. The naturalistic play is really less natural than a romantic or an expressionistic play. That is, shoving a lot of human beings on a stage and letting them say the identical things in a theatre they would say in a drawing room or a saloon does not necessarily make for naturalness. It's what those men and women do not say that usually is most interesting.

"Then I don't think it is the aim of the dramatist to be 'true to life,' but to be true to himself, to his vision, which may be of life treated as a fairy tale, or as a dream. Conceive of life as a huge mass of clay and the dramatist scooping up some of it, creating certain forms with his imagination and art, and then calling in his fellows and saying to them, 'Here you are as godlike beings.'

"It is rather difficult to do that through the naturalistic form. The principal reason why my *Welded* was misunderstood by some was that I erred when I conceived the dialogue against a naturalistic setting. My notion was to have a man and woman, lovers and married, enact their spiritual struggle to possess one the other. I wanted to give the impression of the world shut out, just of two human beings struggling to break through an inner darkness.

"But the sets which I described in my stage directions were so 'natural' that they inevitably conjured up all the unimportant paraphernalia of living, daily existence, to stand between the life of my characters and the lives in the audience."

Eugene O'Neill—The Inner Man
Carol Bird/1924

Reprinted from *Theatre Magazine*, 39 (June 1924), 9, 60.

Interviewing Eugene O'Neill is like extracting testimony from a reluctant witness. In fact, to use the word "interview" in connection with him is to employ almost a misnomer. Certainly it is an inapplicable designation. An interview presupposes a colloquy. A flow of words between two persons. Nothing more erroneous could be circulated about the creator of *Anna Christie, The Hairy Ape* and *Beyond the Horizon* than that he ever was verbose for publication. For that matter, I doubt that he has ever before given out an interview. He shuns publicity as did Mme. Duse and Maude Adams, and follows the habit they established of keeping out of the limelight as much as possible.

Certainly Broadway never sees Eugene O'Neill. He has a place called Brook Farm, at Ridgefield, Connecticut, and most of his time is spent there. On rare occasions, during a rehearsal period of one of his plays, he may be seen around the Provincetown Playhouse in Greenwich Village. But the glittering uptown theatrical district would never call him a mixer.

And yet that simile about "a reluctant witness" is not exactly apt. Reluctance is disinclination. Unwillingness to yield. Eugene O'Neill's uncommunicativeness is not due to any stubborn impulse. He is simply by nature extremely taciturn. Taciturn. Laconic. Reserved. Shy. Four serviceable words to use to describe him. One or two others must be employed. Compassionate, for instance. And it was that magic word—compassion—which opened to me the gates to the inner O'Neill. That hidden self which he does not find easy to reveal.

It was in the little dusty office of the Provincetown Playhouse that I attempted to draw out Eugene O'Neill and get his opinions. These opinions to be broadcasted to the readers of THEATRE MAGAZINE. At this tiny Village theatre, or experimental laboratory, Mr. O'Neill's much-discussed *All God's Chillun Got Wings* was in rehearsal. His dramatic arrangement of Coleridge's *Rime of the Ancient Mariner* was being prepared for its opening night.

Mr. O'Neill, who has been called America's greatest living playwright, entered the musty little room cluttered with papers, and sat down on the edge of a chair. He is a slender, lean-faced man of medium build, with only one outstanding feature—his eyes. They are somber, with a tender melancholy in their dark depths. In repose, with his eyes downcast, his face is ordinary. But, touch a responsive chord, and his countenance is illumined by a slow, rare smile. His eyes soften and glow. A most astounding transformation is wrought in the man.

Now I am almost tempted to delete this entire descriptive paragraph. Upon consideration, I fear that the subject of this interview will be impatient with this prodigal use of words. I am beginning to develop a word complex. I acknowledge their superfluity. It is a feeling carried over from the interview. I have a desire to be concise. Pithy. Direct. O'Neill's impatience with inconsequential words and circumlocution has engulfed me.

Eugene O'Neill fixes me with his somber eyes. I ask him about *All God's Chillun Got Wings,* his play which has brought about such a storm of protest, because it has been misunderstood and believed to be a play dealing with miscegenation. He silently hands me a typewritten statement which was issued sometime ago when the storm first broke. Does he not wish to add something to this? Give it a more timely twist? No. Nothing. The paper crackles loudly in the quiet room. Pregnant silence. More questions. More laconic responses. Waves of silence surge over us.

Silence. Silence. More questions, probings, attempts to secure opinions, statements, anything but monosyllables. Futility! Suddenly, I am overcome with a sense of the ridiculous. Here are two people whose very careers oppose this sort of conduct. A playwright who deals in words. A writer who juggles them daily. Sitting across from each other in silence, apparently overcome with shyness. I long to burst out: "This is funny. What are we afraid of? Why don't we talk easily, naturally?"

I decide to stop dallying. My approach must be direct—must convey to this man that I understand something of his ideals. For, in all the silence, Eugene O'Neill has revealed much. I feel that he is

profoundly compassionate, an idealist, a lover of humanity; but that
he is impatient with superficialities; feels contempt for social veneer.
Perhaps I have gathered something of this from his plays. But sitting
with him in silence has told me much. This surely is genius.
Magnetism. To say little and yet convey to another much of one's
personality. It marks a man as one out of the ordinary. Gives him a
distinct aura.

"You write to arouse the compassion of mankind. You are deeply
interested in humanity."

Eugene O'Neill's look is piercing. His eyes smile and soften. The
illumined look. The sign that the responsive chord has been touched.
After that the way is easy. Though do not imagine that he ever
indulges in prolixity. It is apparent always that Eugene O'Neill will
never be accused of pleonasm. Wordiness is alien to his nature. What
he has to say he says succinctly.

"Yes, I care only for humanity. I wish to arouse compassion. For
the unfortunate. The suffering. The oppressed."

More attempts to draw him out on the subject of inspired writing.
Writing with a purpose. He disclaims any such motives.

"I do not write with a premeditated purpose. I write of life as I see
it. As it exists for many of us. If people leave the theatre after one of
my plays with a feeling of compassion for those less fortunate than
they I am satisfied. I have not written in vain."

But Mr. O'Neill's remarks are even less redundant than they appear
thus quoted. He answers in a word or two. The interviewer must
supply the trimmings—those additional words which round out a
thought. Eugene O'Neill shies from wordiness as from the plague. I
rather imagine that a loquacious person would cause him to writhe.
Or put him to sleep. Or, more likely, sink him into a slough of
indifference. For Eugene O'Neill is indifferent to life's superfluities.
Periphrasis bores him unutterably.

Reminded that he has been charged with writing of only the
sordid, seamy side of life, of poor and sinful wretches, and the futility
of their lives, he insists:

"It is life as I see it. As it exists. People whose ways of living are
bright and easy are dramatized frequently and continuously. Why not
give the public a chance to see how the other fellow lives? Give it an
insight into the under dog's existence, a momentary glimpse of his

burdens, his sufferings, his handicaps? It affords an opportunity for that more fortunate strata of society to see the sort of life which their brothers far down the social scale must face each day. If they are inspired to help those unhappy brothers, the writing and producing of a so-called tragic play is worth while.

"People who have suffered do not need these reminders. They already feel divine compassion. But there are those who have not been touched by misery. These may well suffer, by proxy, for a few hours in a theatre. It will do them good. It will have a humanizing effect. Thus to taste vicariously a bit of life's bitterness.

"As for this type of play having a depressing effect, or accentuating the futility of human endeavor, I do not agree with any such opinion. We should feel exalted to think that there is something—some vital, unquenchable flame in man which makes him triumph over his miseries—over life itself. Dying, he is still victorious. The realization of this should exalt, not depress."

Silence. Stabbed by another direct question:

"Why do you confine your writings to pitiable Anna Christies, blasphemous seamen and the like?"

"Because I find more dramatic material among simple people such as these. They are more direct. In action and utterance. Thus more dramatic. Their lives and sufferings and personalities lend themselves more readily to dramatization. They have not been steeped in the evasions and superficialities which come with social life and inter-course. Their real selves are exposed. They are crude but honest. They are not handicapped by inhibitions. In many ways they are inarticulate. They cannot write of their own problems. So they must often suffer in silence. I like to interpret for them. Dramatize them and thus bring their hardships into the light. Give others a chance to see and help and understand.

"If I write often of seamen, it is because I know and like them so well. I was once one of them. Life on the sea is ideal. The ship for a home. Sailors for friends. The sea for surroundings. Meals provided. A resting-place. No economic pressure. On land, if a sailor goes broke, he will always find a hospitable seamen's home. Tired of one ship he can sign up on another. I like the man of the sea. He is free of social hypocrisy."

Again the conversation swerved to *All God's Chillun Got Wings*.

"It is not a race-problem play," said Mr. O'Neill. "Those who have criticized it have not attempted to understand it. They have lost track of the real issue involved in befuddling irrelevancies. The play's intention is to portray the special lives of individual beings. It is primarily a study of the two principal characters and their tragic struggle for happiness. The real tragedy of *All God's Chillun* is that the woman could not see their "togetherness"—the Oneness of Mankind. She was hemmed in by inhibitions. Ella of the play loved her husband, but could not love him as a woman would a man, though she wanted to, because of her background and her inherited racial prejudice.

"The gabbling sensation-mongers and notoriety hounds have seized upon one incident of the play and distorted it. The hand-kissing scene.The only act of contact between husband and wife. When Ella kisses her husband's hand, it is not a passionate avowal of love, but takes place after she has lost her mind. In her mental confusion, she thinks of him as a little child, much as we are inclined to think of negroes as Uncle Toms or as amusing little children. It is then that she kisses his hand.

"The sensation-mongers clutched at the chance this play afforded to arouse prejudice. But the Negro question, which, it must be remembered, is not an issue of the play, isn't the only one which can arouse prejudice. We are divided by prejudices. Prejudices racial, social, religious. Tracing it, it all goes back, of course, to economic causes. As for *All God's Chillun,* if Harris of the play had been a Japanese and Ella white, and the play had been produced on the Coast, there would have been as great a storm of protest. Or if Harris had been a German, and the play produced in France. Or an Armenian in Turkey. Or a Jew and a Gentile. And these prejudices will exist until we understand the Oneness of Mankind. Life is hard and bitter enough without, in addition, burdening ourselves with prejudices."

At this point rehearsal was announced, and hearing again the drums of silence, I felt that the interruption was not without its advantages. But I left the small Village theatre where Eugene O'Neill is free to try out all the dramatic experiments he chooses with a distinct feeling of having had communion with an unusual man, a distinct personality, a genius, if you will. Eugene O'Neill may be taciturn in speech, but he makes himself heard through his gift of dramatizing human beings, and by projecting his thoughts to those who can hear in the silences.

Back to the Source of Plays

Charles P. Sweeney/1924

Reprinted from the *New York World*, 9 November 1924, 5M.

John D. Rockefeller and Eugene O'Neill have been supposed to be the most difficult American characters to interview. You can't get to Rockefeller, and O'Neill, they say, won't talk.

So much for the credit for having managed to be the audience of one to whom the shyest man in show business directed thirty minutes' conversation about his plays, his point of view on numerous problems of the theatre and himself, following a rehearsal of his newest piece, *Desire Under the Elms,* in the Greenwich Village Theatre Thursday night.

Do you know, you who saw *Anna Christie,* who inspired that superb drama of New York's waterfront? It was Chris Christopherson, 'Gene O'Neill's roommate, on the top floor of a vile gin-mill near Fulton Street and the North River.

"His name was Chris Christopherson," said O'Neill, "and he had been an old deep-water sailor. He was, at the time I knew him, a barge Captain. His end in real life was just one of many of the tragedies that punctuate the history of 'Jimmy the Priest's,' which was the actual name by which my gin-mill rooming house was known.

"Everybody got very drunk at Jimmy's one Christmas Eve, and Chris was very much in the party. He left me about 2 in the morning to go back to the barge. When we roomed together he had no job at all, in which respect we were in the same fix. In trying to make the barge he fell from a plank, and next morning he was found frozen in a great cake of ice between the piles and the dock."

O'Neill was not a guest of Jimmy the Priest from choice or for color.

"Hell, no," said he, "I was flat. The room rent at Jimmy's was $3 a month."

That was during the time this man, today thirty-six years old and acknowledged the foremost of the younger American dramatists, was living the sailor's life so vividly portrayed in *S. S. Glencairn,* the cycle

56

of one-act plays now being presented at the Provincetown Theatre and hailed unanimously as good for a year when it moves uptown into larger quarters.

For the play born of his life in "Jimmy the Priest's," O'Neill was awarded the Pulitzer Prize. And it was the second time this prize had been awarded a play from his pen. It went first for *Beyond the Horizon.*

"I had never heard of the Pulitzer Prize," O'Neill said last night, "until I received a telegram from my wife congratulating me upon winning it. I thought it must be a medal or something and I was very pleased when I learned a thousand dollars went with it, for, believe me, I needed the money."

"O'Neill studied playwriting at Harvard, studied it for a year. But *Bound East for Cardiff,* one of the ones now at the Provincetown and one which many O'Neill followers consider among his best, was written before he ever thought of going to Harvard. That was back in 1914 and shortly after he gave up the sea. At Harvard he wrote a number of plays—and tore them up.

The author of *Emperor Jones, The Hairy Ape, Diff'rent, Gold, All God's Chillun Got Wings,* etc. etc., works hard and pretty much all the time. He has no program, no system, just plugs with a confidence that is rare with folks who have seen so much of agony and despair.

"When I get an idea I put it down," he said, "or I may work on it until I can't see how it will turn out. Then I put it aside and work on something else. Later I may get an idea that picks me up where I left off and I take up the thing and finish it.

"The idea for *Emperor Jones* came from an old circus man I knew. I knew all the circus people. This man, who later was a sparring partner for Jess Willard, had been traveling with a tent show through the West Indies. He told me a story current in Hayti concerning the late President Sam. This was to the effect that Sam had said they'd never get him with a lead bullet; that he would get himself first with a silver one. My friend, by the way, gave me a coin with Sam's features on it, and I still keep it as a pocket piece. This notion about the silver bullet struck me, and I made a note of the story. About six months later I got the idea of the words, but I couldn't see how it could be done on the stage, and I passed it up again. A year elapsed. One day I was reading of the religious feasts in the Congo and the uses to which the drum is put there; how it starts at a normal pulse-beat and is slowly intensified until the heart-beat of every one present corresponds to the frenzied beat of the drum. There was an idea and an experiment. How would this sort of thing work on an audience in a theatre? The effect of the tropical forest on the human imagination was honestly come by. It was the result of my own experience while prospecting for gold in Spanish Honduras. In the first presentation of *The Emperor* with Gilpin in the role, the drum was not handled as skillfully as it might have been, and I think the effect I hoped to get was lost. But in the revival with Paul Robeson playing the Emperor it really worked in accordance with my original scheme."

With *Desire Under the Elms,* which has its premiere at the Greenwich Village Tuesday night, O'Neill will occupy two New York stages, and a new play, finished recently at Provincetown, where O'Neill works, may give him a triple representation during the current season. The name or theme of the new play O'Neill would not reveal. There is another, to be called *The Great God Brown,* upon which he is now working, and he wouldn't talk about that either. Neither would he discuss *Desire Under the Elms* because, he said, to do so might spoil the play for those who go to see it. There's a surprise in it, he did more than broadly intimate. He came right out and said so.

O'Neill wrote a short story once. It was called "To-morrow," and concerned a man, broken and without any reason to hope, who always believed the next day would mark a comeback.

"The man of whom that story was written lived with me at 'Jimmy the Priest's.' He was a graduate of Edinburgh University, and until the beginning of his social decline was a highly valued correspondent of one of the greatest European news agencies. He covered the South African War, for instance. There came an appalling tragedy in his life. The booze got him and he had reached the depths, which, in New York at that time, meant 'Jimmy the Priest's.' One couldn't go any lower. Gorky's Night's Lodging was an ice cream parlor in comparison. But always my friend—at least always when he had had several jolts of liquor—saw a turn in the road to-morrow. He was going to get himself together and get back to work. Well, he did get a job and got fired. Then he realized that this to-morrow never would come. He solved everything by jumping to his death from the bedroom at Jimmy's."

Eugene O'Neill's devotion to the Provincetown Playhouse, the ramshackle projecting room in MacDougal Street, where virtually every one of his plays first saw the floodlights, is an index to a conviction he has about the theatre in America.

"The hope of developing a real spirituality, a real understanding and co-operation between all concerned in the production of plays in this country lies in the development of a repertoire theatre where actors may be assured of experience and permanency," he said. "If actors are to work for a play in the same spirit that animated the Moscow Art Players, where the same player will give the biggest or the least part the same amount of study and enthusiasm, they must be retained throughout the year; they must feel that they are a part of the whole group. The Provincetown group was organized with that idea in mind. The American theatre today finds itself in a blind alley. Everything is set to go on but the actor. He wants to go on but the system blocks the way. He cannot get the experience he needs and wants because there is no place to get it. The whole thing goes back to the landlord system, which virtually rules out plays which could pay a small profit to all concerned, but which, because of the extortionate rents and guarantees demanded by the real estate theatre sharks, it's virtual suicide to offer for production."

Eugene O'Neill Talks of His Own and the Plays of Others

New York Herald Tribune/1924

Reprinted from the *New York Herald Tribune*, 16 November 1924, sec. 7–8, 14.

In these days when the drama is traveling hither and thither by leaps and bounds Eugene O'Neill seems almost an oldtimer. His name and works are thoroughly familiar to the public. Most of them are available now in book form and several have been acted in Europe. The public now indurated to anything and everything new in the theater, accepts his writings with equanimity. Yet how short a time ago it was that he startled to breathlessness. How much he has accomplished in bringing about receptivity, that most healthful sign of a nation's growth!

Certainly the nation owes him a great debt: for being among the authors who jostled the world into recognizing American dramaturgy; for seriously upholding his idea of right and independence and blazing the trail for others; for loosening the stifling tentacles of Puritanism, which still hold on too viciously.

Incidentally, it is worth mentioning here that he was the first American playwright to indicate the worth of authentic blasphemy as a realistic medium. In plays like *Diff'rent* and *The Hairy Ape* the oaths had the force of hell fire. Unfortunately, however, the force of this medium in *What Price Glory* is now being denied the public through the confusion affected by charlatan managers who hoist the unclean on the public and then whine about art for art's sake, or who deliberately attract censorship in order to fill the box office.

As a fitting place to talk of matters having to do with his work, Mr. O'Neill chose the Greenwich Village Theater, where his play, *Desire Under the Elms,* will run, along with the *S.S. Glencairn* at the Provincetown Theater. Such opinions as he presented are here offered in almost the same order as that which they occurred. His speech is somewhat frugal, but intensified; his manner quiet but of piercing directness. The subject of the one-act play seemed a good matter for discussion because Mr. O'Neill's beginnings in the theater came through this brief form of play. It was surprising, therefore, to find that it holds little attraction for him now.

"I am no longer interested in the one-act play," he said. "It is an unsatisfactory form—cannot go far enough. The one-act play, however, is a fine vehicle for something poetical, for something spiritual in feeling that cannot be carried through a long play. In the case of my cycle at the Provincetown Theater the individual plays are complete in themselves, yet the identity of the crew goes through the series and welds the four one-acts into a long play. I do not claim any originality though for this idea, as Schnitzler has already done the same thing in *Anatol*. And doubtless others.

"Many of the characters in my plays were suggested to me by people in real life, especially the sea characters. In special pleading I do not believe. Gorki's *A Night's Lodging*, the great proletarian revolutionary play, is really more wonderful propaganda for the submerged than any other play ever written, simply because it contains no propaganda, but simply shows humanity as it is—truth in terms of human life. As soon as an author slips propaganda into a play every one feels it and the play becomes simply an argument.

"*The Hairy Ape* was propaganda in the sense that it was a symbol of man, who has lost his old harmony with nature, the harmony which he used to have as an animal and has not yet acquired in a spiritual way. Thus, not being able to find it on earth, nor in heaven, he's in the middle, trying to make peace, taking the 'woist punches from bot' of 'em. This idea was expressed in Yank's speech. The public saw just the stoker, not the symbol, and the symbol makes the play either important or just another play. Yank can't go forward, and so he tries to go back. This is what his shaking hands with the gorilla meant. But he can't go back to 'belonging' either. The gorilla kills him. The subject here is the same ancient one that always was and always will be the one subject for drama and that is man and his struggle with his own fate. The struggle used to be with the gods, but is now with himself, his own past, his attempt 'to belong.'"

Mr. O'Neill next made an interesting observation concerning the modern tendency to give more attention to character than to plot.

"The most perfect plotless plays are those of Chekhov. But the newest thing now in playwriting is the opposite of the character play.

It is the expressionistic play. For expressionism denies the value of characterization. As I understand it, expressionism tries to minimize everything on the stage that stands between the author and the audience. It strives to get the author talking directly to the audience. Their theory, as far as I can make it out, is that the character gets in the way. Thus, the audience gets interested in the kind of man he is and what he does instead of the idea. But plenty of people will probably damn me for saying this, because every one has a different idea of expressionism and mine is just what I have acquired through reading about it.

"I personally do not believe that an idea can be readily put over to an audience except through characters. When it sees 'A Man' and 'A Woman'—just abstractions, it loses the human contact by which it identifies itself with the protagonist of the play. An example of this sort of expressionism is *Morn To Midnight,* with character abstractions like 'A Bank Clerk.' This is the point at which I disagree with the theory. I do not believe that the character gets between the author's ideas and the audience. The real contribution of the expressionist has been in the dynamic qualities of his plays. They express something in modern life better than did the old plays. I have something of this method in *The Hairy Ape.* But the character Yank remains a man and every one recognizes him as such.

"I believe that *What Price Glory* is one of the most significant events in the history of our theater. It is a splendid thing that the first fine, true war play should come from the most reactionary country in the world. It is still more wonderful and encouraging to all who love the theater that there should be such a great public for it, because even two years ago it would have been possible only at special matinees or for invited audiences."

Mr. O'Neill's theater habits are highly personalized.

"I hardly ever go to the theater," he states, "although I read all the plays I can get. I don't go to the theater because I can always do a better production in my mind than the one on the stage. I have a better time and I am not bothered by the audience. No one sneezes during the scenes that interest me. Nor do I ever go to see one of my own plays—have seen only three of them since they started coming out. My real reason for this is that I was practically brought up in the theater—in the wings—and I know all the technique of acting. I know everything that every one is doing from the electrician to the stage hands. So I see the machinery going round all the time unless the play is wonderfully acted and produced. Then, too, in my own plays all the time I watch them I am acting all the parts and living them so intensely that by the time the performance is over I am exhausted—as if I had gone through a clothes wringer."

Mr. O'Neill looked up plaintively as if he were even now too tired of talking about his work, and there was nothing left to do but release him.

O'Neill Lifts Curtain on His Early Days

Louis Kalonyme [Louis Kantor]/1924

Reprinted from the *New York Times*, 21 December 1924, sec. 4, 7. Copyright © 1924 by The New York Times Company. Reprinted by permission.

Eugene O'Neill's gallery of lost souls—all the simple, inarticulate hairy apes, dazed and robbed of their muscular conceits by the bewildering realization that they do not "belong" in the society whose very existence is dependent upon their brawn—is, in a multiple sense, autobiographical.

O'Neill's Olsons, Ivans, Yanks, Cockneys, Dutchies and "toffs" like "Smitty the Duke," the Anna Christies, Mat Burkes, Chris Christophersons—all the outcast brethren of "dat ole davil sea"—had their living counterparts. It was with the originals of his dramatic gallery that O'Neill, in his early twenties, bunked and battled.

He bunked with them in the vile forecastles of tramp steamers and cattleboats. He enjoyed with them the sweltering safety of "hotel-liners" and the exhilaration of bucking seas under sail. He roomed with them in dingy boarding houses of sailor towns. He slept with them on the park benches of Buenos Aires. He pulled ropes, sang chanties with them and shared their primitive shore pleasures.

This experience of O'Neill's was begun at a propitious moment. The square-rigger, tall and graceful, was almost a legend—chased into Davy Jones's locker by steam. The old sailors, children of arctic wind and tropical sun, who had worked shattered craft through typhoon and hurricane and who knew all climes and hated all but their own—they, too, were dying out. Their place was being taken by engineers, unskilled laborers "not sailors enough to know the main from the mizzen on a windjammer," and choking, soot-begrimed stokers.

O'Neill's sea plays sprang from this background. His very first plays, in fact, were born of his new experience. Four of these short plays celebrated the adventures of the polyglot forecastle crew of the British tramp steamer, the Glencairn. The Glencairn plays were

64

produced individually about seven years ago at the Provincetown Theatre. O'Neill then was virtually unknown. Since then success has come, and now the Glencairn plays have been revived—for the first time together as O'Neill planned—on the stage of the same Provincetown Theatre.

It was about the originals of the Glencairn characters, also of *The Hairy Ape* and *Anna Christie,* and of his own life among them, that O'Neill talked a few days ago, just before he sailed for Bermuda—his first sea trip, by the way, since he quit being an "able-bodied seaman" on the American Line ships.

O'Neill was 21 when he shipped as an ordinary seaman on a Norwegian bark bound for Buenos Aires. He was bored with life on land, and had just read Conrad's *The Nigger of the Narcissus.* His most recent activity had been to tour the country with his father, the late James O'Neill, famous as the creator of *Monte Cristo.* He wrote a little—poetry. The bark arrived at Buenos Aires after a voyage of sixty-five stormy days. One poem was written during the voyage. All this in the year 1909.

In Buenos Aires O'Neill had his first taste of life ashore. Buenos Aires had a sailor town famous the world over. There was no form of pleasant vice unobtainable in its dives and cafés. O'Neill saw sailors stripped of their pay a half hour after they had left their vessels, fleeced by card sharps or "spanking gals." He saw them polish bottles clean of liquor, saw them stick each other with knives, saw them lying dead in the alleys. Then, his own funds exhausted, he got work with the Singer Sewing Machine Company's branch. But in the evening he usually went to the "Sailor's Opera" for amusement.

The "Sailor's Opera" was a large café to which all seamen automatically went. There the seaman yarned of adventures in strange seas, boasted of his exploits to officially pretty ladies, drank, played cards, fought and wallowed.

"It sure was a madhouse," said O'Neill. "But somehow a regular program was in progress. Every one present was expected to contribute something. If your voice cracked your head usually did, too. Some old sailor might get up and unroll a yarn, another might do a dance, or there would be a heated discussion between, say, Yankee and British sailors as to the respective prowess of their ships. And, if nothing else promise, 'a bit of a harmless fight' usually could be depended upon as the inevitable star feature to round out the evening's entertainment."

It was at this "Sailor's Opera" that O'Neill made the acquaintance of an exquisite young Englishman who was constantly drunk. They agreed to share a room together and did so for several months. The young Englishman was the original of "Smitty the Duke"—the formal hero of the Glencairn cycle.

"When A. [his room-mate] left a café most of its liquor went along with him," said O'Neill. "He was very young, about 25 at the most, and extraordinarily handsome. Blond, almost too beautiful, he was, in appearance, very like Oscar Wilde's description of 'Dorian Gray.' Even his name was as flowery.

"He was the younger son of a traditionally noble British family. He had been through the English public schools, had acquired a university accent, and, finally down in London for good, became one of its lordly young men. He became, for example, an officer in a crack British regiment and joined the usual clubs.

"Then suddenly he messed up his life—pretty conspicuously. Though he didn't have to leave England, he couldn't face life there, couldn't bear the thought of daily reminders of what he'd lost—a lady—and decided to try North America."

Before he shipped back to New York O'Neill had been away to sea to and from Buenos Aires. He had gone on a "bat" while at work ashore, and when it was over went "on the beach" in Buenos Aires. "On the beach" is a sailor's way of saying "down and out," and O'Neill took to the cold benches of the Paseo Colon in Buenos Aires. The Paseo Colon is like our own Battery Park and is located, geographically, in a similar section of the Argentine city.

So that when the dying Yank in Bound East for Cardiff—the final play of the Glencairn cycle—talks with his mate, Driscoll, about "the days we used to sit on the park benches along the Paseo Colon with the vigilantes lookin' hard at us," you catch a glimpse of O'Neill sitting there, too.

And when the same Yank asks Driscoll to remember the "moving pictures in Barracas" (Barracas is a suburb of Buenos Aires), Driscoll remembers without difficulty, adding "so does the piany player. He'll not be forgettin' the black eye I gave him in a hurry."

"Those moving pictures in Barracas," said O'Neill, "were mighty rough stuff. Nothin' was left to the imagination. Every form of perversity was enacted, and, of course, sailors flocked to them. But, save for the usual exceptions, they were not vicious men. They were in the main honest, good-natured, unheroically courageous men trying to pass the time pleasantly."

In making most of his characters, O'Neill said, he took the characteristics of several men and fused them into one individual— that is, a character in his own right and universal. That is true of Yank in *Bound East for Cardiff.*

O'Neill knew many seamen who died at sea, but Yank's end was the typical sailor's death. Outside, fog, damp, gray, ominous; the blasts of the Glencairn's whistle filter into the forecastle, moaning like lost souls. A grim, comfortless forecastle, and stretched on a bunk, a dying sailor, musing how marvelous it would be to be in the middle of the land. It seems to be the inevitable dream of the sailor, his heaven on earth, "never to see the sea no more" and to own a bit of land with a few cows and chickens. Yank sums up the seaman's life in one brief paragraph:

"This sailor life ain't so much to cry about leavin'—just one ship after another, hard work, small pay, and bum grub; and when we git into port, just a drunk endin' up in a fight, and all your money gone, and then ship away again. Never meetin' no nice people; never gittin' outa sailortown, hardly, in any port; travellin' all over the world and never seein' none of it; with no one to care whether you're alive or dead."

There was, however, an actual Driscoll. He had been a stoker on the American Line, when O'Neill was an able-bodied seaman.

"He was a giant of a man, and absurdly strong," said O'Neill. "He thought a whole lot of himself, was a determined individualist. He was very proud of his strength, his capacity for gruelling work. It seemed to give him mental poise to be able to dominate the stoke-hole, do more work than any of his mates.

"The voyage after I quit going to sea," O'Neill explained, "Driscoll shipped on again as usual. I stayed behind at 'Jimmy the Priest's'— a saloon and rooming house at Fulton Street and North River. When the ship returned to New York Driscoll was the first to swing the saloon doors open and bellow for a drink. We could usually calculate the time of the ship's docking from the moment of Driscoll's appearance. Then I drifted away and later I heard that Driscoll had jumped overboard in midocean. None of our mutual sea-mates knew why.

"Driscoll's curious death puzzled me. I concluded something must have shaken his hard-boiled poise, for he wasn't the type who just gave up, and he loved life. Anyway, it was his death that inspired the idea for the Yank of *The Hairy Ape*.

"'Jimmy the Priest's' was the original for 'Johnny the Priest's,' which is the saloon setting for the first act of *Anna Christie*. It was so named because 'Jimmy,' the proprietor, with his pale, thin, clean-shaven face, mild blue eyes and white hair, seemed to be more suited for a cassock than the bartender's apron he wore. Above the saloon were a number of rooms, rented out to seamen, and in one of them lived O'Neill toward the end of his sea experience.

"Jimmy the Priest's certainly was a hell-hole," he said. "It was awful. The house was almost coming down and the principal house-wreckers were vermin. I was absolutely down, financially, those days, and you can get an idea of the kind of room I had when I tell you that the rent was $3 a month. One roommate of mine jumped out of the window. He was an Englishman and had been a star correspondent of an English news syndicate. He covered the Boer War, for example. But all kinds of misfortune had got him, drink, too, and when I knew him he always lived in the land of 'tomorrow.' When he'd get a job on a newspaper he'd last a few days and then get dead drunk on the first week's pay."

This man was the hero of O'Neill's first published story (and last, I believe) entitled "Tomorrow."

"Then," continued O'Neill, "I had Chris Christopherson as a roommate. He had sailed the sea until he was sick of the mention of it. But it was the only work he knew. At the time he was my roommate he was out of work, wouldn't go to sea and spent the time guzzling whisky and razzing the sea. In time, he got a coal barge to captain. One Christmas Eve he got terribly drunk and tottered away about 2 o'clock in the morning for his barge. The next morning he was found frozen on a cake of ice between the piles and the dock. In trying to board the barge he stumbled on the plank and fell over."

Chris Christopherson served as the model for the Chris Christopherson, who is the father of *Anna Christie,* and the sworn enemy of "dat ole davil sea."

O'Neill is not through with the sea yet.

"I have ideas for ten years of steady work in my notebooks," he said.

Fierce Oaths and Blushing Complexes Find No Place in Eugene O'Neill's Talk

Flora Merrill/1925

Reprinted from the *New York World*, 19 July 1925, 4M.

Provincetown, where many of Eugene O'Neill's plays have been written and his early work first produced, will not see the dramatist this summer. His home on the Cape Cod sand dunes is too inaccessible to meet the needs of a new baby. Fresh milk is more easily obtained at Nantucket, and so it is there that Oona O'Neill will take her parents. Born recently at Bermuda, she was given the Gallic name of Oona because it has long been associated with her father's people.

Eugene O'Neill would be a disappointment to those who blush behind their programs at *Desire Under the Elms* and dwell indignantly upon the profanity and frankness of its lines. He doesn't come up to what one could expect of a man who writes "terrible" plays. Though he has made the drab and seamy side of life the background of all his work, there is nothing sordid about the playwright himself. He gives no outward evidence of knowing what life along the waterfronts is like. There's nothing disreputable about him. Oaths do not punctuate his remarks, and he can talk for an hour without mentioning inhibitions. Nor is he the morose, silent, distant person some have painted him. He can, on the contrary, be an animated, easy and entertaining conversationalist. Oona will find in him an ideal playfellow.

So civilized and attractive is this American dramatist it is to be marveled at that he has so successfully escaped being lionized. He is even popular with actors and directors, being notoriously patient and long suffering.

In appearance he is tall and rangy, with well set shoulders and the long, slender hands to which the hackneyed word artistic is commonly applied. It will be his thirty-seventh birthday that he will celebrate this October, yet his black hair is whitening at the temples.

His voice is low pitched, becoming almost inaudible at the end of a
phrase, and it is not the proper organ with which to compete with the
trucks and rumble and squawk up and down Seventh Avenue. The
street's din and heat poured into the small upstairs office of the
Greenwich Village Theatre. Neither, however, disturbed Mr. O'Neill's
good temper, nor did the numerous interruptions of Kenneth
Macgowan, who, coatless, rushed to and fro telling people to go to
the left when he meant the right.

Life, as pictured in the O'Neill plays, is never a joyous affair. He
shows the ugly struggles that go on inside of men. But though he
paints only in charcoal shades, he considers life worth living, and the
human race worth saving.

"The tragedy of life is what makes it worth while," he insisted. "I
think that any life which merits living lies in the effort to realize some
dream, and the higher that dream is the harder it is to realize. Most
decidedly we must all have our dreams. If one hasn't them, one
might as well be dead—one is dead. The only success is in failure.
Any man who has a big enough dream must be a failure and must
accept that as one of the conditions of being alive. If he ever thinks
for a moment that he is a success then he is finished. He stops."

Eugene O'Neill's parentage and early environment had no small
bearing upon his work. He is of the theatre and its people. The son of
James O'Neill, the actor, he early knew the roving life of players and
all that lay behind the scenes. The play with which the elder O'Neill's
name was for so many years synonymous, *The Count of Monte
Cristo,* was of a very different brand from those his son turns out. As
to why he has been unfaithful to the school of good old roaring
melodrama, Eugene O'Neill said:

"I suppose if one accepts the song and dance complete of the
psychoanalyst, it is perfectly natural that having been brought up
around the old conventional theatre, and having identified it with my
father, I should rebel and go in a new direction.

"I think it would be quite amusing, however, to revive *Monte Cristo*
some time, because, as I look back upon all the old romantic melo-
dramas, that was the best, and I should say that Bill Farnum is
probably the present-day actor most fitted to play my father's part."

As to whether the American theatre has progressed further in
playwriting, acting or production, Mr. O'Neill answered:

"I should say it had progressed furthest in production, but also tremendously in playwriting, and in acting not at all, if you leave out one man who is the exception to all rules because he has real genius, and that is John Barrymore. I feel very strongly about the matter of acting in this country, and in my opinion it is impossible to carry on much further until the actors catch up. Under present conditions, there is no very bright prospect of their succeeding."

Many writers who have had their books or plays transported to the screen have upon seeing the result felt none too friendly toward that form of art. In Eugene O'Neill's case, however, the experience was not disheartening.

"*Anna Christie*, the only play of mine to be put on the screen, was a delightful surprise," he said. "I considered it remarkably well acted and directed, and in spirit an absolutely faithful transcription. I would certainly welcome any like treatment of my work either in the films or on the stage."

The public thinks of Eugene O'Neill as a champion of those miscast in life and living on its dregs. Little or no humor livens his work, and the happy ending is as foreign to him as it is in reality. Since he dramatizes hunks of unsugarcoated life, it would seem unlikely that he is ambitious to depart from this field of realism and suppressed emotions in which he is so successful a forerunner. He laughs at the idea that he is a subtle propagandist or has a mission, and insists that other fields in the drama do interest him.

"Of course, a satiric comedy is the only kind I would want to write," he said, "but I certainly hope to do one such comedy. Maybe within the next two seasons they will be surprised to find that I have. At present I am three plays ahead, two of which will be produced next season. They are *The Great God Brown,* and *The Fountain,* which Lionel Barrymore was to do but won't be able to under present circumstances. Therefore we will put them both on here or at the Provincetown Theatre. I am not saying what the other play is as it may not be produced until later. There is still another play that I hope to finish this summer. It's a woman's play inasmuch as the important role is for an actress as it was in *Anna Christie*.

"I have no ambition to go out of my field and become a novelist," he stated emphatically. "I feel that a carpenter should stick to his trade. I don't hold with these novelists who suddenly decide they will write a play. I think it takes years of intensive, hard work to learn your medium if you want to be any good in it. In my opinion, the drama is a darn sight harder medium than the novel because it is concentrated. The only way I would want to write a novel would be if I had seven or eight years to devote to doing ten, all of which I would throw away before I should think I could possibly write one decent book. That is what I did with plays. I must have thrown away a dozen when I first started. Yet I knew the theatre, having been born in it.

"I don't mean I was born in a dressing room, but it was in a hotel on Broadway at the corner of 43d Street. At that time it was a quiet uptown hotel and they still haven't changed that particular part—the old section of the Cadillac. Every time I go past I look up, because the room was on the fourth floor, third window from Broadway on the 43d Street side. I can remember my father pointing it out to me."

Eugene O'Neill grinned and added: "*Desire* is playing about fifty yards from there!

"Although I have spent a good deal of time here and ought to be used to the city," he continued, "I have never written a line in New York. It's too jarring, too hectic.

"I don't consider the settings I give my plays old fashioned. The oil lamps and scows are what are closest to the soil and sea. They are still a part of modern life. After all, a farm is a farm even now. It hasn't changed so much."

When asked who were the great American playwrights of to-day, he promptly replied:

"There are none. What's more, I don't believe there is any great playwright in the world, with the possible exception of Hauptmann. The last great one died with Strindberg in 1912—that is the last undeniably great playwright, because some think Hauptmann is, and some think he isn't."

Concerning the kind of plays he himself likes to see, O'Neill said:

"I am interested in any sort of play that I hear is good, but I seldom go to the theatre. I know that all the worthwhile plays will be published, so I wait and read them. I prefer judging them that way, because I can visualize an ideal production. Actors generally get between me and the performance. That is, I catch myself recognizing the technique all the time. I don't mean that I blame them, but having been brought up among actors I recognize what they are

doing when they put over a point. The mechanics of acting stop me
from seeing the play. Therefore, I never go to one unless I hear it is
very well acted; but I read them all.

"Musical comedies are, of course, the exception. I go to them to
get a laugh."

In telling what he likes best and least in his own work Eugene
O'Neill was singularly free from affectation or conceit.

"I like *Desire*," he remarked; "*The Hairy Ape* and *The Emperor
Jones.*"

At this point he smiled and said quite clearly:

"I liked *All God's Chillun Got Wings.*

"Out of the old strictly naturalistic plays," he continued, "I liked
The Straw very much, though it failed after two weeks here in New
York. The only one-act play of mine that I am fond of is *The Moon of
the Caribbees*. I am least satisfied with *The First Man* and am by no
means pleased with *Anna Christie*. It was too easy to do. I could go
on and do *Anna Christies* all my life. It doesn't go deep enough. It
was written during a certain stage of development and at the time
was the thing I was doing, but I wouldn't want to go back to it now."

Eugene O'Neill: Writer of Synthetic Drama

Malcolm Cowley/1926

Reprinted from *Brentano's Book Chat*, 5 (July/August 1926), 17–21.

Once, when I lived in the vague district which borders Greenwich Village on the south, I knew a kindly, a conscientious bootlegger. Spanish Willie was his name, but he preferred to be addressed as Mr. Fernandez. He was ungrammatical, polite, and had a strong religious sense; in fact he worshipped several gods. Haig and Haig were two of these; the others were Man-of-War, Al Smith and Eugene O'Neill. Whenever I paid him a visit, he used to say:

"Gee, that guy O'Neill is a regular prince."

Then he would stumble to the sink and wash two glasses. "Tell you, Malcolm, I feel blue today. The Brooklyn boys is after me. I losted two grand on the ponies. But yesterday my nag comes in and I win about fifteen hundred smackers, so I guess we stands about even on the series. I want you should taste some of my sacramental wine. Did you hear that Gene was in town?"

"Gene who?"

"Why Gene O'Neill, of course. You know Gene, don't you? He's a regular prince. The boys tell me he's coming round to see me tonight. Sure, take another glass. I maybe wouldn't have it, only the police captain is a square shooter.

"You see, I was rolling the barrel in, yesterday evening it was, and three bulls sees me and holds me up for a hundred and fifty bucks. But I went round to see the captain, and he says to the bulls, he says, what sort of crooks is youse guys anyway? I want you to play straight, he says, and he made them give the money back, all but thirty dollars that he let them keep for theirselves. Ten bucks apiece, that's square enough. Listen . . . there's some bloke at the door. Why Gene, good evening. It's a treat to see you."

Eugene O'Neill, the author of *Beyond the Horizon, Emperor Jones, Anna Christie* and *The Hairy Ape*; the winner of two Pulitzer prizes; the hope of the American drama; the subject of profound

essays in Japanese, Czech, Italian and all the Scandinavian
tongues:—Mr. O'Neill himself came strolling through the dingy and
double-bolted door. Having brushed some of the cockroaches away,
he sat at Spanish Willie's table. "I'm glad to hear that you're feeling
better, Will," he said.

"Aw, Gene, that cough wasn't so much. I oughta knowed better
than to sleep in the gutter all night. Say, I just got some fine Scotch
off the boat. Won't you have a drink on me?"

"Sorry, Will, I'm not drinking tonight."

I felt that the invitation to a drink, and the refusal, were a formula
of politeness which had been repeated a dozen times. Meanwhile I
was observing O'Neill as he twisted his long nervous hands above the
table. There was no trace of patronage in his manner. No slang, no
artificial breeziness, no effort to talk down to his host. He was just as
grammatical, just as considerate as if he were holding a conversation
with Shakespeare or the Prince of Wales. Perhaps this was the reason
why all the West Side gorillas worshiped him, and even attended his
plays.

Years before, when finding fifty cents to buy a dinner was his
greatest financial problem, one of the gangsters noticed that he was
shivering in an extremely shabby overcoat. "You shouldn't dress like
that, Gene," he said. "Tell you what. You make a trip up the
Avenue—right away. Go to any store you like, pick out any overcoat
you want, and tell me which one it is. That's all. I'll hand you over
the coat tomorrow evening."

O'Neill thanked the amiable shoplifter, but did not accept his offer.

This evening in Spanish Willie's, he was talking about the old
scenes which both of them had known. I wish I could report their
conversation. Every time I try, the words seem to lose their magic.
They were speaking of ships and docks and crimes and politics; of
gangsters, sailors, stevedores, ward politicians and square-shooting
black gamblers—all the figures of that life which seethed between
wharves and crimping houses, between dance halls and saloons; all
the glamour of a Manhattan which is almost totally unknown. I sat in
silence, listening. The Elevated went rumbling past, while the empty
glasses shivered on the table. Finally it was time for him to go.

"Well, you saw him again. Ain't he a regular prince?" asked
Spanish Willie.

It was during the autumn of 1917 that I saw O'Neill for the first time. I had just debarked in New York with a gorgeous uniform, a collection of souvenirs from the front, and fully $.65 in cash. My friends met me at the boat. They led me first to the Provincetown Players, to improve my mind, and then to the back room of the Hell Hole, where my little fortune could be spent to the best advantage.

To enter this back room, you tapped at a door three times, and were inspected through a slit by Louie, the waiter. After this ceremony, which foreshadowed prohibition, you were allowed to choose a table and drink sour beer for five cents a glass. Meanwhile your friends would be describing the suspicious characters who lounged about the room. So-and-so was a pickpocket, So-and-so wrote plays, and the little man with a dark, pleasant face had five notches on his gun. The proprietor kept a pig in the cellar, nobody knew why. There was an upstairs, a place of mystery to which nobody was ever admitted. It was said that a crazy woman went wandering through the deserted rooms. It was said that during the last ten years the saloon had never been closed for an hour. It was also said that Eugene O'Neill . . . but first let us try to describe the situation.

Or even better, let us try to photograph his memories as they must have existed at the time. The picture would show an extraordinary jumble of impressions, without much chronological sequence. There was the large comfortable house in New London, near the sea, where he spent his boyhood. The melodramatic grandeur of his father in the rôle of Monte Cristo. Himself as a young actor in the same play. His voyages before the mast, with fadeaway views of the wharves at Buenos Ayres. Some of his first plays were written at sea, in a minute, almost unintelligible script, on such stray bits of paper as he could find in the forecastle.

The film of his memories continues to unroll. There is a period of some months in a tuberculosis sanitarium, where he gathered the material which was later to be used in *The Straw*. There is another period spent in cheap lodging houses along the North River. There is a year at Harvard, studying dramatic technique with George Pierce Baker. Finally a succession of calmer years spent on Cape Cod and in New York.

With these years the preparatory stage of his career had come to an end. He had written perhaps a dozen short plays of the sea, and

more than half of these had appeared on the stage. Shortly the
Provincetown Players would produce *Moon of the Caribbees,* the
first play in which he departed entirely from the conventional
technique of the theatre, the first play which properly belongs with his
later work.

It was also among the first of his plays to attract the attention of
Broadway managers. And the people who chattered their way
between the Hell Hole and the Provincetown Players were repeating
a story which bore on this point. I refuse to vouch for its accuracy.
However, it seems that Mr. Belasco had requested Mr. O'Neill to
come to his office. And it seems that Mr. O'Neill had sent word to Mr.
Belasco that if Mr. Belasco wished to see him, he, Eugene O'Neill,
could be found in the back room of the Hell Hole any afternoon
between four and six.

To recapture the meaning of the story as it impressed us in 1917,
you must remember that in those days David Belasco represented the
ruling tradition in the American theatre. In those days no tragedy
could be expected to succeed, and no tragedy by an American
author could even be produced. The American drama, as we think of
it today, was a hope seen faintly, somewhere in the future.

The change was produced by a combination of several elements.
The little theatre movement was one of these. The influence of
foreign dramatists was another. A third element, due rather to books
and magazines than to the stage, was the general education of the
public taste. However, the element of personality was probably the
most important of all. Without the personal talent of Eugene O'Neill,
the revolution in the American drama might never have taken place.

One event deserves to be remembered, because it was a crisis both
in his own career and in the history of the theatre. Some time in
1919, *Beyond the Horizon* was produced uptown for special
matinees. The critics praised it highly and predicted its early death. Of
course a tragedy of American life could never succeed. But somehow
the public came. The play moved to another theatre. It was given
regularly for evening performances. Each week the end of its run was
expected, and each week its audience increased. Before it was finally
withdrawn, it had been played 144 times on Broadway, had won the
Pulitzer prize, and had stimulated other American playwrights to

break the conventions of the theatre. The new American drama was under way.

In all probability you are familiar with O'Neill's later work. Even if you never attended his plays, and even if you never read their published versions, which apart from their connection with the stage are important as literature; even without this first-hand knowledge, you must at least have followed their fortunes through the newspapers—which of his plays succeeded on the stage, and which of them the public failed to understand; what the critics thought of one, and what the censors reported about another. I'll take such knowledge of his plays for granted, and make no attempt to analyze them here. However, I should like to repeat, as nearly as I can remember, some of his comments on his own work.

Thus, when he spoke of *Moon of the Caribbees*:—"This was my first real break with theatrical traditions. Once I had taken this initial step, the other plays followed logically."

Of *Emperor Jones*:—"When this play was produced in Germany, it was called 'expressionistic,' as if I had been trying to imitate Werfel or Hasenclever. As a matter of fact I had never heard of expressionism until long after the play was written. Its technique grew naturally out of my own problems."

Of *Anna Christie*:—"It was written just before I finished *Emperor Jones*, and the characters were people I had known years before. I never liked it so well as some of my other plays. In telling the story I deliberately employed all the Broadway tricks which I had learned in my stage training. Using the same technique, and with my own experience as a basis I could turn out dozens of plays like *Anna Christie*, but I never cared to try. It is too easy."

Too easy . . . the words are significant. His whole history as a dramatist has been a search for more difficult problems. Writing about standard theatrical characters was too easy; he preferred the difficult search for real people who had never been described. It was also too easy to follow the conventional technique of the stage. Throwing it over, he developed a technique of his own; in fact he developed a new technique for each of his plays.

Very early in his career he had learned to tell the dramatic story of man's rebellion against his environment, a theme which is the basis of almost all his plays. But simply to tell the story was too easy. He began to expand its meaning and to make the emotions deeper. At the same time the language of his characters became simplified and "stylized," as witness his comments on *Desire Under the Elms:*—

"I never intended that the language of the play should be a record of what the characters actually said. I wanted to express what they felt subconsciously. And I was trying to write a synthetic dialogue which should be, in a way, the distilled essence of New England. . . . The farmhouse plays an actual part in the drama; the old elms too; they might almost be given in the list of characters."

Thus, inanimate objects are made to take their part in the action. And the people he describes acquire a significance outside themselves; they tend to become the symbols of certain elements in man's nature. In *The Great God Brown,* even the names of his characters are full of allusions:—"Dion Anthony is Dionysius and Anthony, a pagan god and a Christian saint. As his character develops, the pagan part of him dies away, and he becomes a Christian saint under the mask of a Christian devil. Margaret is a character whose name recalls the Marguerite of Faust. As for Cybel, she is of course Cybele, the earth goddess."

Personally I think that he is mistaken in some of these later tendencies. I believe that stylization belongs to the technique of painting or poetry rather than of the stage, and I disapprove of symbolism in all its forms. However, this judgment is merely personal. And it is more than a personal judgment to say that whether O'Neill is right or wrong, he ranks definitely above the other American dramatists. Of all the thousands who write for our stage, he is the only one who belongs not to his country alone, but to the world.

A Eugene O'Neill Miscellany
New York Sun/1928

Reprinted from the *New York Sun*, 12 January 1928, 31.

The personal side of Eugene O'Neill has seldom been brought before that public which regards him as the greatest of the American playwrights. The reason, of course, is that he is thoroughly uninterested in being exploited. His life was done into a concise little biography several years ago and that, O'Neill feels, is that. At least he won't have to repeat the essential facts of his career over and over again when these facts are available in handy book form.

The Theatre Guild's production of *Marco Millions* on Monday night at the Guild and the revelation on January 23 of another O'Neill play, *Strange Interlude,* at the John Golden, has revived a chronic interest in the man. His shyness is now proverbial. People who know anything at all about the theater know that he writes what he pleases and lets the producing theater worry about its production. He doesn't haunt rehearsals, nor does he indulge in routine cant about "my meaning."

To answer some of the questions which have remained more or less obscure in previous stories on him, a list of impertinent, personal questions was prepared and gone over with him. The questions and the answers follow:

Did you, like other playwrights, look on Broadway with a yearning to see your plays produced?

His answer to that is a flat "No." His explanation is that when he began writing plays he knew enough about Broadway to know that he would not find immediate production there. So he didn't try to convince Broadway. It must be remembered that O'Neill's father was James O'Neill, a well-known actor, so from boyhood he had a keen knowledge of the theater, inside and out.

Who is your literary idol?
The answer to that is in one word—Nietzsche.

How long have you had the idea for *Marco Millions?*

"The desire to write a play on Marco Polo developed some years ago when I was reading material before writing *The Fountain.* So much of that material referred to Marco Polo that I got the idea then."

About *Strange Interlude*—did he have the idea for a long time?

"For three years, and I worked harder on it than on any other play I've ever written."

Going on by way of explanation, he said that the Guild was unable to include *Marco Millions* on last year's schedule because of the production of *Juarez and Maximilian,* a great effort. He also said that *Strange Interlude* was not submitted to any one else and that Lawrence Langner, a member of the board of managers of the Guild, read six acts of it in Bermuda last spring and that the finished draft was immediately sent to the Guild and accepted for production.

A personal question asked the places where he lived in his days of early manhood around New York.

"In my boyhood the family stopped at the Cadillac Hotel, Forty-third street and Broadway. It was then the Barrett House. I was born there. We later stopped at other hotels on the West Side—the Empire, the Belleclaire and the Lucerne. Still later the family stopped at the Prince George Hotel.

"In my sailor days I always stayed, when in New York, at Jimmy the Priest's, on Fulton Street, near West—opposite Washington Market.

"Some time after that I stayed at the old Garden Hotel, on the northeast corner of Madison avenue and Twenty-seventh street. It's torn down now. The circus men who stayed there I knew very well. Not only the circus men, but the poultry men, the horse breeders and all others who displayed their wares at the old Madison Square Garden. Used to meet them all in the bar. One of my old chums was Volo, the Volitant, a bicycle rider whose specialty was in precipitating himself down a steep incline and turning a loop or so in the air. Volo is now a megaphone man on one of the Broadway sightseeing buses. Billy Clark is his real name. Jack Croak was another. He used to work on the ticket wagon of the Willard Shows. He's now with the Walter L. Main circus, I believe. There was good food at the Garden, and it was a good place."

Asked whether he felt that his plays had been the subject of much stupid criticism and if the critics knew what he was driving at, he answered:

"My answer is—what do you mean by critics? They can be divided into three classes: Play Reporters, Professional Funny Men and the men with the proper background or real knowledge of the theater of all time to entitle them to be critics. The play reporters just happen to be people who have the job of reporting what happens during the evening, the story of the play and who played the parts. I have always found that these people reported the stories of my plays fairly accurately. The Professional Funny Men are beneath contempt. What they say is only of importance to their own strutting vanities. From the real critics I have always had a feeling that they saw what I was trying to do and whether they praised or blamed, they caught the point.".

How does he regard his own plays? Which are the favorites?

"I don't regard *Anna Christie* as highly as some others do. *The First Man* I don't like. The ones I like least are those which come nearest a strict, realistic technic."

His favorites are the plays which show what he wants to feel is his growth. *Moon of the Caribbees, Emperor Jones, The Hairy Ape* (a great favorite), *The Straw* (which he feels is the best of all his naturalistic plays) and *All God's Chillun Got Wings* are the chosen few. O'Neill thinks *All God's Chillun* is a lot better than it ever had credit for being, for he resented the publicity which attended the New York production and remembers, with something of a glow of pride, that when the play was produced in California, away from the hubbub of racial prejudices, it achieved a success on its own merits.

Of the more recent plays, O'Neill is particularly partial to *Desire Under the Elms, The Great God Brown, Marco Millions* and *Strange Interlude* (of course) and at the moment the greater part of his devotion is for the unproduced *Lazarus Laughed*.

Realism Doomed, O'Neill Believes

Richard Watts, Jr./1928

Reprinted from the *New York Herald Tribune,* 5 February 1928, sec. 7, 2.

At the outset you might as well be informed that this is intended as no interview with Eugene O'Neill: no portrait of the man, and no pseudo-survey of his genius. These negative explanations having been given, it may be added that the accompanying essay was originally intended as a combination of the first two forms, but that somewhere about midway in his talk with the author of *Strange Interlude,* this observer suddenly forgot that he was supposed to be obtaining an interview and became so interested in conversing with a charming gentleman that he failed to ask what are known as leading questions.

As a sort of obeisance to the regulations of the Interviewers' Union I should at least tell you, however, that the eminent Mr. O'Neill is dark and distinguished looking, with slowly graying temples, and that he seems sensitive, rather shy, reserved, but completely without tem-peramental mannerisms. These concessions to the requirements of journalistic writing having been made as hastily as possible, I trust I may now explain certain ideas that came from a casual conversation with America's First Playwright.

In the first place, a number of spectators of the dramatist's supreme achievement, *Strange Interlude,* have been discerned wondering audibly if the play would not have been equally effective if divorced from its device of the glorified aside. To O'Neill the idea seems absurd. Without the audible expression of the characters' thoughts, the tremendous scene at the beginning of the second section, where Nina and her four lovers sit around the table and consider their respective fates, would be meaningless, and the exposition in the first act without effect. The only episode in the play that might not be seriously hurt by loss of the new soliloquies would be the act in which the mother tells Nina of madness in her husband's family.

As for the influence of his play's new technique on the future of

84

stage writing, O'Neill, despite his confidence in the form, has little to say. He does believe, however, that so-called realism in the theater is doomed and that it will not be many years before playwrights realize it. Though something of a modernist, he is able to call upon the past as witness. So great a dramatist as Ibsen turned, in his greatest dramas, to a symbolism that was hardly realistic and Strindberg never bothered himself overmuch about this matter of minor verisimilitude.

The son of a famous actor, O'Neill is, himself, highly interested in acting. He confesses that this preoccupation with thespian technique makes play-going difficult for him. Becoming interested in the methods and tricks of the players he is likely to neglect the quality of the drama he is supposed to be observing. This concern, however, has numerous advantages when he is watching the rehearsal of one of his own plays. In *Strange Interlude*, for example, it resulted in making the playing version considerably shorter than the published form, for he would frequently see how the actors were putting over his ideas so completely that he did not require dialogue to complete the projection of their thoughts.

It has sometimes been declared by his detractors that O'Neill's writing of plays that showed scant regard for the ordinary stage limitations of time, space and manner was, among other things, a lazy man's method of dramatization. Though I am sure it was not intended as conscious rebuttal, the playwright did offer a denial of the charge when he told of some of the difficulties of composing *Strange Interlude*. For one thing, he had to make the first section end on a fairly conclusive note and still provide his play with the carry-over quality that would bring the audience back after supper hour. Second, not just one, but four of his characters were complex figures whose reactions had to be thought out with endless care and insight. The result was that he spent no less than 300 working days on the play, an unusually long time for so serious a worker.

There is one criticism of his method of inscribing the thoughts of his characters to which Mr. O'Neill objects. That is the objection that a man's subconscious thoughts would not be so articulate, so lacking in irrelevancies, so neglectful of the realization that one's reactions may be in visual images, even in sound or smell, rather than in carefully ordered sentences. O'Neill, of course, realizes this, but he points out that his expression of the subconscious is intended as no more "realistic" in form than is his spoken dialogue. Discarding the irrelevancies and the lack of articulateness, he endeavors to express the inner feelings dramatically and honestly, rather than with a mere regard for the technical form they take—whether in sound, or sight, or feeling.

At the present moment O'Neill has in mind a new play, to be called *Dynamo,* which, while of a more normal length than *Strange Interlude,* will combine something of the methods of that greatest of American drama and of his *Lazarus Laughed.* It will not employ masks to express states of soul, but it will employ sound and mass in the manner of the latter play. The work is outlined in his mind, but he has so far written no word of it. He expects, however, that, after *Strange Interlude,* it will be fairly simple, not only because it will be comparatively brief, but also because in it only one of the characters will be complex enough to cause difficulties in the writing.

Among the notable things about Eugene O'Neill is the fact that he is one playwright who does not pretend that he never sees the notices of his plays. He reads them and is interested in them, and heaven knows, he has his likes and dislikes among the local critics. It is only fair to everybody to add that these judgments of his are not necessarily based on the degree of enthusiasm expressed for his works, even though he would object to being used as a sort of injured Belgium in a war between rival reviewers.

Though the matter of actors and their technique worries him, he has a profound admiration for the work of Max Reinhardt's players and, in particular, for the distinguished Alexander Moissi. For the difficult leading role in his *Lazarus Laughed,* a part that requires an actor with a most remarkable vocal quality, he can imagine only Moissi or Chaliapin. He can think of no American actor qualified.

This as yet unproduced play, which is to be done next month by the Pasadena Community Theater, is one of the most difficult works to produce that one can well imagine. In each scene there are forty-nine gradations of masks, which must be changed from Jewish to Greek to Roman. But O'Neill thinks this complication is a help as well as obstacle to production. Whether intended as Greek or Roman a crowd of stage supers is ordinarily likely to look nothing but American, while by the use of masks it is possible to achieve the appearance of the various nationalities. Likewise the muffled voices coming through the masks aid in providing the sound of a mob in action. I supply these examples to show that O'Neill's supposed stage eccentricities should not conceal from any one that everything he does is guided by an amazingly sure sense of theater.

O'Neill as the Stage Never Sees Him

Montiville Morris Hansford/1930

Reprinted from the *Boston Evening Transcript*, 22 March 1930, sec. 4, 5–6.

As it is easy to catch and record the physical reactions of the creative genius to life's stimuli, so it is extremely difficult to interpret the more elusive mind. Eugene O'Neill is a brilliant example of more than one warring element—warring in the restless sense, the sense of incompleteness, a realization, evidently, on his part that life does not and cannot give the ultimate satisfaction. Conscious of this, O'Neill is often intolerant, and at times strangely gentle and quiescent. Often with his two small children, he is quizzically paternal; but in all these moods he is obviously aloof. So aloof, now and then, so abstract and remote in thought, that surrounding friends, wife and children, noise, conversation, all these appear to fade from him, and he explores shoreless seas of speculation, the while he sits in an easy chair in his own library. He is difficult to put in print.

Intimate knowlede of O'Neill leaves one with a strange sense of the inadequateness of life, the disappointment of action, the shadow of an age-old and eternal tragedy, groping, hoping, perhaps. One must admit, however reluctantly, that this sense is always present in talking to him, no matter how trivial the subject. Furthermore, in his presence, one feels the utter futility of talk—even about anything. The very looks of the man offer one food for pessimistic reflection. When he talks, there is a feeling of brooding finality, just around the corner, too elusive to capture, but almost hauled into sight, which leaves the listener, the average mind, in an unsatisfactory mood. Even in the ordinary subjects of household conversation, O'Neill's negatives and affirmatives leave one hanging on an edge of something, suspecting that they are mere figures of speech, a sop to persons who are compelled to live in a world of yes and no. I have talked to him by the hour, played with him, lived in the same house, yet, were I to meet him on the street today, I would wonder whether I had ever known him—would wonder what new tortures contracted his brows, what adventurous roaming he had done since we parted. So, it is difficult to catch the spirit of such a man and confine it long enough to write it down. However, his mechanical and physical side, gestures and reactions to daily phenomena, are all quite apparent to, and easily caught by, the observant person in the course of more than a casual association. These I shall dwell upon somewhat, in the hope that snatches of the man's mind may break through and shine for a moment. With his plays, I have nothing to do. I never saw one of them. Knowing the man somehow eliminates any great desire to see and hear his work. I have read most of the one-act plays and at least three of the longer ones. I was constantly with him during the period of *The Great God Brown, Lazarus Laughed, Strange Interlude*, the years 1924 to 1927, all spent in Bermuda.

One of O'Neill's characteristics is the extreme variance between his two selves—the mental and the physical. The connection is quite rusty. His muscles are controlled, of course, by an unusually deliberate mind, and they answer accordingly. Consequently, O'Neill is a slow mover. His brain is also a slow mover when it comes to quick thinking, though in an average crisis, his hesitation might not be noticed. But, generally, he will be the very last, in a gathering of friends, to agree on any action, such as going for a swim or on an island picnic, simply because he is still thinking it over after the others have decided. This characteristic is often embarrassing to strangers, who get the idea that he is unsocial. But this is scarcely true, though in some cases O'Neill would rather stay quietly at home. He is shy of meeting with strangers, unless he knows beforehand just what is going to happen. He hangs back from being introduced to people and does everything in his power to side-step certain associations. However, to make up for this, he is always glad to meet people who are doing worthwhile things, probably feeling a certain sympathy with them which eases the situation. His very few close friends are always welcome—men and women before whom he can call things by their right names and be understood, and especially in the presence of whom he can take a book, get up from his chair, walk about and stretch himself—the latter one of his favorite gestures.

Quite noticeable is O'Neill's helplessness in a rapid conversational bout—those quick-firing and snappy moments when smart stuff is being juggled back and forth. In such situations he is dumb, and he will look around upon the assembly in a sort of bewilderment, as if wondering what it is all about. In ordinary conversation, however, among a small and select company, he is delightfully entertaining: especially when he can hold the talk down to one subject long enough to come to some definite understanding about it. But rapid small talk is foreign to his tongue. Interruptions leave him stranded. If he is interrupted while talking he will leave off and keep perfectly quiet, while the conversation veers around other matters, and then as quietly resume where he left off. Often he tries to get into a linguistic battle, and sometimes a few words will issue from his lips, but he immediately takes refuge in silence until a more opportune moment arrives. This characteristic will strike the observant person quite forcibly, and I have noted carefully his inability to cope with rapid or even extremely flexible conversation in a mixed company. This is caused, probably, by his unusual ability to concentrate. He possesses this to a high degree. When thoroughly immersed in a book, it requires some moments before he can be brought back to the present.

Financial success, in recent years, has probably had an appreciable effect on O'Neill's attitude to society. At one time he was a Socialist and belonged to that select crowd of reformers who lived in Greenwich Village. Unlike many of them, he must have developed the climbing notion, and soon broke away from many of his old haunts and associations. Socialists, in those days, meant much more that they do now. His friends in the old days have often remarked this change and spoken of it to me. It probably reduces itself to the age-old answer: when luxuries can be had, they are not to be passed by for a mere whim or theory, and O'Neill likes to bask in an easy chair as much as anybody. But he has not always been tolerant of even the moderately wealthy class. Whether he is conscious of this transition is doubtful; probably he thinks he is just the same man. But the fact is that he enjoys the many comforts of life which, formerly, he did not have, could not have, and—for these very reasons—did not believe in. Not an exceptional phenomenon, surely. Yet this change is all the more significant in a man of O'Neill's many stage preachments, especially in his earlier works before financial success set in. It is scarcely probable that the change will have much effect on his future work, for, after all, your creative genius is a supreme actor, either in fact or in thought, and O'Neill has an odd way of always dealing with elementals. Such a phase may be only transient as so many of O'Neill's gropings are.

Viewed from the standpoint of production of work, O'Neill is a supreme play machine. He expresses himself in the dreams of his puppets, and probably enjoys it more than any other modern writer. He is entirely wrapped up in his work. His bedroom, where he always writes, his little playbook and his fountain pen are his gods. Their lure is irresistible. He once told me that he always had several plays seething in his head, ready to be put to paper. And a good illustration lies in the fact that even while writing *Lazarus Laughed*, he had *Strange Interlude* clamoring for expression. I well remember the day *Lazarus Laughed* was finished, a long, lazy afternoon at Belle-vue, Paget, a Bermuda estate which he had leased for the season. He came down from his bedroom in his bathing suit and joined me for a walk to the beach. "Well," said he, "I've just written the last curtain on *Lazarus*." At this statement, I pictured a few days, if not weeks, of rest and boating, swimming and general relaxation. When I expressed as much, he said, "No, I've just begun another play." This was *Strange Interlude*. He began to write it practically on the next sheet of paper after the final page of *Lazarus Laughed*. Such switching of the mind from one big work to another, within a few moments, is an example of concentration not often met. He never said another word to me about *Strange Interlude,* and I saw him almost daily during the entire writing of it. Indeed, he never spoke of any of his plays to me except, one time in speaking of the West Indies, he said that *Moon of the Caribbees* was founded on a fact. Most of his conversation hinges on current events, particularly sports and various adventures. He seldom speaks of plays.

Like most creative workers, O'Neill is difficult. He flits from mood to mood with ease and, often, embarrassing results. He is good-hearted almost to a fault, can easily be imposed on, and he has an old-fashioned attitude to many things, seemingly quite at variance with the modern world. He has admirers from all parts of the earth; letters arrive for him, some of them taken up with long discussions of a particular play; others are written in a wildly fantastic mood, showing an effort by the writer to chime in and bid for a sympathetic understanding—two great souls meeting at last, etc. These letters he pores over as seriously as if they were the very backbone of fame. With such a deliberate mind, there is nothing that does not enthrall him, and he is naturally curious to read what people think of him. I recall a rather pathetic incident about such letters, during the winter of *Lazarus Laughed*. Some unknown admirer wrote to him in extravagant terms about one of his plays. It was a woman, and evidently in dire straits both mentally and economically. The letter attracted him, for it was written in a devil-may-care style, but under all there was an atmosphere of forced acceptance of conditions for which she had never wished—the usual stone wall against which to batter the tender head. And she was poor, her home was bleak, unhappy and altogether unlovely. Coupled to these matters, winter was coming on, and she had no coat in which to brave the weather. It is characteristic of the man that he sent the coat—a simple solution, he evidently reasoned. But it shows how he thinks about things. He is the kind of man who would look at a beggar twice, if not three times before passing on, with his hand going deeper into his pocket with each look.

To the casual onlooker, O'Neill appears to drift along more or less easily, at least in the several minor activities of daily life. It is only for the more intimate associate to note the turmoil within, those moods that are barely kept under the surface. His mental slumps inspire one with a great desire to take a walk, get away. He is best left alone at such times. Yet, in some respects, he is most comical. Coming slowly down the back stairs to join a group on the porch at Bellevue, I have watched him stand for two minutes, trying, evidently, to decide upon which chair to sit, and wondering (certainly by his expression) what sort of human beings were these gathered together. Often there comes to his face an expression of astonishment, even on seeing his own family, as if undecided just where this or that child fitted into the general scheme of things. This characteristic is always apparent and impresses one with the feeling that O'Neill is continually undergoing a sort of physical helplessness, as if his mind did not know what to do with his body.

Such large production of plays means rather strict adherence to a daily program of work, and O'Neill almost follows union rules when writing. He does all his work in long-hand, in a small loose-leaf book. His handwriting is extremely difficult to read, and often the typist is compelled to use a strong reading glass laid over the page while transcribing his plays. He usually works from breakfast (about 9 o'clock) until 1 o'clock, at which hour he lunches and then begins to play. In Bermuda, his chief sport was swimming and he did a quarter to a half mile in the water every day for the entire winter and summer. Long exposure to the sun and salt had turned his body to a shade of light leather. He made a striking figure, standing on the beach in the brilliant tropical sunlight. In later months, during the latter part of the *Strange Interlude* period which he finished at Spithead, his evenings were spent on the beautiful cement plaza in front of the house, overlooking Hamilton Harbor and the Great Sound, the sky blazing with stars. There, surrounded by a small group of friends, he would talk about every subject under the sun, from prize-fights to astronomy, with special reference to British critics, who seemed to think that if O'Neill lived long enough, he would grow up and at last write a play. This attitude on their part never failed to exasperate O'Neill. Generally, he admitted that most of his critics were right. Indeed, I have rarely seen a playwright more open to suggestions from the critics. He discusses such matters quite freely with insight and sympathy for their point of view.

Apart from the work of writing plays, O'Neill lives in what may be called the vernacular. There is no mollycoddling in his conversation. With his intimates, he cracks out his words with a tang of the lumberjack; he likes slang, and now and then he touches up his phrases with the terms of the New York Eastsider or the extremely descriptive words of the sporting world, yet with never a suggestion of the vulgar. As he is at ease in small talk among close friends, so in a strange company he usually confines his talk to one person and is rather careful in his speech. Reticent and modest along some lines almost to a painful degree, in the years I have known him I have never heard him utter an off-color phrase. To those who know him well, this characteristic is a sort of standing joke.

These few personal characteristics of the man may convey to the reader some slight news of O'Neill's daily round. With all his strange antics, his difficult moods, his good heart, unusual gentleness and fighting tempers, he stands, an angular figure against the fabric of life. I may be wrong about it, but I alway feel that everything on earth is eternally new to O'Neill: that every time he sits in a chair it is the first

chair he ever sat in, and that he gives thanks that somebody invented
the chair for that special moment—that when he gets up he forgets
the chair immediately, and that he goes through this same process
with everything with which he comes in contact. He loves good food,
is a fine eater, and he approaches a lamb stew in exactly the same
mood as the chair. I have been in his dining-room, with a small group
of friends, and O'Neill would grace the head of the table clad in an
undershirt, canvas trousers and barefooted. Calm, silent and con-
templative—all with that childish wonder showing in his face, as if
this were really the very first dinner he ever attended and the lamb
stew and fish the first that had ever been cooked. Furthermore, I
believe that the man never feels quite at home with anybody, and
certainly nobody ever feels at home with him, and this in spite of the
fact that he can never do enough for his friends.

In thinking over O'Neill's many-sided equipment, the one outstanding impression is that he does not belong anywhere; that the
warring elements within are too much for him; that he is forever
tortured by a tragic wanderlust that has neither beginning nor end.
There is no doubt that O'Neill often approaches things almost from
the child's standpoint, and with all his vast experience with life—and
I sometimes think that this item about him is very much exaggerated—he exhibits a trust entirely too spontaneous for business purposes, and that he has been, and is, a victim of life, not an aggressor.
His aggressiveness shows in his plays, perhaps, but not in the man.
And from this viewpoint it is easy to understand why he is often
buffeted by a reality of which he is surely unconscious. He purchased
a beautiful home in Bermuda, rebuilt much of it, dreamed awhile
under the tropic sun and stars, even saying that, at last, he had found
the ideal resting place. But this resting place was a mere passing
thought in a man whose thoughts can not be bounded by countries,
and soon he was up and away, questing again, who knows where?
All one knows about O'Neill is that his tracks are large across the
world of play-writing.

Out of Provincetown:
A Memoir of Eugene O'Neill
Harry Kemp/1930

Reprinted from *Theatre Magazine*, 51 (April 1930), 22–23, 60.

The beach and bay of Provincetown was a golden wealth of sunlight and bright, dancing waves. On the porch of a cottage, in the open day, sat a group of writers and artists who were planning an organization subsequently to be known as the Provincetown Players. Susan Glaspell, Mary Heaton Vorse, Hutchins Hapgood, Neith Boyce, and several others. Dominating them sat George Cram Cook, their future director, a huge-bodied man, eager and kindly. He was thoughtfully twisting an iron-gray lock that stood out from the mane of hair over his forehead—a characteristic gesture of his.

Shyly and diffidently there approached a new member to join them. All the rest had achieved somewhat in the artistic and literary worlds. This young fellow was as yet utterly unknown, except that he was the son of James O'Neill, the old-time actor who won fame and fortune by playing *Monte Cristo*.

The young O'Neill was dressed slackly like a sailor who had just jumped ship. Dark and taciturn, he favored the portrait of Edgar Allan Poe. The same handsome moroseness was there. If his large, brown eyes had not burned so penetratively, they might have seemed furtive.

It was easy to see that, at first contact, the group were dubious of their new member's ability and doubtful of his future worth to them. Nowadays they will hardly recall that reaction. All like to have been in on a winner.

O'Neill had come to town trampishly with an older man for companion and mentor—a remarkable person everybody knew as "Terry"—Terry Carlin, the anarchist philosopher; a man already close upon seventy, but tall and straight and lithe-bodied as any Indian.

The way O'Neill arrived was, even by our unconventional group, taken for no remarkable augury. He had been a sailor, it was said. He was evidently one of those half-baked youngsters who persisted in believing in their genius despite an equipment pitiably scant of education and general culture. That he proffered us a book of one-act plays for perusal, for the printing of which he admitted he had somehow paid, did not materially forward his case. That, too, was the usual stunt of people without ability.

O'Neill was not given to talk about himself. What we learned from him about himself had to be pried out of him.

Jack Reed, the radical newspaperman now buried within the walls of the Kremlin, was a member of the Provincetown Players. He had a house in Provincetown for the season. At one of our meetings, held at his place, Eugene O'Neill won less favor by reading a play that was frightfully bad, trite and full of the most preposterous hokum. It was, as I remember, something about an American movie man who financed a Mexican revolution for the sake of filming its battles. One of the scenes depicted the hero's compelling the commanding generals on both sides—both being in his hire—to wage a battle all over again because it had not been fought the way he liked it!

At the next meeting something decidedly clicked. O'Neill, wearing an old sweater and cotton trousers, sat motionless in a wicker chair, while he delivered in his low, deep, slightly monotonous but compelling voice the lines of a one-act play about seamen in a ship's fo'c'stle, the climax being the death of one of them in his bunk. We heard the actual speech of men who go to sea; we shared the reality of their lives; we felt the motion and windy, wave-beaten urge of a ship. This time no one doubted that here was a genuine playwright.

Eugene O'Neill and his elder mentor, Terry Carlin, took up quarters in a place of four small rooms over the general grocery store of John Francis. In those days the rush of summerers had not set in and run up rent to exorbitant figures. The rent O'Neill paid for his place was not much. His rooms were sketchily furnished. There were two beds, a Morris chair, several kitchen chairs, a kitchen table, a small sitting-room table, a three-burner oil stove for cooking. The back windows gave on a magnificent view of bay and harbor.

The calibre of the young playwright was soon manifest. He proved to be a hard-working, solitary being. In the midst of a party he kept that aura of a being apart. When he spoke it was hesitatingly and haltingly. It was only when he drank that he expressed himself fluently. Then he was worth listening to. He never made small talk for the sake of conversation; when he had nothing to say he fell into a silence. Participants of that silence were frequently embarrassed, because, with saying nothing, O'Neill looked straight through those in his presence.

We soon learned that, though O'Neill was poor, he was not destitute. His father, it seemed, sent him a very small allowance— enough to keep him under shelter and alive. The rift between father and son came because the son refused to be an actor. He was determined to become a playwright. The father was proud of the traditions of the stage and thought no profession nobler.

The tentative but robust efforts of the Provincetown Players' first summer had been brought to a close. After much debate whether such a move held wisdom, the group decided to have a winter in New York. They transformed a first-floor apartment on Macdougal Street into a tiny theatre.

O'Neill, remaining behind to finish a one-act play or two, belatedly followed. That winter all his plays attracted notice and excited comment. Cook openly proclaimed that the theatre was for the young playwright to do what he willed with: that he was the greatest asset of the organization. "It's all for 'Gene!'" George Cram Cook used to say proudly. O'Neill was outspoken, too. He was glad to be one of them. But the moment they ceased to keep pace with his growth he would frankly part company and go on.

When storms of debate and disagreement broke at meetings, O'Neill seldom grew excited. When he wished to assemble emphasis, however, his was a forceful command and use of simple, scaring epithet that rivaled the speech of the coal-heavers and seamen he wrote about.

After several winters of success, we moved our theatre south a few doors to a place slightly larger. There we had our own restaurant over the theatre. One of our chief hang-outs, outside of our restaurant, was a place named the Golden Swan, but called popularly the Hell-Hole, an old-fashioned saloon on the southeast corner of Fourth Street and Sixth Avenue. It was headquarters for the Hudson Dusters. It had three back rooms where we went. The last back room was where the gangsters throve. There O'Neill soon quietly grew dominant over the most desperate characters, drinking with them and studying them when drink brought their mental and spiritual guards down. He drew on the tales of their rich, crude adventures for his plays.

The gangsters grew agog as children over their new friends. We found them sweet-natured and gentle except when riled. They straightway liked us. They treated the women with respect. O'Neill they would have died for. Occasionally there were fights. When O'Neill got mixed in a fight his fists were skilled and accurate. He never quarreled. When a quarrel was thrust upon him he met it, head-on.

The managers began to get after O'Neill. He wasn't at all anxious to be taken up by them. Those were the days when the Happy Ending prevailed and dramatists were solemnly informed by those who held the power that the public would not tolerate the tragic dénouement.

One night Belasco sat on our front bench. He sensed earlier than any of the regulars the coming greatness of O'Neill. He tried to get in touch with him. It was no use; O'Neill was not to be reached. O'Neill and his associates, though they conceded its excellence in many respects, avoided like death the influence of Broadway, whose judgment of art came through the box-office. Belasco's pursuit of O'Neill grew hotter. Letters, special delivery letters, telegrams. One night the Belasco office sought the Provincetown Players on the phone. The theatre downstairs was closed. Christine, the gorgeous, the flaming-haired, who ran our restaurant, got the message on the extension wire. Christine had a droll sense of humor. No, she didn't know where Mr. O'Neill at that late hour was to be found, but they might try the Golden Swan!

Lefty, the bartender, swung onto the telephone at the Hell-Hole. Mr. Belasco wished to see Mr. O'Neill at his studio that night. It was important. No kidding. O'Neill sent back word from his back room, where he was listening to stories from the Hudson Dusters, that if Mr. Belasco wished to see him, *his* studio was the third back room of the Hell-Hole!

Several summers followed in Provincetown, rich in growth for all of us, notably so for Eugene O'Neill. He had grown to be dominant among us. He made no effort to achieve this position. It fell to him naturally. Up there in the dunes, under a summer sky, we spent most of our time in the open. O'Neill, most of any. He was strong and athletically built, but once he had had a sharp touch of consumption. He bronzed in the sun like one of Provincetown's dark-hued Portuguese fishermen. He was a superb swimmer. Often we would glimpse him far out in the bay, sliding effortlessly along, half the length of the harbor.

Despite his meagre income, O'Neill welcomed occasional guests. The strangest characters. One, a sailor, when on one of his deep-sea drunks, dove headlong through a window down a flight of stairs, landing on the roof of a porch below, unhurt. And one night, during the progress of a drinking bout, the breaking of crockery went on in O'Neill's place till dawn. It developed that they agreed on seeing a green mouse in a corner and the game was trying to hit it. They threw all the dishes and saucers and cups. Then they threw the pieces—and the pieces of the pieces. No one was able to hit the green mouse.

It was late that fall when my wife and I were enabled to get away from Provincetown to New York, through my receipt of a check for three poems, from Charles Agnew MacLane, editor of the *Popular Magazine*. I felt ever so boastful, successful, and proud. This was the one time I detected the slightest buckling-under where O'Neill was concerned. Frightfully caught, he confessed; he wondered to me if he might not sell a story to MacLane? I told him I'd go and ask Mac-Lane. He suggested the story he later used in his one-act play, *In the Zone*. I spoke to MacLane about it on reaching New York. By then O'Neill had clenched himself to fresh resolution and never wrote the suggested story.

O'Neill spent many cold months there in those Provincetown rooms, into which leaked all the winter winds. Before my wife and I departed, I saw him sitting with his legs stretched out over an oil stove, his feet placed on a chair opposite. He wore an overcoat. Blankets were wrapped about his legs. He was writing away on a pad in his painstakingly minute script. He reached down to limber up his cold-stiff fingers over the oil-stove.

O'Neill had a long play ready for the Provincetown Players, *The Emperor Jones*. George Cram Cook, seeing in this play his opportunity to try his mettle as a producer, went apart to think the production over. O'Neill followed him to his retreat.

"I'm glad you came, 'Gene. Now we can talk over several points that—"

"Jig!" 'Gene cut in. "You're a rotten producer, and I came to tell you that I've reached a place where I must have more competent direction."

"At least, 'Gene, you're brutally frank!" gulped George Cram Cook.

Arthur Hopkins was called in. *The Emperor Jones* proved a sensation. O'Neill was made. The Provincetown Players, as if it had achieved the purpose Fate meant for it, now began to drop apart as an organization. The old group dissolved. O'Neill went on.

Successful, the great playwright did not desert Provincetown. He bought a large house there, several difficult miles across the toilsome dunes that separate that town from the ocean. The house he bought was formerly a Coast Guard station that had been given up because of the sea's threatened invasion. After it had been abandoned by the Government, the ocean changed its mind and stopped digging away the beach, to heap up new ramparts.

The playwright married. He brought his wife to the abandoned Coast Guard station. His only communion with the outside world was by wagon and team, for cars couldn't come there through the slack sand.

The watch-tower of the house became the studio of the dramatist. Access to the tower was up a flight of steep, ladder-like stairs through a trap door. There, with all the sky and ocean about, he wrote play after play. His fame grew. Fortune took the hand of Fame. Yet O'Neill did not change. He bore the test. He did not vary his life of hard work and outdoor living. Sometimes he relaxed by going on a jamboree, but the ocean was his real playmate. He swam far out, labeling for a superstition the legend that no one could swim there safely. He procured an Eskimo kayak and paddled against the horizon. He would drift and write, naked except for trunks. Once he spied a fishing-boat lying to, far off shore. He made to it in his flimsy craft, seeking fresh fish for his table. The astonished, perturbed captain swore at him furiously for risking his life for a mess of fish and gave none.

I have never seen O'Neill's imperturbability shaken. And only once have I heard of its being shaken—and the story came from himself.

There is a story back of this story. Philadelphia Jack O'Brien had been teaching me about boxing and fighters at his gym. I was planning a prize-fighter's novel. I suggested to O'Neill that he write a play revolving around the career of a prize-fighter.

Just before the Dempsey-Firpo fight O'Neill had me in mind, and he invited me and my wife to accompany him to the big spectacle. My wife and I couldn't scrape up the fare at the moment. I proffered some excuse, though the big lure was also held before me of meeting Dempsey after the fight. Helen MacKellar, the actress, had arranged a meeting for O'Neill with Dempsey then.

Returned to Provincetown, O'Neill told me of the fight. Of how he found himself "behaving like any other real American," standing up on his seat and yelling ferociously.

When he came to, he saw he'd snatched a derby from one man's head and broken it over the head of another—neither man noticing the action—"nearly a million people were crazy—literally—for about five minutes!"

"How about seeing Dempsey after the fight, 'Gene?"

"Oh, yes! When Jack came in at the door, the first thing we noticed was his black eye. 'How'd you get the black eye, Jack?' Helen MacKellar asked. 'Aw, Helen!' sheepishly answered the champion, 'I forgot to duck!'"

Said O'Neill further: "As he stood framed in the doorway, I thought I was seeing my Hairy Ape in real life. But after we got to talking, apart in a corner, I found him a fine, good-natured gentleman. Dempsey didn't know me from Adam.

"We asked him why he had gone in and just slugged. He answered he wanted to show he could swap blow for blow; that he'd made it a point of pride to wade right in and exchange blows like fighting a bum on a street corner."

While O'Neill was telling me all this, we ourselves were having afternoon tea at Frank Shay's.

"So you like Dempsey?"

"A splendid chap! He taught me his peculiar weave and that short jolt to the chin of his—like this!" practically volunteered O'Neill. And I caught a short right to the jaw.

But his wife was having a weather-eye on us. "'Gene!" she called shrilly, "stop that!"

We had been stiffening the tea, of course, with something else.

Since then O'Neill has stopped drinking entirely, convinced that alcohol is no friend to creative writing—is nobody's friend and soon a bad master.

And Fortune is his slave and Fame is subserviently holding his stirrup.

The Boulevards After Dark
Ward Morehouse/1930

Reprinted from the *New York Sun*, 14 May 1930, 24.

PARIS, May 3.—In France, four hours by train from Paris, is a chateau, gray, isolated and austere, encircled by a beautiful wood and near the River Loire. It is there that America's First Dramatist, Eugene O'Neill, absent for two and a half years from American shores, has found the tranquillity afforded him nowhere else. And it is there that he is working on the play which he considers the most ambitious effort of his career.

At the chateau two Americans, Mr. and Mrs. Eugene O'Neill (Carlotta Monterey), keep house, thirty-five rooms of it, including two eighteenth-century towers. A hundred miles and more separate them from the Place Vendome and the whirr of Paris. Their isolation discourages Americans who might be inclined to pop in. Their nearest neighbor is a French peasant, and he isn't really near.

I've just returned from the O'Neills and the chateau country of this republic and am imprisoned once more at a typewriter near the Etoile, with the Eiffel Tower, from my window, a blurry spire against the Parisian sky. This account is submitted as a report of my findings—of the life in Touraine of Eugene O'Neill and his bride of last July, of Eugene O'Neill at 41. . . . The theater has finally made Eugene O'Neill a rich man. And, after a two-day visit with him, I have the feeling that he's also a happy man.

To get to the O'Neills you take a 3:30 train out of Paris, a fast jumpy train. Eugene O'Neill had written on to London that he'd meet that train, and so he did, but because of the station maze or because of our mutual ineptness, we missed each other. So, after ten minutes of desperate and distracted pantomime, I found myself flung aboard another train, a smaller and jumpier one. It bore me to a village, where I was deposited in front of a deserted station. It was raining and getting dark.

The chateau? Monsieur O'Neill? The only villager in sight couldn't parley Anglais, but he indicated a road that stretched away toward the horizon. So up that road I started. I finally reached a farmhouse, where a peasant was working with a scythe at the edge of the field. Surely he had heard of M. O'Neill—or hadn't *Strange Interlude* got out this far? Surely he'd heard of his chateau? I scribbled the name. "Ah, oui!" he said, and dropped the scythe in the excitement. He, too, pointed to that roadway. Brightly I proffered some francs. He understood that. Well, it seems that this Touraine farmer had a friend and that his friend had a barn, and to this barn we went. The tremendous door was flung open and there, warm and snug, was one of those tiny French cars. In ten minutes, after a wild zig-zag whirl over the squashy highway, I was standing on the doorstep of the chateau, the foreign home of the Eugene O'Neills.

Mr. O'Neill, the forty-one-year-old father of a sophomore at Yale, is grayer than when I last saw him. He's a nervous man and probably always was. Shy, too. Or until he gets pretty well acquainted. He has no small talk and probably never has had. Tall, lean and apparently muscular and always, to my notion, faintly resembling Phil Dunning.

His life in France is nicely routined. At 8:30 A.M. he's in his workroom. He writes always in long hand, using dozens of pencils. His handwriting is fascinatingly minute; so fine, in fact, that from first glance at a page of his dialogue you feel that a microscope would be necessary for the reading of it. He labors there, feet outstretched and with manuscript propped up before him, from 8:30 until 1:30. At that hour he joins Mrs. O'Neill at luncheon. He seldom works in the afternoon. He saves his afternoons for bicycle riding, for roaming his magnificent forty acres with his two dogs, a Gordon setter and a Dalmatian coach dog; for swimming in the concrete pool which he recently built and for roaring over the uncongested French roads in his Bugatti racer. He's a fool about motoring and always was. To him the Bugatti is a joy. When let out it will do 106. In the evening Playwright O'Neill reads. He tells me that he hasn't had a drink in four years. His favorite beverage is Coca Cola. Mrs. O'Neill buys it by the case.

Eugene O'Neill is a dramatist who can slave away in the country, where it's quiet, but he can't write in the city. Never could. His forty plays, long and short, were done in such places as France, Bermuda and Old Peaked Hill Bar, Provincetown. At the chateau there are no distractions and during the new Broadway season, certainly within the next six months, he'll send to New York, and to the Theater

Guild, the manuscript of the American drama which causes him to shut himself in his tower study for about forty hours out of every week.

Seated before an open fire in the large, high-ceilinged living room, Eugene O'Neill, who's seen but few New Yorkers and fewer newspaper men since he started travels that were to take him to China and back, talked of himself and his writings. He talked slowly and thoughtfully. It was nearly midnight. Two candles flickered on the table behind us.

"If I had any idea," he said, "that I'd have to repeat myself, that I had to stand still, I'd quit writing plays. I'd call it a day. I write primarily for myself, because it is a pleasure and it would cease to be that if I started repeating. I could have gone on forever with plays like *Anna Christie,* or with the expressionism of *The Hairy Ape,* but I'm interested in trying to do better things.

"Now, this new play of mine is the hardest thing I've ever tried. God knows, it's the most ambitious. It is an American play, in four acts, and represents a development of my technic. I've done the first draft. I'll do a second, then lay that aside and start on something else. Later I'll come back to it, and perhaps I may have something. I don't want to talk of its content. That hurt me with *Dynamo.* I just want to finish it, call a stenographer from Paris, and then mail it to the Guild. I've been at work on it for a year. Carlotta seems to think it's all right." (*"Wonderful,"* was the word Mrs. O'Neill used to me.)

The dramatist-son of a grand old actor sipped his beverage and sat gazing at the burning wood chunks.

"You see," he said, "I've found out something. I've found out that I ought to take more time. Looking back to *Dynamo,* I did eighteen long plays in eleven years. That's too much. If I could go back I'd destroy some of these plays, say, four of them—*Gold, The First Man, The Fountain* and *Welded.* I've written, I think, forty plays—twenty long and twenty short. In my note book I have ideas for thirty plays, perhaps thirty-two. That's work for a lifetime."

"Would you," I asked, "destroy *Dynamo?*"

"No, but I'd rewrite it. *Dynamo* had in it the makings of a fine play, but I did it too fast. And it was silly of me to mention a trilogy. And I wasn't surprised that they jumped me about it—that was but natural after *Strange Interlude.*"

He paused. "The play of mine," he said, "for which I have the

greatest affection is *The Great God Brown*. Next, *The Hairy Ape* and
then *Strange Interlude*. My favorite short play is *The Moon of the
Caribbees*. I think the best writing I've done for the theater was in
Lazarus Laughed."

"And about your actors?"

"I've been remarkably lucky, I think, in the matter of actors. Certainly the performance of Walter Huston in *Desire Under the Elms*
was tremendous. Exactly what I had in mind. And there were
splendid performances by Paul Robeson in *The Emperor Jones* and
by Lynn Fontanne in *Strange Interlude*."

Being a dramatist, either one whose plays have never emerged
from the dust heap of a managerial desk, or one whose plays have
brought international renown, is not without its bothers. Eugene
O'Neill isn't given to explosions, but when on the subject of
plagiarism suits he comes pretty close to it. He waxes hot; almost
bitter.

"It's like going," he said, "to a garbage can for diamonds. . . . Take
the case of *Strange Interlude*. That damn fool suit is not only an
annoyance but an expense. Such suits as this don't come to anything
but when they're thrown out you never collect costs. With *Interlude*
we were about to sell it to talking pictures for $75,000 and of that I
would have had half. The preposterous suit held up the sale." And to
calm himself he took another drink—a soft one.

. . . It was well after midnight. I was shown to a bedroom at the
end of a long corridor. A tall candle flickered at the bedside. There is
no electricity at the chateau—it would be out of place, unthinkable!
Lamps and candles. I slept despite the quiet and at 8:30 A.M. the
butler was in the room with orange juice. He didn't bring the
morning paper. You can't have the calm of the chateau country and
also get the box scores.

Now, as to the home life of Genie, as his wife calls him, and the
actress that New York knew as Carlotta Monterey: They have a corps
of servants. If there's one thing cheap in France (and I doubt it) it's
hired help. The O'Neills keep a butler, a chef, a housemaid, a
personal maid for Mrs. O'Neill, a gardener and a chauffeur. The
chauffeur, who is also a mechanic, gets the highest wage—$45 a
month.

The O'Neills go to Paris but seldom, and then on business. They motor always. They get London and Paris on their radio, which is to be found in the summer salon, the room with the Florentine ceiling. They've seen few Americans in the past year. Their present guest is Mrs. Theresa Renner, attractive wife of a physician of Shanghai, who attended the playwright when he was ill in China. Mrs. Renner accepted the O'Neills' invitation and came all the way from Shanghai, fourteen days, via the trans-Siberian railway. The American guests at the chateau have been Lillian Gish, George Jean Nathan, Theresa Helburn and Helen Westley. Miss Westley was, seemingly, a little bewildered by it all. I don't think she understood how the O'Neills can live where they do. I don't think she likes France.

The chateau was rented from an old French family on a three-year lease. When that lease expires Mr. and Mrs. O'Neill will pay off the help, pack up their things and take a boat back to America. At least, they think they will.

"I have not had," he said, "any idea of living over here permanently. Nothing like that. No nonsense such as renouncing America. There's such a thing as being sensibly patriotic. But living away from America has been a good way to get to know how to see things that you couldn't see before."

And so that is how I found the O'Neills in France. They were standing at the doorway, he was clad in a heavy sweater and she was trim and smart in Parisian sport clothes, when the chauffeur whirled through the driveway in Carlotta's magnificent French car. Eugene O'Neill extended his hand and grinned. "Yes," he said, "tell them we're coming back. And I may even get there for rehearsals."

The door of the tonneau slammed. The engine roared. The great car shot forward and I was off for the Tours train, which was to take me back to the boulevards and bewilderments of the city known as Paris.

Exile Made Him Appreciate U.S., O'Neill Admits

Ernest K. Lindley/1931

Reprinted from the *New York Herald Tribune*, 22 May 1931, 19.

Eugene O'Neill, who ended a voluntary exile of three years by slipping into the port unnoticed on Sunday, three weeks after the arrival of his latest and longest play, *Mourning Becomes Electra,* had been heralded at the Theater Guild, emerged yesterday for an interview.

He returned filled with "appreciation of American superiorities." He thinks the rebirth of the theater is coming in America, not in Europe—the European theater is "flat." In another year, when the lease on his French chateau has expired, he is coming to America to live and work. He has his work planned for five years ahead—he is going to carry forward the experiments with masks, which he began in *The Great God Brown.* He is eager to see how his new trilogy, on which he has been "working like a Trappist monk for a year and a half," is received. Each performance will require two separate evenings; the play contains neither masks nor the asides which gave length to *Strange Interlude.*

Since he left America he has wandered in the Orient, fled from "snoopers" in Shanghai, been divorced by the second Mrs. O'Neill and married Carlotta Monterey, the actress; lived in the chateau in Touraine, in the Canaries and Switzerland. *Strange Interlude* has had its astonishing run, and *Dynamo,* announced as the first play of a trilogy, was received with such indifference that many critics proclaimed that O'Neill was on the downgrade.

Outwardly, O'Neill seemed unchanged yesterday as he sat behind a desk in the offices of the Theater Guild, gradually but constantly shifting his position, smiling shyly, recurrently lowering his deep-set eyes, his low, sad voice hesitating over his simple answers.

He was asked if he intended to return to the Chateau de Plessis in Touraine.

"We're going back after the play has been put on," he replied. "We have a lease with about a year to run. After that we're coming back here."

"Where?"

"Oh, somewhere where there's sunshine. It has been raining in France for fifteen months, nine days out of ten. It's a beautiful country but a terrible climate."

"You want some place where you can work better?" it was suggested.

"Oh, I've been able to work everywhere. We're living in the country there. Its just like other country. After a while you feel you want to come back."

"Do you feel that you've derived any benefit from living abroad—been able to see America any more clearly, for example?"

"I feel that is the greatest benefit I have derived from living abroad. It has enabled me to see America more clearly—also to appreciate it more.

"I mean, to see the qualities we have that they don't have," he went on, in response to several questions. "Most people who travel abroad get the sort of snobbish idea that they are coming in contact with something superior. I don't feel that way. I have talked with a great many people in the theater over there—I don't mean the critics, but the people who are working in it. They feel that it is flat, tired out. They feel that we have something dynamic, and that if we can get their cultural background the rebirth of the theater is not going to happen over there—in Europe—but here. So do I."

"Did you see much of the French drama?"

"Yes, I saw a good deal of it. It was mostly pretty dead and not so well directed or so well acted as over here."

Mr. O'Neill smiled. "I know that sounds like patriotic ballyhoo," he said, "but it isn't. I went over there with the opposite opinion—I think before long they'll all be coming over here."

The discussion turned to Mourning Becomes Electra.

The author explained that it is three separate plays about the same people over a period of two years from 1865 to 1867. The setting, a New England seaport town, where clipper ships were built before the Civil War. There are three important women characters and three important men characters. The first play is called Homecoming, the second *The Hunted* and the third *The Haunted*. The first play has four acts, the second five and the third four.

"The scenery is very simple," Mr. O'Neill explained. "Six or seven sets. One scene is on a ship, it is true, but it's a very simple ship. A good many of them use the exterior of a Colonial house with steps and six pillars. Every play moves from the exterior to the interior, comes back to the exterior again and then goes back to the interior. It's a sort of a formula.

"Yes, there are three tragedies—cumulative."

"Is each complete?" he was asked.

"I've tried very hard to get the right compromise," he replied. "Each play takes a very definite part of the lives of the people, which causes the next part. I've tried to give the idea that each one has to follow—granting the first part the other has to happen. I've tried to get the idea of Fate into it. Not exactly the Greek idea, but Fate more from the point of view of modern psychology. I hope that any one who sees the second play, for example, will want to see the first as much as the third."

His own scheme for producing the play, he said, is to have a preliminary week for the critics—the first play on Monday and Tuesday, the second on Wednesday and Thursday and the third on Friday and Saturday. After that he would have the plays given in rotation, one week at a time.

"I don't know whether the Guild is going to agree to that," he added.

The rehearsals are to begin August 17, and the director and part of the cast will be chosen within a few days.

"There are no asides in the play," he replied to the next question. "I started off using asides. Then I thought of using masks. But I got rid of both. I found they got in the way."

"You have become convinced that the aside is not good dramatic technique?"

"No," he replied. "But these people are intense, people with lots of will power. You see what they want from their actions. I don't think the soliloquy will work except in rare instances. *Interlude* was about people who don't know what they want, don't know how to get it."

Mr. O'Neill said he had the vague idea for the play for about five years. "Was it the magnitude of the idea which caused you to make it three different plays?"

"No, a trilogy was the idea from the beginning."

"Why?"

"You have to keep yourself interested in something," he replied, "to go on.

"My personal interest in the theater is to see just how much can be done with it—not only for my sake, but for everybody's sake. The more it is pushed out, the more can be done with it. That's why I am interested in seeing how this play is received."

"Do you care?" he was asked.

He raised his voice for the first time: "Of course I care. I've been working like a Trappist monk for a year and a half."

He was reminded that George Jean Nathan, dramatic critic, had testified recently that he had given O'Neill a great deal of advice concerning his plays, and that usually it had been rejected.

"His only suggestion so far concerning this one," he replied, "is the removal of one line he doesn't like—I think I shall leave that in."

"Then the play is finished, except for such changes as you may want to make in rehearsals?"

"I've written all of it in long-hand three times. I think that's enough."

If this play should go over, would his next be even longer?

"They all look to me like single-evening plays," he replied. "I have my work planned for at least five years. When I get to thinking about some of them, they may stretch out. But you very seldom get an idea for a trilogy."

"Wasn't Dynamo to have been the first play of a trilogy?

"No," he asserted. "That was not to have been a trilogy at all. I called it that. But it was really three plays about the same subject—Dynamo was misunderstood, partly because I wrote letters about it, in which I misunderstood it myself, before I had finished the play."

If not a longer play, in what direction would he look for new ventures in the drama?

"One of my principal obsessions is the reintroduction of masks as a medium in the theater. One of my next plays is to be a play of masks. My idea about masks is that they can be made acceptable to the

modern audience—as they were in ancient times—but in a new
sense. People do recognize, from their knowledge of the new
psychology, that every one wears a mask—I don't mean only one,
but thousands of them. I believe people will come to accept them in
the theater. I don't think *The Great God Brown* had a long run
merely because it was a novelty."

As soon as the preliminary conferences on *Mourning Becomes
Electra* have been finished Mr. and Mrs. O'Neill will go to San
Francisco to pass the early part of the summer with her relatives. No,
he would not do any work for the "talkies."

"An emphatic 'not.' I don't mean I have a snooty attitude toward
them. I have only seen two and I don't know anything about them. I
think it will be more fun to do my own work."

O'Neill Picks America as His Future Workshop
Richard Watts, Jr./1931

Reprinted from the New York Herald Tribune, 27 September 1931, sec. 8, 1.

Patriotism, Eugene O'Neill would tell you, is the last refuge of the traveler. Returning to America after three pleasant years abroad, three years which probably were the most mellow and satisfying of his brooding existence, he finds his native land both stimulating and exciting. Europe and the Orient were delightful and his residence in that lovely chateau of his just outside of Tours was a strikingly happy one. America, however, is to him the land of vividness and gusto, the most vigorous and invigorating of nations, the place in which to live and work if one is concerned at all with keeping in touch with the epic dramatic trends of the chaotic modern civilization.

For one thing, it happens, he believes that the local theater, for all of its frailties, provides the one living and growing drama in present day culture. The English stage is facile, but uncreative; the French is generally decadent and moribund, the German is concerned chiefly with tricks of production and the Russian is the victim of a narrow censorship, ruinous to genuine artistic creation. From such a general indictment he would, to a certain extent, exclude the Irish. O'Casey is to him the greatest of living dramatists, and he regards Yeats as the one great poet of our time.

Even in Ireland, however, the European dramatic decadence has left its mark. In rejecting O'Casey's last play, the Abbey Theater of Dublin revealed sadly but conclusively that it had lost something of the fighting spirit which caused it to produce the masterpieces of Synge in the days when theatergoers were interested enough in the drama to throw things when they got mad. Even the embattled Irish theater has grown a bit flabby.

In the current Russian theater there is, Mr. O'Neill says, at least one reason for optimism. The spirit of the actors has gained everything in vigor, intelligence and integrity which government consorship tends to destroy among authors and producers. A Russian stage which

113

lived up to the level of the Russian actor would be incomparable. He admits the importance to the Muscovite drama of the earnest, crusading zeal which goes into the Soviet writing for the theater, and he sees the possibility of the emergence of a mighty zealot who might write great plays, not only despite but also because of the current insistence on the drama as a communist tract. The real creative artist is, however, smothered by government supervision.

Mr. O'Neill's plays are enormously popular in Russia, but even he has suffered from the censor's grim-eyed work. In *Desire Under the Elms,* his central character is, you may remember, given to numerous and eloquent speeches addressed to the Deity. Since, however, God has been abolished in the Union of Soviet Socialist Republics, the lines on the subject were stricken from the play and the central character thereupon became minor in importance. A vast section of the point of the work was lost, too, but at least the drama-loving Muscovites were spared the shock of hearing about Divine Providence.

Last year in Paris the Kamerny Theater of Moscow presented its production of *All God's Chillun* and a less emasculated *Desire.* O'Neill was enchanted with the results. For one thing, he found that the actor who blacked up and played his Negro hero in the play about miscegenation captured the quality he was striving for with considerably more comprehension and completeness than even Paul Robeson, who had the role in the original production, ever managed, though the role was practically written for him. Mr. O'Neill admired, too, the spirit which caused the actor who had played the leading part in *All God's Chillun Got Wings* to perform as an extra the following evening in *Desire Under the Elms.*

At this point it strikes me that this report of Mr. O'Neill has, in its refusal to quote from its subject directly, something of the quality which used to be found in accounts of a vague and mysterious White House Spokesman. It should be noted, therefore, that this is not intended as an "interview" with the First Playwright. It is merely intended as an effort to express, in a rather free-handed way, a number of the ideas expressed by Mr. O'Neill in an utterly informal conversation which had about it nothing, I fear, of the air of a prosecutor grilling a suspect.

Of all the genuinely distinguished writing men of our time, it is probable that only Eugene O'Neill and William Butler Yeats live up to one's hopes for their physical appearance. The bronzed, handsome, graying Mr. O'Neill is pretty much the ideal of what a great, melancholy and brooding playwright should look like, just as the fine, ecstatic brow of Yeats gives to its possessor the ideal manner and appearance of an Olympian poet.

Anyway, getting back to the subject of the O'Neill viewpoint, his concern with the question of the cinema should be recorded. In the first place, he must certainly be one of the few authors in the world who has ever been satisfied with the picturization of his work. The silent screen version of *Anna Christie*, in which Blanche Sweet played the title role many years ago, strikes him as being a fine and faithful work. He did not see the Greta Garbo, or garrulous, version because some friends had come to him with unpleasant reports. He is convinced that the screen, handicapped as it is by censorship and the need to be excessively popular in its efforts, has little chance of being a distinguished art form until the cost of production is reduced enormously.

At the same time, the cinema as a dramatic method appeals to him greatly. In the pre-vitaphone days he even wrote film adaptations of *The Hairy Ape* and *Desire Under the Elms* in which he changed their plot details to fit in with the requirements of the medium. Now he has an even more ambitious idea in mind. He is contemplating a version of his *Lazarus Laughed* in which only the actor playing Lazarus should appear on the stage, while the rest of the production should be cinema. He believes that this would make the difficult production feasible and that, in addition, it would be helpful to the mood of the play in showing its protagonist as the one live person in a world of marionettes.

O'Neill Plots a Course for the Drama

S. J. Woolf/1931

Reprinted from the *New York Times Magazine*, 4 October 1931, 6. Copyright © 1931 by The New York Times Company. Reprinted by permission.

Having voyaged beyond the horizon, Eugene O'Neill has returned to this country to write his plays here. "It is well to travel occasionally, but if a man wants to write about his country he must live in it," he said. "The tempo, the attitude, the psychology of Europe are different, and one unconsciously absorbs these things. An author is of necessity influenced by his surroundings. To write of Americans, one must live in America, breathe its atmosphere, experience its reactions, live its kind of life, and feel the pulse of the people."

He spoke softly, almost shyly, as he slouched in a chair in a cubbyhole of a room piled high with newspapers—the theatrical office of a friend. Through an open door typewriters clicked. Errand boys appeared with packages. The business end of the theatre was everywhere in evidence. Yet he was remote from it all. It was like meeting a musician in a piano factory, a poet in a printing plant.

Mr. O'Neill is very different from what one expects him to be, more fragile, more tenuous, more apart. Behind his quiet manner there is a tenseness of nerves, which his long, thin fingers emphasized as they beat a tattoo on his thigh or dug themselves into the palms of his hands. His clothes, immaculately cared for, hung well on his tall, thin figure; his black hair, graying at the temples, was carefully combed, and his four-in-hand was meticulously tied about a well-fitting collar.

His forehead and eyes dominate his face. It would be easy to make a caricature of him with straight lines until one came to the eyes, but curves alone would express them, circles of intense darkness. About them is a furtive sadness, which seemed puzzlingly familiar. It is the same sadness one sees in the faded daguerreotypes of Poe.

Forty-three years ago James O'Neill, the father of Eugene, was one of the idols of the American stage. As the innocent Edmond Dantes who eventually escapes from prison, becomes the Count of Monte

116

Cristo and wreaks vengeance on his enemies, he was thrilling the theatregoing public. While Niblo's Garden was still a theatre on lower Broadway, while long-haired, fur-coated actors congregated about the Union Square Theatre, the elder O'Neill was nightly ripping the sack in which he had been thrown into a canvas ocean.

"I can still see my father," said the playwright, "dripping with salt and sawdust, climbing on a stool behind the swinging profile of dashing waves. It was then that the calcium lights in the gallery played on his long beard and tattered clothes, as with arms out-stretched he declared that the world was his.

"This was a signal for the house to burst into a deafening applause that overwhelmed the noise of the storm manufactured backstage. It was an artificial age, an age ashamed of its own feelings, and the theatre reflected its thoughts. Virtue always triumphed and vice always got its just deserts. It accepted nothing half-way; a man was either a hero or a villain, and a woman was either virtuous or vile."

The Two Orphans, Rosedale and *Paul Kauvar* were in their heyday, and a young man, Belasco by name, had begun to direct at the old Madison Square Theatre when Eugene Gladstone O'Neill was born in a corner room on the third floor of the old hotel which still stands at Forty-third Street and Broadway. The Barrett House of those days was a family hostelry fully half a mile above the most northerly of New York's theatres. Horse-bells jangled as bobbing yellow street cars trailed past brownstone residences and frame buildings which were just beginning to be turned to business purposes. The Great White Way was still an avenue of comparative darkness lighted in the Sum-mer by a solitary sign at Twenty-second Street advertising the breezes which swept Manhattan Beach. The rest of its diagonal course was illuminated by gas lamps. On the stage, romance held full sway. Margaret Mather in *Article 47* and Fanny Davenport in *Fedora* brought forth many a tear from the unmade-up eyes of their corseted, bustled audiences, while the flowing mustaches of Lester Wallack, Harry Montague and Maurice Barrymore caused hearts to flutter behind their whalebone armor.

In this atmosphere young O'Neill grew up. For seven years he was taken around the country as his father arose each night from the waves. Then his schooling began and continued until he was 19, when he was dismissed from Princeton for what in his own words was "general hell raising." He wanted to live, to see the world. Although his first job as secretary of a mail order house gave him much leisure, it afforded him no opportunity to roam. Then he made a trip to Honduras in search of gold; and subsequently he accepted a position in his father's theatrical company as assistant manager. But hot trips on stuffy trains to small towns palled on him. Above the rattle of gravel in bags, used to simulate the raging storm, he heard the call of the sea and, deserting the painted ocean for the real, he set sail on a Norwegian bark for Buenos Aires.

In the Argentine he tried his hand at various commercial ventures; he was a clerk for the Westinghouse Company, he attempted to sell sewing machines, and even worked in a packing house. He was a failure at everything and spent months hanging around the waterfront with beachcombers and stokers. Again he set sail, this time for Africa, but as he had no money he was not permitted to land and returned on the cattle steamer on which he had arrived. He finally shipped on a tramp for New York and lived here in a longshoreman's dive.

"About this time," he told me, "vaudeville was extremely popular, and my father decided to put on a tabloid version of *The Count of Monte Cristo*. He offered me one of the smaller parts and for a season we traveled all over the country, appearing twice a day, between a trained-horse act and a group of flying acrobats. That was my only actual acting experience, for when the season ended and my family went to our Summer home in New London I got a job as a reporter in that city."

But his health failed and he had to go to a sanitarium; it was there that he began to write plays. Upon his recovery he took a course at Harvard under Professor Baker. About fifteen years ago that strange erratic genius, George Cram Cook, was conducting a theatre in a crude building on a wharf in Provincetown and there produced one of O'Neill's plays. When the Provincetown Players came here, O'Neill came with them, and in the old barn in Macdougal Street, with its diminutive stage and its wooden benches, many of his plays had their first showing.

"One of the things I regret," he said, "is the passing of the experimental group theatre where innovations are tried out by men and women who are inspired with real ideals. The Provincetown Players and the old Washington Square Theatre have no successors today.

There are commercial managers who are doing now the same things that they were doing ten years ago. But that is the usual story of commercial producers. They are invariably ten years behind the times and never do they credit their public with as much sense or taste as it has. They are afraid to put on good plays for fear the audience will not appreciate them, with the result that many an able man is compelled to write trash to their order so that he may live. In the meantime, plays produced with the certainty that they will be box office successes, prove failures."

"Is this particularly true of this country?" I asked.

"I would not say it was," he replied. "The theatre is dead as far as England and France are concerned. In Germany it has become a prop for the glorification of the theatrical director and plays are written or changed so as to give him a chance to display his technical skill.

"In Russia there is a real renaissance of the theatre. It is a new country with new ideas, and tradition does not bind it, nor does commercialism throttle it. New men get a chance and new ideas are tried out, and the box office does not play the leading part. The result is that to my mind the most interesting work that is being done today in the theatre is in Russia.

"That does not mean that the same thing could not be done here. I believe that we have the best directors, the best writers, the best actors and the best scenic artists in the world right in this country, but all of them are going along each in his own way. If all this talent could be collected and made to work together I am certain that productions could be given here that would be unequaled."

From a silver case he took a cork-tipped cigarette, a particularly mild kind, he told me, and for a few minutes he smoked in silence. I wished that he, like his characters in *Strange Interlude,* would express his thoughts, but he did not. Instead the telephone rang and somebody wanted free tickets for an opening performance. In the next room the machinery of theatrical production kept up its endless grind, while he, a master craftsman of the theatre, seemed oblivious of it all.

The afternoon sun, until then kept out of the room by tall buildings on the other side of the street, at last found a space between them through which it could pass. Suddenly he looked up and smiled. It was a boyish smile and an awkward one—as if he had just become aware of his long lapse into silence. Then, pointing to a drawing of Shaw that was hanging on the opposite wall, he remarked: "I wish they would take that down; the old gentleman seems to be laughing at me."

The mask was off. He was himself again, and I asked him what progress he had noted in the theatre since he had begun writing.

"The greatest change that I see is the fact that now the playwright has secured for himself the right to say anything he chooses.

"Up to a comparatively short time ago, as late as the time when Clyde Fitch and his school were popular, for three acts an author would build up a thesis and then in the fourth act proceed to knock over what he had constructed. The managers felt that they knew what the public would accept and the plays had to conform to their ideas. The very fact that I was brought up in the theatre made me hate this artificiality and this slavish acceptance of these traditions.

"After *Beyond the Horizon* had made a success downtown it was with much uncertainty that a manager put it on in a Broadway theatre. He believed in the play, but he feared his public. The public accepted it, even though I did not kick over in the last act all that I had done in the previous ones. The play was carried to its logical conclusion. The tragedy of Robert Mayo brought an exultation and an urge on the part of the audience toward more life.

"That is one of my favorite plays," he went on. "So is *The Great God Brown*, so *Strange Interlude*. There are others, however, that I should like to destroy."

"Which are they?" I asked.

"You probably never saw them," he replied. "They are those which the public would not accept. But that is not the reason I would do it. I now realize that they are not good plays."

Eugene O'Neill

George Jean Nathan/1932

Reprinted from *The Intimate Notebooks of George Jean Nathan* (New York: Alfred A. Knopf, 1932), 21–38; collected in *The World of George Jean Nathan* (New York: Knopf, 1952), 30–43. Reprinted by permission of Associated University Presses.

In all the many years of our friendship, I have heard Eugene O'Neill laugh aloud once and only once. We were walking, after dinner one evening in July, up the long, lonely road just beyond the château he was then living and working in at Saint Antoine du Rocher in Touraine. In the country, men who live in cities generally find themselves talking out of character. If they are sober, sedate fellows in the city, they become orally frisky in the country; if they are flippant in the city, they become more or less solemn and even wistful at the smell of flowers and manure. Their discourse alters with the scene. O'Neill, who in the city—for he is essentially a man of cities despite his inability to write save a cow is mooing or a sea is swishing beneath his window—has the mien and the conversational *élan* of an embalmer, presently proceeded thus: "When Princeton, after kicking my tail out of place as an undergraduate because I was too accurate a shot with an Anheuser-Busch beer-bottle, and hit a window in Woodrow Wilson's house right where it lived, some years later suddenly got proud of its old beer-bottle heaver but magnanimously allowed Yale to claim the hoodlum for its own with an honorary degree, I found myself in New Haven late one night viewing a number of old boys of the class of 1880 or thereabouts having a hot reunion with themselves. Three of them in particular, that I ran across on one of the street-corners, were so grandly stewed that I had to stand still and watch them. One of them, it appeared, was president of a big bank in New York; another was vice-president of one of the big railroads; and the third was a United States Senator. After playing leap-frog for about ten minutes, during which one of them fell down and rolled half-way into a sewer, the three, singing barber-shop songs at the top of their lungs, wobbled across the street to the opposite corner where there was a mail-box. With a lot of grunts and after much steaming and puffing, the bank president and the vice-president of the big railroad got down on their knees and hoisted their old classmate, the Senator, up on their shoulders in a line with the slit in the mail-box. Whereupon the Senator proceeded to use the mail-box for a purpose generally reserved for telegraph poles and the sides of barns."

The boisterous roar that followed his recollection of the scene marked, as I have said, the only time within my knowledge of O'Neill that he has laughed outright at anything. In all the years I have known him, the most that has ever issued from him has been a quiet little chuckle and I have only, in all that time, heard him chuckle twice, once in New York when he indulged in a reminiscence of the wonderful free-lunch that he and his brother Jim used to get with a five-cent glass of beer (and live on) in a saloon opposite the old Madison Square Garden, and once at Le Plessis, in France, when he handed me a newspaper article in Spanish, treating of the time he once spent in Buenos Aires during his sailor days, asked me to translate it for him, and I inserted several imaginary paragraphs describing in rich detail his great proficiency as a tango dancer. He is constitutionally the antithesis of *l'homme qui rit*. Nothing even faintly amuses him, unless it be the remembrance of his dead brother's gift for Rabelaisian monkeyshines, the singing (in a voice capable of just three notes, all sour) of old barroom ballads, or remembered tales of his father, the late James O'Neill who, during the years when he was a matinée idol, used to parade Fourteenth Street at high noon daily—after at least three hours spent in dolling himself up—by way of giving the girls a treat, and who always made it a practise on Sundays to get to church half an hour late by way of staging an effective entrance for himself.

Contrary to finding amusement in the world, O'Neill finds endlessly the materials for indignation. The body of his dramatic writing reflects him more closely, I venture to say, than that of any other playwright in the present-day American theatre. Let the dramatic critic of some yokel newspaper in some yokel town that he has never even heard of write that he isn't all he should be as a dramatist, and he lets out a vituperative blast of such volume that, once done, he finds himself completely exhausted. Several times I myself have been denounced, if somewhat more politely, for expressed opinions on his work. Once, he let me read the manuscript of his play, *Welded,* in which he had great faith. When I reported to him that all I could discern in it was some very third-rate Strindberg, he sharply observed that I couldn't conceivably understand any such play as I had never been married, put on his hat, walked out and didn't let me hear from him for two months afterward. When, several years later, he sent me the manuscript of *Lazarus Laughed* and I wrote to him that I didn't care for it, he replied in the next mail that my judgment of it couldn't be taken seriously by him because I was lacking in all religious feeling and was therefore prejudiced against any such play, and that it was really a masterpiece whatever I thought about it. On this occasion, he was so disgusted with my critical gifts that he didn't write to me again for three months. The same thing happened in the case of *Dynamo,* which in a preliminary manuscript reading struck me as being close to caricature. Even after the play was produced and almost unanimously condemned, he stuck to his loyalty toward it and to his conviction that all the critics were dolts. "It maybe wasn't all it should have been," he subsequently admitted to me, "because I was going through a lot of trouble in family matters when I was writing it, but just the same you're dead wrong about it." And—I happened to be visiting him at the time—he sulked for the rest of the day and condescended only to exchange a curt goodnight with me at bed-time. If a newspaper or any other kind of photographer snaps him without his formal permission, he seethes. If he gets a letter with something in it that displeases him, he mutters sourly over it for twenty-four hours. The petty nuisances and annoyances that every man suffers and quickly dismisses from mind and attention cause him something bordering on acute agony.

After many years of being very hard up, his plays gradually began to make him money. But real money came only with the tremendous success, both as a performed play and published book, of *Strange Interlude,* which netted him close to a half-million dollars. Since boyhood, he had had just two wishes: one, to have some shirts tailored by a first-class London shirt-maker and, two, to own a carriage dog such as he had seen loping after the rigs of the rich in his youngster days. His greatest satisfaction in *Strange Interlude* was that it had made the gratification of the two wishes possible.

He has a dislike of meeting people that amounts almost to a terror.

Even with his few close friends he is generally so taciturn that it is sometimes necessary to go over and poke him to make certain that he is neither asleep nor dead. He sits glumly for hours at a time without opening his mouth, brooding deeply over some undecipherable concern which, upon ultimate revelation, turns out to be a worried speculation as to whether his wife has ordered spaghetti, his favorite dish, for dinner for him that night. Having sat at different tables with him countless times, I have, with rare exception, heard him during the course of a meal say more than two words and they have invariably been—in reply to an inquiry as to whether he would care for any more of this or that—"Why sure." The way to lose O'Neill's friendship is to ask him for oral expressions of opinion on anything (if he feels like expressing an opinion, he will write a letter, and a satisfactorily long one), or to introduce him to any man other than one who knows a great deal about professional sports and who will confine his conversation to that subject. The one great admiration that he has temporarily achieved for any man in the last four years was for Sparrow Robertson, the chief sporting writer of the Paris *Herald,* whom he met just once and found to be "a grand bird." He has a greater respect for Sean O'Casey, but beyond that an aversion to most men of his own profession, asserting that the majority of them are not worth the powder to blow them up, and of all those whom he has met in later years only W. S. Maugham and H. R. Lenormand have any interest for him. He goes to a theatre about once in every five years and then only in Europe because he has heard that some play of his is being done there in a language that he cannot understand. I have known him on only one occasion really to admit that he had been in a theatre. That was when the Russian Tairoff did *All God's Chillun* in Russian in Paris several years ago. He professed to have found it the best production of any of his plays that he had ever seen. "But," I protested, "you don't know a word of Russian. How could *you* tell?" He looked at me pityingly. "You should have seen the way Tairoff's wife, in the rôle of the girl, brushed those books off the table in that scene in the last act!" he replied with grave seriousness.

Displaying outwardly all the glow and effervescence of a magnum of ice water, he is internally given to huge enthusiasms of all sorts and varieties. Whatever piece of work he happens currently to be working

on arouses him to such a pitch of incalescence over its virtues that he
will go around all day wreathed in broad, mysterious smiles. And
when O'Neill thus smiles, it is as if any other man stood gleefully on
his head, waved his arms and legs and let out a bellow that shook the
heavens. Familiar with all his longer, as well as with a number of his
shorter plays, since their manuscript infancy, I recall only one time
when doubt over a script that he was writing assailed him. In all the
other cases he was as excited over their merits as a child of the
wealthy anticipating on Christmas Eve the gifts he was certain to get.
The one exception was a trilogy which he had undertaken. "Would
to God," he wrote me, "that this damned trilogy of mine were off of
my neck! I'm beginning to hate it and curse the day I ever conceived
such an idea. The notion haunts me that I've bitten off a good deal
more that I can chew. On my return, the first two acts of the first play
struck me as not right, so I've started to rewrite them. And so it goes
on! It looks as if the rest of my life was doomed to be spent rewriting
the damned thing. I honestly feel very low about it and am anxious
to get done with it and free my mind from the obsession of it and get
on to something else. When these two acts are done, for better or
worse, I'm going to call quits. I don't think I can go through the
ordeal of typing it myself now. I'm too fed up. Think it wiser to get it
typed. It would bore me so that before the end I would probably
burn it."

   But not so usually. Confidence generally permeates his being,
warming him to the very toes. He says nothing, or at best very little,
but the mysterious smiles embroider his features. Of *The Straw,* he
informed me, "I have complete confidence in my own valuation of
it." *Where the Cross Is Made,* was "great fun to write, theatrically
very thrilling, an amusing experiment in treating the audience as
insane.""I would like to stand or fall"—in each instance—"by
*Bound East for Cardiff, The Long Voyage Home, The Moon of the
Caribbees, Beyond the Horizon, The Straw* and *Gold,*" he wrote me.
Each of these plays, he duly announced, was "my sincerest effort and
was written purely for its own sake." Of *All God's Chillun Got
Wings*—"Well, I've got it done and I'm immensely pleased with it!"
Of *Desire Under the Elms*—"Its poetical vision illuminating even the
most sordid and mean blind alleys of life—that is my justification as a
dramatist!" Of *Marco Millions*—"there's a whole lot of poetical

beauty in it and fine writing." *The Great God Brown* was "a
devastating, crucifying new one." *Lazarus Laughed* was "far the best
play I've ever written." Of *Dynamo*—"I thoroughly disagree with you
about the play. It is *not* far, far below me, I'm sure of that! Wait and
see! It will come into its own some day when it isn't judged as a
symbolical trilogy with a message to good Americans about what's
wrong with them and what to do about it. I think you're wrong this
time—as wrong as about *Lazarus Laughed*. Not that you're not right
about the excessiveness of the stage directions, but then I thought
you knew that my scripts get drastically weeded out in that respect
when I read proof and that I always let them slide as they first occur
to me until then. A slovenly method, perhaps, but the way I've
always worked. Then again, I don't think it's fair to take the speeches
of a lot of admittedly inarticulate characters in a particular play as
expressions of the general underlying theme of a trilogy—which I
obviously never intended them to be." Indeed, even in the case of
the latest trilogy, *Mourning Becomes Electra,* about which there were
the preliminary doubts already recorded, I received, when the play at
length was finished, this comment: "It has been one hell of a job!
Let's hope the result in some measure justifies the labor I've put in.
To get enough of Clytemnestra in Christine, of Electra in Lavinia, of
Orestes in Orin, etc., and yet keep them American primarily; to
conjure a Greek fate out of the Mannons themselves (without calling
in the aid of even a Puritan Old Testament God) that would convince
a modern audience without religion or moral ethics; to prevent the
surface melodrama of the plot from overwhelming the real drama; to
contrive murders that escape cops and courtroom scenes; and finally
to keep myself out of it and shun the many opportunities for
effusions of personal writing anent life and fate—all this has made the
going tough and the way long! And even now it's done I don't know
quite what I've got. All I *do* know is that after reading it all through, in
spite of my familiarity with every page, it leaves me moved and
disturbed spiritually, and I have a feeling of there being real size in it,
quite apart from its length; a sense of having had a valid dramatic
experience with intense tortured passions beyond the ambition or
scope of other modern plays. As for the separate parts, each play,
each act, seem better than I hoped. And that's that."

Wherever he happens to be at the moment happens enthusiastically also to be the place of all places for him to be and forever live in. Provincetown was "ideal, quiet and the only place where I could ever work." When in Bermuda, he wrote me, "I didn't start this letter with any view of boring you by an expounding of inner principles. It was rather to recommend Bermuda to you as a place to 'take the waters' in case you're planning a Spring vacation. The climate is grand. The German bottled beer and English bottled ale are both excellent. And the swimming is wonderful, if you like such, which I do above everything. It has proved a profitable Winter resort for me. I've gotten more work done that in the corresponding season up North in many years." When at Belgrade Lakes, in Maine, he sent me a postcard: "There's tranquility here. A place to think and work if ever there was one! Ideal for me." "Well, after a week in London," he wrote, "I am strong for it. It seems to me that if it were possible for me to live contented in any city this would be the one. There is something so self-assuredly nerveless about it. Of course, the weather has been unexpectedly fine—warm and sunny every day—and that helps. In short, I've been happier here since I left New York than ever in my life before." While he was living in Guéthary in the Basque country, I received the following: "The Basque country and the Basques hit me right where I belong! According to present plans and inclinations it is here that I shall settle down to make a home for the rest of my days. Europe has meant a tremendous lot to me, more that I ever hoped it could. I've felt a deep sense of peace here, a real enjoyment in just living from day to day, that I've never known before. For more than the obvious financial reasons, I've come to the conclusion that anyone doing creative work is a frightful sap to waste the amount of energy required to beat life in the U.S.A. when over here one can have just that more strength to put into one's job." When he was in Indo-China, this arrived: "This is the place! There is nothing more beautiful and interesting in the world. It is grand!" Settled for several years in Touraine, he wrote: "This is the place for me! The most beautiful part of France. Here is the ideal place to live and work!" During a motor trip through Spain, I received three postcards from him at different times. One, from Madrid, conveyed this message: "I've never seen a more beautiful spot. It would be a great place to work in." One, from Granada, this: "Spain is most interesting and I'm darn glad we picked it out for a vacation.

Granada is quiet, peaceful and immensely attractive. What a place to
live and work in!" One, from Malaga, this: "This is the best place I
have ever struck in Europe—really good stuff! It'd be a swell place to
live and work in." Returned to New York again, he said to me, "Why
I ever left here, damned if I know. There's life and vitality here. It's
the place for ideas! This is the spot for me and my work." His present
passion is for a small island off the Georgia coast. "The best place to
live and work I've ever found!"

O'Neill and Sinclair Lewis are alike in one respect. Both have
naturally a boyish quality, an innocent artlessness in a number of
directions, that will doubtless remain with them to their last years. In it
lies much of their charm. Lewis is as excited over a party as any
débutante, and a trip to Hoboken on the ferry works him up to a
degree of delight comparable only to Robert Fulton's first sensation
when he saw his steamboat actually working. O'Neill, for all his
solemn exterior, gets an unparalleled pleasure from splashing around
in a swimming pool and making funny gurgling noises, from putting
on the fancily colored dressing gowns he bought several years ago in
China, from singing raucous duets with a crony—"Rosie, You Are
My Posy" and "'Twas Christmas in the Harem" are two of his
favorites,—from lying on the ground and letting Blemie, his pet dog,
crawl over him, the meanwhile tickling him on the bottom, from
watches with bells in them, from the idea that one day he may master
the accordion and be as proficient a performer as the vaudeville
headliner, Phil Baker, and from drinking enormous glasses of Coca-
Cola and making everyone believe it is straight whiskey. When his
very lovely wife, Carlotta, comes down to dinner in some particularly
striking gown, his face lights up like a county fair. She knows well the
effect it has on him and quietly lays in a constantly replenished
wardrobe for his relish. "Do you like it?" she will delicately ask on
each occasion. And, though his infinite satisfaction is clearly to be
perceived, like a little boy who doesn't want to give in and admit
anything too quickly, he will invariably mumble, "Well, it's pretty, but
I like blue better."

Years ago, he was a drinker of parts. In fact, there were times when
he went on benders that lasted a whole month and times when he
slept next to the bung-hole of a whiskey barrel at Jimmy the Priest's
and when Jimmy, the proprietor, coming to work the next morning,

found the barrel one-eighth gone. About four or five years ago, however, he hoisted himself onto the water-wagon and has since sat thereon with an almost Puritanical splendor and tenacity. Like many another reformed bibber, he now views the wine-cup with a superior dudgeon and is on occasion not averse to delivering himself of eloquent harangues against it and its evils. It is not easy to forget his pious indignation when Barrett Clark once ventured to mention his old drinking bouts to him. "Altogether too much damned nonsense has been written since the beginning of time about the dissipation of artists!" he exploded. "Why, there are fifty times more real drunkards among the Bohemians who play at art, and probably more than that among the people who never think about art at all. The artist drinks, when he drinks at all [note the whimsy of that *at all*], for relaxation, forgetfulness, excitement, for any purpose except his art!" So today, it is Coca-Cola, followed by Kalak, with a vengeance.

O'Neill is very slow in making friends. He tests a potential friendship much after the technique of a fisherman, trying out various personal and metaphysical lines, flies and worms to determine what kind of fish the stranger is and to what degree, personally or philosophically, he resembles a sucker. Once he has made a friend for himself, that man remains a friend, in his eyes, until Hell freezes. In all the world I suppose that there are not more than five men at the very most whom O'Neill really regards as friends, and at least three of these are relics of his early more or less disreputable days in Greenwich Village and the adjacent gin-mills. I had known him for exactly ten years until we got to the point where we called each other by our first names.

He has done much of his more recent writing in an enormous chair that he had manufactured for himself in England. It is a cross between a dentist's and a barber's chair, with all sorts of pull-in and pull-out contrivances attached to it and with a couple of small shelves for reference books. A board is so arranged that it can be manoeuvred in front of him and on it he rests his pad. Stripped to the waist—he never works, if he can help it, with anything on above his navel—and with his legs stretched out to their full length, he writes everything in long hand and his chirography is so minute that it takes a magnifying glass for average eyes comfortably to read it.

I have never known him to tell a smoking-car story and, if someone happens to venture one while he is around, he sits silent and wide-eyed at its conclusion, as if he couldn't possibly understand it and wonders just what the point is. As for himself, he has just one story and will repeat it, to his apparent own infinite amusement, on the slightest provocation. It is the venerable one known as "The Old Bean," and concerns the braggadocio of an old souse who, despite all the dire catastrophes that befall him, imagines that the tremendous shrewdness of his intellect allows him on all occasions to get the best of everyone else. It is a long story, lasting at least an hour if related at top speed, and I have heard it from him regularly twice a year. Once, telling it to me again and embroidering its details, it occupied the entire time it took us to walk the seven miles from Le Plessis to Tours. The sole other occasion for unwonted loquacity on his part is the reminiscence of his vagrant New York days at the dive known as the Hell Hole and at Jimmy the Priest's where, with a pot-companion named Joe Smith, he shared a room—which they always referred to as "the garbage flat"—for the fine sum of three dollars a month. His particular comrades at Jimmy's, in addition to Joe, included a number of odoriferous colored gentlemen, a press-agent for Paine's Fireworks named Jimmy Beith, and one Major Adams, a red-nosed inebriate of sixty-odd who had been cashiered years before from the British army. This fraternity, hardly ever with more than fifty cents at a time in its combined treasury, subsisted on raw whiskey for breakfast and on what free lunch it could cabbage off the end of the bar during the rest of the day. From time to time, other habitués of the place were accepted into the fold, including an old sea captain named Chris Christopherson, whom O'Neill in later years incorporated name and all into his play, Anna Christie, a sailor named Driscoll, whose name suggested to him the Driscoll of Bound East for Cardiff, The Moon of the Caribbees and In the Zone, and a septuagenarian miser who had lived in a small, bare room above the saloon for twenty-two years, who never could persuade himself to throw away a newspaper and who could hardly find room enough to sleep on the floor for the enormous stacks of accumulated copies of the New York Times. The favorite tipple of the brotherhood, when one or another of the members—usually O'Neill, who at intervals would contrive to cozen a dollar out of his father—managed in some way to get hold of the price, was, aside from the breakfast rye,

Benedictine drunk by the tumblerful. But such treats were rare and makeshifts were necessary. Alcohol mixed with camphor was found—after one got used to the taste—to have a pretty effect. Varnish diluted with water was also discovered to have its points. And there were days when even wood alcohol mixed in small doses with sarsaparilla, with just a soupçon of benzine to give it a certain bouquet, was good enough, in the brothers' view, for any man who wasn't a sissy.

For weeks on end, the brotherhood would sit, or lie, in Jimmy's without stirring out for even a moment's breath of air. That is, all save the Major, who had a hobby for collecting old and wholly useless books of all descriptions, which he never read, and for attending funerals. If he came home any evening without at least three frowzy books garnered from God knows where or without having attended at least two funerals of persons entirely unknown to him, he would mope for the rest of the night and would regain his cheer only after he had drunk a half dozen or so toasts to His Majesty, the King, in beakers of varnish. It was apparently not the royal toasts, however, that caused the Major's demise, but something ponderously diagnosed by a hastily summoned neighborhood medico as "malicious liver complaint." The Major's funeral was a gala affair, with the remaining brotherhood so melancholiously but none the less richly in its cups that no fewer than three of the mourners lost their balance and tumbled into the grave on top of their late brother's coffin.

Nor was it the nature of the brotherhood's refreshments that unwound the mortal coil of Brother Beith. Learning one night, while full of Pond's extract mixed with one-eighth whiskey and three-eighths gasoline, that his dear wife, whom he had forgotten all about in the fifteen years he hadn't laid eyes on her, had run off with a fellow in South Africa, he committed suicide by jumping out of one of Jimmy's upper windows. Beith's suicide, together with certain personal emotional misfortunes in an encounter with Cupid, weighed upon O'Neill's mind and—now it may be told—a month or so after Beith took his life the man who was to become the first of American dramatists attempted, with an overdose of veronal, to follow suit. When, one afternoon at two o'clock—the conventional hour for rising and having whiskey breakfast—O'Neill failed to stir, failed even to respond to the brothers' nudges, pokes and peremptory kicks, an

ambulance was quickly summoned and our friend was carted off at a
gallop to Bellevue. With the brothers grouped solicitously about his
cot, two interns worked over him for an hour before he again gave
signs of life. Three hours later, the dose of veronal not having been so
large as he believed, O'Neill was back in the world once more and,
with a whoop of joy, the brothers put on their hats and moved
mysteriously toward the door. "We'll be back soon," they observed
significantly—and were gone. Four hours later, they reappeared, all
beautifully and magnificently drunk. It developed that they had
rushed to O'Neill's father and had got fifty dollars from him to pay
the hospital fee for his son's resuscitation. "You dirty bums!" groaned
O'Neill, with what vocal strength he could muster. "How much you
got left?" Thirty-two dollars, they reluctantly informed him. "All right,
divide!" he insisted. And with his sixteen dollars safe in hand, he
rolled over, grinned satisfiedly, and went happily and peacefully to
sleep.

We were sitting one late Summer afternoon about two years ago in
my rooms in the Avenue Maréchal Foch, in Paris, looking out at the
merry-go-round of motor cars in the Etoile and at the Arc de
Triomphe in the sinking sun. I asked him—his reflective mood
seemed to inspire the question—what he would like more than anything else out of life.
    "The Nobel Prize?" I hinted out of the side of my apéritif glass.
    "On careful consideration—and no sour grapes about it because I
have had no hopes—I think the Nobel Prize, until you become very
old and childlike, costs more than it's worth. It's an anchor around
one's neck that one would never be able to shake off," he answered,
gulping his tea.
    "A more intelligent critical appraisal of your work?" I smiled.
    His ears, as is their wont when critics and criticism are mentioned,
stood setter-like and challenging on end. "I expect denunciation! It's
generally sure to come. But I'm getting awfully callous to the braying,
for or against. When they knock me, what the devil!, they're really
boosting me with their wholesale condemnations, for the reaction
against such nonsense will come soon enough. These tea-pot
turmoils at least keep me shaken up and convinced I'm on my way to
something. I know enough history to realize that no one worth a

damn *ever* escaped them—so it gives me hope. When I'm generally approved of, I begin to look in the mirror very skeptically and contemplate taking up some other career I might succeed at. So it's all tonic."

He finished his tea.

"I'll tell you what I want and it's the God's truth. I want just what I've now at last and for the first time in my life got! Life has certainly changed for me in the last year or so and for the first time in God knows how long I feel as if it had something to give me as a living being quite outside of the life in my work. The last time I saw you I told you I was happy. A rash statement, but I now make it again with a tenfold emphasis. And, believe me, it has stood tests that would have wrecked it if it wasn't the genuine article. I feel younger and more pepped up with the old zest for living and working than I've ever felt since I started working. I may seem to slop over a bit, but you don't know into what a bog of tedium and life-sickness I was sinking. I was living on my work as a fellow does on his nerves sometimes, and sooner or later my work would certainly have been sapped of its life because you can't keep on that way forever, even if you put up the strongest of bluffs to yourself and the world in general. Now I feel as if I'd tapped a new life and could rush up all the reserves of energy in the world to back up my work. Honestly, it's a sort of miracle to me, I'd become so resigned to the worst. So be a little indulgent and don't mind my unloading a little of the pop-eyed wonder of it at you!"

At this point Carlotta, his wife, came in, put her arm around him and kissed him.

"Where've you been?" he asked, his face suddenly lapsing again into that perverse little-boy expression.

Carlotta gave him another little kiss.

"I've been shopping for dresses, Genie dear," she said. "Blue ones."

O'Neill Is Eager to See Cohan in *Ah, Wilderness!*

Richard Watts, Jr./1933

Reprinted from the *New York Herald Tribune*, 9 September 1933, 7.

Eugene O'Neill, looking bronzed and healthy after his year-and-a-half stay on his island estate, Casa Genotta, off the coast of Georgia, is back in town watching the rehearsals of his latest play, *Ah, Wilderness!*, which is being produced by the Theater Guild with George M. Cohan as the most distinguished member of the cast. In his hotel suite yesterday Mr. O'Neill, in his shy and reticent manner, was enormously enthusiastic over the fact that Mr. Cohan was to appear in a play of his.

As a matter of fact, the signing of Mr. Cohan was the culmination of a long-time determination on the part of the author of *Strange Interlude* and *Mourning Becomes Electra*. When he wrote *Marco Millions* a few years ago it was his earnest desire that the composer of "Over There," who was nominated by Percy Hammond as the nation's First Actor, should create the role of the go-getting Venetian Babbitt that was the O'Neill conception of the mighty traveler Marco Polo. But Mr. Cohan was unavailable at the time, and the playwright has ever since planned to have him in a drama of his.

Although their fathers were friends, it was not until the first rehearsal of *Ah, Wilderness!* that the two distinguished men of the American theater met. It is obvious that they got on perfectly from the time of their introduction.

"I cannot overemphasize," said Mr. O'Neill, "how delighted I am at having Mr. Cohan in a play of mine at last. I think he likes the comedy, too. But he did tell me that one of the things which first attracted him to it was the fact that the first act takes place on July 4. I really didn't mean the setting as a shrewd device to lure Mr. Cohan to a part I wanted him for, but I realize now that he was amused at the connection the date has with his own career."

One thing which pleases him with Mr. Cohan's acceptance of the part is that, although the leading role, it is not in any sense planned as a vehicle for starring. In the work, the First Actor has the part of the father of the leading juvenile, played by Elisha Cook, Jr. Incidentally, *Ah, Wilderness!*—the title of which, as has been widely heralded, is taken from Omar's idea of Paradise enow—is described by its author as "a comedy of recollection." Its action takes place in what Mr. O'Neill described as "a large small town, not very far from New York, in the year 1906." "The setting has been described as New England," he said, "but it is New England only if you will accept the southern part of Connecticut as belonging spirtually to that part of the country. I call the work a comedy because it is on the whole more gay than grave, but as Mr. Cohan says, it is and it isn't a comedy in the usual sense."

Mr. O'Neill emphasized the fact that he by no means intended his play as a satiric treatment of life in the first decade of the twentieth century. In truth it is a nostalgic picture of the America of its day. "Perhaps," he said, "it is because I am growing old that I begin to look back fondly on my youthful days in a part of the country that was my one real home in those times."

The writing is naturalistic in form, and there will be no technical innovations in the story-telling. *Ah, Wilderness!* will be, among other things, that novelty in an O'Neill play—a drama that starts at 8 p.m. and ends at 11.

Ah, Wilderness! was written in six weeks, between drafts of another play, *Days Without End*, which will be the Guild's following production.

"I wrote six drafts of *Days Without End*," Mr. O'Neill said, "and it was just after I had made the third of them that I woke up one morning with the idea of a comedy. Only once before, in the case of *Desire Under the Elms*, has a plot idea come to me so easily, so I put aside the graver drama and went to work on the new plot. I wrote it more easily than I have written any other of my works and then back to *Days Without End*."

Days Without End will be more serious and dramatic in quality, but it does not end with a tragic or defeatist note. The central character, contrary to the fate of many O'Neill heroes, wins through to success and happiness. In this second drama the author will go back to the use of masks, but this time there will be but one of them, worn by the central character. The setting will be modern New York.

After *Ah, Wilderness!* and *Days Without End* Mr. O'Neill will return
to a limited use of the *Strange Interlude* technique of asides repre-
senting the secret thoughts of the characters. In a drama which he
plans to call *The Life of Bessie Bowen,* the protagonist will speak her
thoughts, but the other characters will confine themselves to the
conventional manner of stage speech.

"I do not plan to confine myself to any one type of technique,"
Mr. O'Neill said. "Rather I plan to use the method, whether it be
naturalism or symbolism, that happens to fit in with the sort of drama
I am writing. The characters in *Strange Interlude,* for example, were
neurotics, and they had to be portrayed in a form which would
suggest that quality, a quality of writing which could not be used in
dealing with such comparatively simple people as appeared in some
of the earlier dramas."

Mr. O'Neill has no suggestions concerning the coming trends in the
American theater. Quietly ensconced on his Georgia island, he has
seen neither play nor motion picture in several years. Relaxation he
finds in fishing, in reading detective stories and in occasional
activities concerned with editing *The American Spectator*—a job
which he takes rather lightly, chiefly because, one gathers, he wants
George Jean Nathan to have all the fun of handling the publication.
In reading he is interested in the work of newspaper sports writers
when he is not perusing tales of imaginary crimes. An enthusiast for
the work of such commentators as W. O. McGeehan, Don Skene and
Sparrow Robertson, he feels that there is more style and gusto in this
branch of newspaper writing than in any other form.

He has not yet seen the coming picture version of *The Emperor
Jones,* but plans to do so as soon as it has been released publicly. As
a matter of fact, though, he is not as interested in the cinema now
that it has gone in for dialogue as he was when it was a pantomimic
medium. The silent version of *Anna Christie,* made a dozen years
ago, he still regards as a faithful and satisfying version of the original.
As for *The Emperor Jones,* the outline he has heard pleases him, as
does the bit of additional dialogue which was given to him to read,
and he is frankly more interested in it than he is in the operatic version of the play, presented at the Metropolitan last season.

The Recluse of Sea Island

George Jean Nathan/1935

Reprinted from George Jean Nathan, *The Theatre of the Moment* (New York: Alfred A. Knopf, 1936), pp. 196–207, by permission of Associated University Presses. Originally published in *Redbook Magazine*, 65 (August 1935), 34–37, 71.

If there is one thing in all the world that is utterly and completely distasteful to the foremost figure in the American theatre it is the theatre. He ventures to enter one not more than once in every seven or eight years and each time loudly and indignantly swears off for the rest of his life. Something seems always to happen to him when he goes to a theatre that increases doubly his prefatory misgivings. When he went eight years ago, in Paris, to see a production by the eminent Russian director, Tairov, of his own *All God's Chillun Got Wings*—in the new and modernly equipped Théâtre Pigalle—he went upon the invitation of Baron Rothschild, whose interest and liberality had made the reformed Pigalle possible. Arriving in the box that had been set aside for him, he was cordially received by two gentlemen, both of them charming in the warmth of their manner and reception. To one of them he took, as he subsequently expressed it, an immediate "shine," though he is by nature notoriously a very aloof person and one given to few acquaintances and even fewer friends. To this one, he devoted his whole attention for the evening, listening with close and genial interest to everything he had to say and periodically and impatiently shushing aside the other, who from time to time would seek, timidly and politely, to edge in with a suggestion or passing word. As he was leaving the theatre, he addressed a sotto voce query to his companion of the evening. "Who *is* that other guy?" he demanded. "That—why that's your host, Baron Rothschild," replied the other. A look of grieved concern seized O'Neill's countenance. "Good God, then, who are you?" "I," returned the other, "I'm Jack Campbell, a reporter for the Paris *Herald.*"

It took O'Neill a week to recover his equanimity. "That's what happens," he subsequently said to me, "when I go to the theatre."

A year ago—seven years after the contretemps noted—he again took a chance on the theatre, this time in New York. The exhibit was the *Continental Varieties* and the motivating force behind his excursion was the presence in the show of Escudero, the Spanish dancer. (It was an enthusiasm for the dancer's art on the part of his wife, Carlotta, that on this occasion weaned him from his theatrical prejudice.) He sat glumly through the first part of the program, hoarsely muttering to himself, and finally succeeded in persuading his wife to get out of the place as quickly as possible. When he got back to his hotel, he discovered that he had left his favorite muffler in the theatre, and the next day he began sneezing with a terrible cold. "You see!" he told me. "Never again!"

O'Neill's whimsical annoyance with the institution that has made possible his eminence and his great worldly success has become such that, during the long period when he is engaged in the writing of one of his plays, he has struck a bargain with his wife never under any circumstances to allow the theatre or anything in any way connected with it to be mentioned in his hearing. Any letter that may come to him containing any news of things theatrical, whether directly concerning him or not, is not to be shown to him. Nothing in newspapers or magazines having to do with the theatre is to be read by him or to him. "It wouldn't be so bad if the theatre was any good," he argues when reproached for his isolation, "but as it stands—outside of Russia, maybe—it only gets in the way of your temper and any serious attempt you want to make toward good work." Whereupon he grunts, slowly lights a cigarette, gazes with wrinkled brow at its tip for a full minute to see that it is burning properly, moves to a chair in a far corner, deposits himself therein, and maintains a grim and majestic silence until he feels certain that the subject is safely changed for the rest of the day.

But the theatre is not the only thing from which O'Neill remains steadfastly sequestered. He elects, in these years, as in many of those that have gone before, to lead an existence completely removed from what the rest of us are pleased to allude to as "life." The major part of his year is spent in his lovely house, walled in from the outside world, on that little plot of land off the coast of Georgia known as Sea Island. There he lives with devoted Carlotta and a few servants— notably Mlle. Edna, a colored cook of uncommon virtuosity; there he

works and broods from nine in the mornings until ten at nights, with
time out only for meals, a bit of gardening, a solo swim in the sea and
a run up and down the deserted beach; there he has his entire being.
Two months in the year, when the weather gets bad on the island, he
spends in a quiet Adirondack camp, many miles away from the
nearest railroad station, or in some other such isolated spot. Perhaps
a week in New York then—incognito in a closely guarded hotel
suite—to consult with his dentist, to steal off to the six-day bicycle
races, for which he has had a long-standing affection, to guzzle some
of Luchow's Edelbräu, and to repeat endlessly to me that he simply
can't understand how any man can live in New York and not go
crazy—and back again promptly to Sea Island.

On his last year's visit to New York, he, Sean O'Casey, the finest of
the Irish playwrights, and I lunched together in his hotel rooms.
O'Casey and I, before joining him, had coached ourselves in a plot to
take him to task, with a great show of indignation on our parts, for his
burial of himself from all contact with the world and his fellowmen.
Slowly and, we thought, with a pretty histrionic skill, we edged
against his self-defence with lush arguments as to the necessity of an
artist's—and particularly a dramatist's—mingling with the stream of
life if he is to comprehend it and interpret its depths and mutations.
As the hours passed, O'Neill began to indicate, first, a mild restlessness, then a growing mood of irritation, and finally an open, hot
rebellion. Jumping out of his chair—and if there is any previous
record of his ever having got out of a chair with an alacrity greater
than that customarily displayed by a stock company Richelieu, no
one who knows him is privy to the fact—he confronted both of us
and, his face flushed, made what is the longest speech that he has
made in all the many years I have known him.

"What you fellows have been saying," he exploded, "is damned
rot! That mingling with people and life that you talk about, far from
giving anything to an artist, simply takes things away from him,
damned valuable things. If he hasn't everything in himself, he is no
good. The life outside him can steal from him but it can't contribute a
thing to him, unless he is a rank second-rater. You talk of the thrill of
cities, as against the so-called loneliness and stagnation of the
country. What is the thrill? A lot of meaningless noise, a lot of crowd-
ing bores, a lot of awful smells, a swirl of excited nothingness. You

talk of the thrill of a city's beauty. Well (pointing out of the window), look at those skyscrapers! What are they; what do they stand for? Nothing but a lot of children's blocks! Do you mean to say that they've got anything to do with the great soul of humanity, with humanity's deep, underlying essence, and hopes, and fate? You're both bughouse!"

Whereupon he bestowed upon each of us a black and completely disgusted look, turned his back on us, and abruptly left the room. O'Casey and I exchanged a significant and self-congratulatory wink. In about ten minutes O'Neill returned, resplendent in some new-fangled slacks that he had bought that morning. Immediately O'Casey and I launched into a lavish encomium not only of the slacks but of his general sartorial taste and even magnificence. A forgiving grin spread over O'Neill's features. The admiration of his slacks tickled him. But suddenly he caught himself and the frown again stole over his face. "Just the same," he informed us, "about that other stuff, you're both nuts!"

His thorough and firmly rooted belief in the value of isolation, indeed, is such that already he is beginning to show signs of finding his lonely island too close to the borderland of the American world and is beginning, with his wife, to study the atlas for some more distant and less penetrable hideaway.

It is not to be gathered from all of this, however, that O'Neill, despite the legend that has come to be attached to him by persons who haven't the faintest inkling of what he is really like, is not an enviably happy and richly contented man. Of all the men who are near to my knowledge and friendship, he seems to me the most happy and the most contented, and by far. The legend to the contrary has its tentacles in a variety of vacuums. First, because his physiognomy happens to have been cast by God in a tragic mould, like Henry Irving's, and because, like Groucho Marx, his expression happens naturally to be grave and even melancholy, he is held to be a tragic, grave and melancholy man. The truth about him is that, while hardly a persistently jocund one, he is fundamentally a cheerful and at times even a waggish fellow, with a taste for low barroom chatter, bordello anecdotes, rough songs and other such forms of healthy obscenity. Secondly, his complete isolation of himself has given rise to the theory that he is a misanthrope, one who hates his fellowman and is just this side of being an eater of babies. While it is true that he cares nothing for people in the mass and goes to extremes to avoid having anything to do with them, he likes nothing better than to be with one of his few close friends, on which occasions he is as happy and sportive as a small boy. Every now and again, further, he will encounter, either by accident or in the course of what may be timidly alluded to as his public life, a stranger—like the Paris reporter referred to—toward whom he will wax warmly friendly and sympathetic. H.R. Lenormand, the French dramatist, is one such; Vincent Youmans, the American song writer, is another; and George Boll, a Southern real estate operator, is still another. Such men, although they do not penetrate deeply into his existence, are highly agreeable company to him, and he is very fond of them.

A third source of the legend of his persistent misery is the memory of the theoretical very hard time he had of it when he first began to write plays and the extreme difficulty he encountered in gaining a hearing for his work and the slightest recognition of his talents. This, for all the popularity of the legend, is utter nonsense. While he was studying at college and shortly thereafter, he wrote a number of plays, both short and long, but, appreciating that they were not worth a hoot, he promptly destroyed all of them and would not, before their extinction, allow even his closest cronies to read them. All, that is, with one exception: a three-act farce-comedy which he rather fancied for a spell—lasting approximately three or four months—after which period he read it again, concluded that his first opinion of it was deplorably uncritical, and burned it instanter. When he began to write plays in real earnest, he experienced, the theorists should know, no lack of outside sympathy and even enthusiasm. It is true that the professional theatre was not interested in those earliest plays, for they were one-act plays and the American professional theatre has never been much interested in one-act plays, whether O'Neill's or anyone else's. But he did not lack an immediate production of these one-acters in the little theatre, notably the Provincetown, which promptly grabbed up any and everything he turned out. And it was not long before little theatres all over the land were playing his one-acters, and the more intelligent and receptive editors were eagerly buying them for magazine publication.

What is more, the moment he turned to the longer form of drama, the professional theatre at once opened its doors to him. John D. Williams read the manuscript of *Beyond the Horizon* just two hours after it was put into his hands, immediately telephoned to O'Neill that he liked it enormously, and told him that he would produce it as soon as he could gather together a worthy cast, which he duly did. This *Beyond the Horizon* was his first long play, if we omit those he wrote and himself destroyed, and the very first professional theatre man who read it quickly accepted it for production. Both *The Emperor Jones* and *The Straw,* which followed it, were produced by the Provincetowners, but it must not be forgotten that O'Neill was a member of that producing group, and a very enthusiastic member, to boot, and that he gave his plays to it in both friendship and pride. *Gold,* which, like the two plays cited, was also produced in 1921, received its professional theatre presentation by the same John D. Williams who gave *Beyond the Horizon* a hearing. And, as in the other instance, Williams was the first producer to whom the manuscript was submitted. *Anna Christie* was produced in its original draft (known as *Chris Christopherson*) by the veteran professional manager, Mr. George C. Tyler. When it failed after a very brief showing in Philadelphia, O'Neill rewrote it. Edgar Selwyn, of the then conspicuous Selwyn firm, read the revised script—it was sent to him first—and reported that he could see no play in it. The same afternoon it went to Arthur Hopkins, who immediately accepted it for production. All of which is the true, if not generally recognized, story of O'Neill's "difficult early days" and the "awful time he had to get any sort of a hearing."

The paradoxical aversion of the first among American playwrights from the theatre is equalled only by his similarly paradoxical aversion from actors. While he freely allows that there are some competent members of the profession—he has an affection for George M. Cohan, a very considerable respect for Walter Huston, and a tender memory for the late Louis Wolheim, all three of whom have acted in his plays—he has only a large and raucous snort for the overwhelming majority. In this respect, he shares with a certain school of criticism the conviction that an actor is a creature who has missed his profession. One of O'Neill's most acute sources of embarrassment with actors may be expressed in his own words. "A lot of them seem to get away with it all right during the early part of a play, but then—

pop!—out comes the fairy touch, the falsetto voice, the fancy little gesture, the roll of the hip—and the play goes blooie."

One of O'Neill's sorest spots is the criticism that is made in certain quarters of his fondness for the use of masks in his plays and the allegation that they only confuse matters and make his plays doubly difficult for an audience. His favorite answer is: "Well, I used them in *The Great God Brown* and it seemed to confuse matters so much and to make the play so doubly difficult for an audience that the play ran for eight months in New York alone!"

For his fellow playwrights, O'Neill has little respect, save for three— or maybe four: Lenormand, Maugham and O'Casey—and, lately, Maxwell Anderson. He confesses that the greatest influence upon his work is Strindberg. "He is the greatest influence on any playwright who is worth anything today, whether the playwright admits it or not," he adds. It is torture to him to write a letter. He will shy from the task for days and then, more often than not, will entrust the job to his wife who, incidentally, is no mean literata in that department. He is not at full ease and at peace with himself unless he can live near the sea. Most of his life has been spent either upon it or at its borders. When he is removed from it, he must have at least a river, a lake, or some body of water near by. His present work-room in his house on Sea Island is built to resemble a cabin on a schooner; its windows look out upon the Atlantic and it is full of ship models and records of the sea and of the ships that have sailed the seas. Yet never once, in all the years I have known him, have I ever heard him use so much as one nautical term in conversation. That discourse, as the reader has doubtless ere now perceived, offers in general a distinct contrast, as is so often the case with writers, to O'Neill's literary self. As against the formality of his writings, with their frequent poetic overtone, it is free, easy, colloquial, and often négligé, which makes him the surprised delight of any interviewer who, approaching an audience with him, foresees a painful session with a gloomy pundit. And as the cast of his spoken words denies all of the usual pretensions of *homo literarum,* so his private reading pleasure, self-critically confessed, indicates his unaffected simplicity. O'Neill reads every mystery and detective novel immediately it appears on the stands.

A last word and we drop the curtain, for the time being at least, on this strange, this oddly self-sufficient, this genuinely engaging fellow.

Just as he detests every phase of public life, so he detests—as one such phase—being written about. That is, as a person apart from his work. When I wrote to his wife that I was going to confect this chapter on him, she replied that, while it was agreeable to her to have someone who knew him well dispel "the school-boy legends that have gone their ridiculous and dull way into print" and to have him pictured somewhat more faithfully than one who, at the age of fifteen months, leapt directly from his perambulator into a barroom, where legend has had him remain ever since, nevertheless "Gene doesn't at all cheer at the idea!!" The two exclamation marks are hers. O'Neill, in short, the most widely discussed figure in the American theatre, finds such discussion, including this, gratuitously obnoxious. He wants, dammit, to be left alone.

Eugene O'Neill Undramatic over Honor of Nobel Prize

Seattle Daily Times/1936

Reprinted from the *Seattle Daily Times*, 12 November 1936, 1,
14, by permission of *The Seattle Times*.

Eugene O'Neill, the playwright, who with his wife came to Seattle
recently to reside for the winter, was awarded the Nobel Prize for
Letters today, an Associated Press dispatch from Stockholm reported.

The prize O'Neill will receive in conjunction with the award will
approximate $45,000. The amount of the 1935 prize, which was not
awarded, has been added to the 1936 sum.

ONE THURSDAY MORNING

Time—Today.

Place—A house on Magnolia Bluff.

Characters

Eugene O'Neill.

Carlotta Monterey O'Neill.

Dr. Sophus Keith Winther.

A reporter.

(The scene is set in a well-furnished living room. A cheerful fire
blazes in the hearth and outside the fog curtains the view of the
Sound. The playwright is found seated on a large green velvet
davenport. He is wearing a gray sweater and flannels. Beside him is
his wife, dressed in a red sweater suit and wearing a pair of gray
suede shoes she received this morning from London. Dr. Winther
stands before the fireplace and a reporter is perched on a chair.)

Reporter: How did you hear about the award Mr. O'Neill?

O'Neill (with a smile at his wife)**:** My wife told me. She woke me
up this morning to tell me.

Mrs. O'Neill: Dr. Winther woke me up to tell me about it.

Dr. Winther: The Associated Press woke me up to tell me.

Reporter: Were you surprised, Mr. O'Neill?

O'Neill (who is in a good humor): Well, not exactly. I've had telegrams of congratulations from New York this week—just on rumor. But I didn't know for sure. I didn't think they would award it to an American again so soon. And then I thought if they did it would go to Dreiser—he deserves it.

Reporter: Do you know what particular play it was awarded for?

O'Neill: No. I don't know. I don't know how they fix that.

Mrs. O'Neill: I hope it was for *Electra. Electra* is my favorite. I feel so strongly personally about it. We went through such a horrible time with it. Gene used to want to tear it up. When he was through he felt as if he never wanted to write another play.

Reporter: What is your favorite play—of the ones you have written, Mr. O'Neill?

O'Neill: I received the most personal satisfaction from *Electra*—you know that is Carlotta's play. As far as writing goes, I was most pleased with *The Great God Brown* and next *The Hairy Ape*.

Reporter: What is the subject of your next play—the one you are working on now?

O'Neill: Oh, it's a tremendous thing. It tells the story of an American family from 1806 to 1932. It takes them from the East Coast to the West Coast, back to the East Coast and ends in the Middle West.

Reporter: Is that why you're here in the West—to get atmosphere?

O'Neill: Something like that. I have to live in a place before I can write about it. I have to have the feeling of living there. Of course, the western part of the play takes place in 1870, but I'm going to travel all around the West. Just looking and talking to tradespeople—that's the way I get the feel.

Reporter: It's a very long play, isn't it?

O'Neill: Oh, yes. It goes on forever. I feel like I've been writing it forever. I started out with four plays and now it's eight plays and it might be nine plays—that's a luckier number, anyway.

Reporter: How will it be produced?

O'Neill: I hope it will start next October. With one play a season, people can go on seeing it forever. And when all eight plays are produced I hope they will run them all off on successive nights—that ought to knock the audiences cold. They'll never want to see another play.

Reporter: Do you always live in the places you write plays about?

O'Neill: Yes—but I don't always write plays about the places I live. I'll never write a play about the South. You know, we lived in Georgia. We went there for the climate. Now, I'll try it here. In Georgia you sweat half the year—and there aren't any union hours for sweating. I wrote part of this play half naked with bookkeeper's black sleeves on my arms, blotters under my hand and I sat on a bath towel.

Reporter: Do you go to see your plays, Mr. O'Neill?

O'Neill: Never. After I get through with seven or eight weeks of rehearsal I never want to see or hear of the play again. It's on its own.

Mrs. O'Neill: We go through torture until the first night. That night we stay home and walk the floor and then it's all over.

O'Neill: An Impression
Theresa Helburn/1936

Reprinted from the *Saturday Review of Literature*, 15 (21 November 1936), 10.

I remember the first time Eugene O'Neill came to dinner with me. It was the evening of the day Lindbergh flew the Atlantic. We had meant to talk of plays and production problems but we were, of course, like everyone else, under the spell of that adventure and we talked instead of what lay behind the apparent simplicity of that amazing flight, behind its clean-cut success, its almost poetic precision. I can imagine no one more sensitive to all its implications than O'Neill with his sense of the romantic and the dramatic, with his memories of lonely nights at sea and his knowledge of stark realities. That I have so often, since then, bracketed the two men in my mind, may be, of course, purely fortuitous but it is not without reason. For I have often thought that Gene is a good deal of a lone eagle in his chosen field—daring new and, God knows, long enough flights on his dramatic Pegasus; and that he has in himself to a high degree the singleness of purpose, the capacity for profound preparation, the courage, and the intense conviction that have been subsequently associated with the great flier. He has also a simplicity, a directness, a dread of empty adulation and noisy crowds, a passionate desire for privacy.

O'Neill is a very shy person. He is also a very real one. Alone with him you realize your own shyness. For you cannot keep on the surface very long; after a certain amount of banter you must either dig deep or be silent. Not that he is always serious company, far from it. He has a quick perception of humorous angles and a rich response to any sort of natural humor. The quality of his humor is evident from his comedies; the homely fun of *Ah, Wilderness!* and the satiric philosophic comedy of *Marco Millions.* He has not much use for sophisticated badinage. And like all shy people he is at his best with

Theresa Helburn (1867–1959) was a member of the Board of Managers of the Theatre Guild and one of the Guild's founders.

one other person. I always have the feeling, when he is in a group, that some very valuable time is being wasted.

I like most to think of O'Neill out-of-doors. Of all the times I have seen him, he seemed most at ease walking against a strong breeze on the endless beach that borders his Georgia house. Against the turbulence of sea and wind he talked freely, easily, with a sense of relaxation I seldom feel in him. It was as if the tumult without stilled the tumult within. Indoors—especially after he has been working—one feels the dynamo still turning—driving and wearing him down. And in the theatre I have the sense that he is armoured against the constant pricks and arrows that the ordeal of rehearsal holds for a sensitive artist. But he sits quiet and impassive in the front row, hour after hour, and to every question from actor or director he responds without a second's hesitation and with complete assurance. Here is one playwright who has spent so much time on the preparation of his script, has built his structure so carefully from its foundation, that he knows the right position of every brick from every angle. Never a doubt as to what anyone of his characters is thinking or feeling at any moment; never an ambiguity about a motive or a reading. To the director's suggestions he answers quickly "yes" or "no." To suggestions of changes he usually answers "no." But not arbitrarily, nor is that the end. He evidently considers them all for some time seriously and frequently returns the next day having found a way to meet a suggested change that has dramatic value without damaging the fabric of his play. It is the same about cuts. He almost never makes them on the spur of the moment. He listens to the director's ideas but he takes his script home and brings it back the next day cut or not cut, as the case may be, according to his leisured judgment. People have called O'Neill stubborn in rehearsal but it is the stubbornness of inner conviction, a most valuable quality in a medium so easily the prey of contrived effects and emotional tricks as the theatre. And it is a not impractical conviction; it is founded on long experience and an expert sense of "theatre"—the rightful heritage perhaps of an actor's son. But O'Neill doesn't like compromise. Often we have said to him "Gene, the audience won't stand for that." To which he has replied "The audience will stand for anything provided we do it well enough."

He certainly doesn't spare himself in trying to do his share of the

work well. The mere physical effort in the preparation of his MSS
would dismay the average playwright, accustomed to hasty drafts and
efficient secretaries. His preliminary notes often fill what would be a
good-sized volume in print, and all written by hand in perfect handwriting so fine that even with glasses I have to strain to read it. Many
a playwright says to himself, "No matter how much I rewrite whoever
is going to produce my play will want a lot of changes, so what's the
use of doing too much work now?" There is something to be said for
this point of view, for managers often fancy themselves as vicarious
playwrights. Nevertheless, there is probably more to be said for the
managers since a great many plays are, as submitted, far from ready
for production. Perhaps it is better theatre policy to work on final
versions with director or producer or both. Many writers are greatly
helped by this sort of collaboration and it frequently results in a well-
rounded production—far better than would have been otherwise
possible.

But O'Neill is more than a playwright, he is a dramatist. When,
after long preliminary preparation, he has finished a draft, he puts it
away for at least three months. During that time he travels or works
on something else or perhaps just stays at home with his books, his
wife, and his ocean. Then he takes it out, reads it with a fresh
perspective, and starts to work again. Usually three drafts are written
in a year or more and all in that perfect long hand. When it finally
gets to the typist all she must need is a reading glass! And when it
gets to the producer he can take it or leave it. It is ready for
rehearsal—the changes made in work are only minor ones.

O'Neill is the only playwright I know who does not want to have
his plays tried out on the road. That certainly shows an inner
sureness rare in the theatre. Only once did we persuade him to such
a course; that was with *Ah, Wilderness!*—so full of comedy we felt it
only fair to the actors to test out the laughs and get the pace of the
play before the ordeal of a New York first night. Gene finally acceded
but for a long while refused to come himself to Pittsburgh. However,
he finally showed up at a mid-week performance and then returned
at once to New York, more than ever convinced, I am sure, that the
trip had been unnecessary for everyone concerned.

The joy that all Gene's friends feel in the Nobel award is the
greater that it should come now when he is at work on the most

difficult project of his career, a series of eight plays, a picture of American life over six generations.

Last March I went to stay in the lovely house on the coast of Georgia that Carlotta O'Neill, with her rare gift for combining beauty with comfort, had devised for Gene's protection and isolation. In his study, built like the master cabin of an old sailing vessel, its windows overlooking the sea, Gene sketched for me the plan of his dramatic "comédie humaine" and I was amazed at the amount of work involved: the preliminary research, the endless notes, the detailed scenarios that had preceded the draft of a single play. Were it anyone but Gene I would doubt the achievement of it. But again and again O'Neill has attempted the impossible in the theatre and come through on top; not a reason in the world to doubt his doing it again.

O'Neill Turns West to New Horizons

Richard L. Neuberger/1936

Reprinted from the *New York Times Magazine*, 22 November
1936, 6, 23. Copyright © 1936 by The New York Times Company. Reprinted by permission.

SEATTLE.

On the sundown rim of the continent the second citizen of the United
States to win the Nobel Prize for Literature is combining a long-
postponed vacation with the searching out of new background for his
latest dramatic undertaking. Eugene O'Neill has come to the Pacific
Northwest to rest. He has come also to gather material on the
settlement of the Oregon country in the Eighteen Sixties and the
Eighteen Seventies when the first transcontinental railroad was being
pushed across the Rocky Mountain Divide.

He receives his greatest honor at the start of a new chapter in his
career. The message telling him of the award clicked over the telegraph wires only a few days after he had ridden a transcontinental
train westward beneath those same wires. He is about to begin a
cycle of eight plays dealing with the history and the psychology of an
American family from 1806 until 1932. He plans to trace the family's
migration from New England to the Pacific Northwest and then back
to the Central States. In Oregon and Washington the playwright
hopes to obtain the background and setting for the years between
1857 and 1880, a period in his play which will be motivated by the
family's going from Cape Cod to Puget Sound via the stormy
passage around Cape Horn. Each of the eight plays, he says, will be
complete in and of itself, so that it can be seen as a separate entity.
He contemplates writing two of the plays a year.

His stay in the Far West may be longer than the time required to
accumulate the material for his latest project. He intends to sell his
home in Georgia and take up permanent residence on the Pacific
Coast; he has not yet decided, however, whether it will be in
Northern California, Oregon or Washington.

He is certain it will not be in a large city. "You can't concentrate
and work in a metropolis," he explains. He is eager to get away from

the heat and humidity of the South, and says this is one of the reasons for his presence on the fir-bordered slopes of Puget Sound.

From a long, English-style house overlooking Puget Sound O'Neill gazes down to the sea as it breaks on the ramparts of Magnolia Bluff. His study window frames a picture of the Olympic Mountains across the sound, rising like snowy watchtowers from the Pacific. Lofty fir trees dot the yard and surrounding slopes. In this picturesque setting last week O'Neill learned of his Nobel award—a distinction which only Sinclair Lewis in this country shares with him. Here he discussed present-day matters.

People are the clay with which O'Neill models his plays, and he frequently recollects small incidents to illustrate his remarks and his writings. To him the study of human beings and their behavior is fascinating. He seldom forgets any occurrence that seems to indicate the reasons for people's actions and habits.

Laughing, he told of the unfamiliarity of people with the theatre in some parts of the country where he has lived. "When a legitimate play is presented," he said, "the promoters herald it as being with actual living actors." But to him the situation has also a grave aspect. He considers it unfortunate that relatively few of the American people have had opportunity to participate in or to enjoy the theatre.

"I think that the WPA theatre projects may ultimately be the answer to this problem," he said. "Take one of my own plays, for example. It will be presented in New York; then the Theatre Guild will take it on a road trip. After that it's dead. If you want to see a revival, you have to go to Europe. I think other playwrights will tell you the same thing.

"The WPA theatre projects can change this," he continued. "They have the opportunity to bring legitimate stage productions to every community in America, whether that community be rural or urban. The WPA units can present important plays before audiences that never before have seen an actual stage production. The possibilities in this respect are thrilling."

O'Neill believes that one of the chief functions of the government theatre project should be the development of new actors and writers. "This program should try to find young talent, both on the footboards and at the typewriter. I hope those in charge will give every advantage to actors and writers who are just starting out. They should be encouraged and helped."

He sees in the WPA program a partial recognition of the fact that the art theatre cannot exist without subsidy and assistance. "Heretofore the American idea of the theatre has been dictated by business considerations," he said. "Millionaires gave money for art museums, grand opera and archeological expeditions, but the theatre budget had to balance. Relatively little of their money went to the theatre."

He added that the paying of union wages to stagehands, the high cost of traveling units and similar expenses made it almost impossible for the art theatre to exist without financial aid. He believes the WPA units are translating into action the fact that the government has an obligation to give a reasonable amount of encouragement and assistance to cultural undertakings.

Since the World War, O'Neill thinks, the theatre has extended the sphere of cultural influence. For a time the American theatre was only a place of entertainment. "Amusement is important," he said. "Do not underestimate it. But culture is also significant. I believe the theatre as a cultural influence dates from the Washington Square Players in 1914 and the Provincetown Players in 1916. These groups helped make it possible to present serious dramas."

Shortly after that period O'Neill wrote Beyond the Horizon. It was a tragedy of American life with a tragic conclusion. It ran successfully on Broadway for half a year. He thinks the work of the Washington Square and the Provincetown groups was responsible for the reception accorded Beyond the Horizon. In his opinion, "These theatrical pioneers helped to introduce culture into the pattern of the stage."

He does not mean to imply that in the old American theatre there was no culture. He looks back with admiration to the time of Booth, when stock companies in various large cities exchanged their notable stars. But between that period and the coming of the Washington Square group amusement superseded culture on the stage, he believes.

The experience of Eugene O'Neill with the theatre does not date from his own activities. His father was James O'Neill, the famous portrayer of the Count of Monte Cristo of Dumas's great novel. The young O'Neill, almost from his birth—at Forty-third and Broadway in New York City on Oct. 16, 1888—was brought into intimate contact with the world of the drama.

As a small boy Eugene accompanied his father on stock tours. They traveled on clattering old day-coaches and slept in family hotels. Looking out across the mound to the distant mountain, O'Neill recalled that the last time he was in Seattle was during one of his father's *Monte Cristo* trips. He remembers those years as clearly as his latest fishing excursion. He smilingly recollects his filling in at one town for an acting player. "I was a punk actor," he says.

O'Neill hopes the WPA projects will help to revive some of the culture and the color of the period of his father and Booth. He believes the government program should include a resurrection of the classics—Shakespeare, the Restoration comedy, the Elizabethan drama. "The WPA units are, and can be, a real educational influence," he said. "By reviving the use of the old playwrights, and by bringing forth the best of the new ones, they can become invaluable to our national life."

Although O'Neill has spent much of his time on the coast of Georgia and in the inland waterways of Washington, he has not lost contact with the dynamic political events of recent months. He is enthusiastic over President Roosevelt's overwhelming re-election. He thinks the nation has gone ahead under the New Deal, and regards the President as a great democratic leader.

The Nobel Prize man is optimistic over the future of liberty in America. "The results of the recent election indicate that the people intend to preserve their freedom," he commented. In the same spirit, he believes there should be complete liberty and latitude in the government's theatre units. "Once let censorship creep in, and the good of the program has been almost nullified."

His winning of the latest prize is only one more experience in a life vivid with adventures and undertakings. He has been a seaman, a secretary in a mail order firm and a newspaper reporter. He has prospected for gold in Honduras and sailed on ships to many an out-of-the-way port. Into plays set as far apart as the jungles of *The Emperor Jones* and the waterfront of *Anna Christie,* he has woven the pattern of his own experiences. It seems particularly appropriate that he should receive word of his award within sight of the sea he knows so well.

He still loves the wilds and the woodlands. Fishing trips on Puget Sound have assumed an important place on his schedule. Clad in an old sweater and slacks, he likes to skim over the choppy bay in the motor boat of one of his friends. He likes to watch the American of the backwoods and the American of the great farm areas. He still remembers the companions of his boyhood adventures. On his list of "must" tasks is an attempt to find in Oregon an old prospector he knew in Central America years ago.

At home O'Neill is quiet and affable. He pokes the blazing fire on the hearth and smiles, "It's good to hear the logs crackle again. After the heat of the South I don't mind even this fog." He pointed out through the French doors of the big living room to where a quilt of clouds was beginning to shroud the Sound.

He is meticulous and neat. He writes in fine penciled handwriting. After a fishing trip he changes his outdoor garments for a tight-fitting double-breasted suit with shirt and tie to blend with it. He opens his package of cigarettes sharply and squarely, carefully pulling away the frayed edges of tinfoil and cellophane. He remembers minute details: In discussing the people of the South, he recalled the effect of the late Huey Long's speeches on the villagers he knew in Georgia; he even recollected some of the Kingfish's remarks verbatim.

O'Neill is curious about his new surroundings. He asks questions about the country, the people, the fishing, the climate. He wants to visit Bonneville and Grand Coulee Dams. He intends to match his fishing skill against the Chinook salmon of the Columbia River. One of his first acts on arriving in Seattle was to drive over the winding road to the glacier-flanked ramparts of Mount Rainier.

He looks like his pictures. His lean, wiry build gives the impression of added height. His sparse hair is becoming gray, and so is his mustache. He has a sharp profile, and his chin turns a ninety-degree angle. He appears tense and active and seems to find it difficult to relax. But he is not stilted or aloof, and he laughs amiably when an anecdote amuses him. He is a devoted reader, and two or three volumes on the table beside him, including histories of the Northwest, were placed with bookmarks.

Approval for his plays interests O'Neill more than plaudits for him as their author. He is going to Sweden to receive the premier award in literature, but will not be able to attend the Nobel festival there on Dec. 10. First he must look after such commonplace affairs as disposing of his home in Georgia. Then—and he gazes down toward the choppy waters below his home—there is that matter of fishing and boat trips, and perhaps fighting it out in the Columbia with a seventy-five-pound Chinook.

He is the winner of the Nobel Prize, but he also is the boy who left Princeton for adventure in the fo'c'sle and the gold fields. Perhaps that is why he is as quick to tell you about boating on the Sound as he is to discuss the cultural aspects of the Federal Government's theatre program.

Eugene O'Neill Lets Us in on Why
The Iceman Cometh
Earl Wilson/1946

Reprinted from the *New York Post*, 2 August 1946, 4, 36, by permission of the *New York Post*.

Out on the sun-sprayed patio of a high-up apartment in the east 80s—an apartment rich with 10,000 books—I sat with Eugene O'Neill, the tall, gray playwright, while he made jokes poking pins in Eugene O'Neill.

"How long a play will *The Iceman* be?" I asked the shy 57-year-old genius with the fencerail frame.

I wondered whether it'd be a longie.

You remember *Strange Interlude*—5:30 to 11 p.m.—one hour out for dinner? He supposedly has another new play that could run from 8 a.m. to midnight. A boss of mine used to say "Wilson, you don't write the best stories, but you write the longest." Well, O'Neill writes the longest plays—and the best.

"The Iceman," he said, using the pet name for *The Iceman Cometh*, the play that brings him back to the Theatre Guild and Broadway in October for the first time in 12 years, "would have run for four hours, with a dinner intermission.

"But it won't now.

"Look at the problems of taxi-cabs and getting dinner in an hour.

"Everybody would have come back wanting to eat the author.

"To ROAST him and eat him."

"So the play"—and I may as well tell you it's about Death, about 14 men and 3 tarts waiting for the Iceman, meaning Death—"will open at 8 and come down at half-past 11," O'Neill said. His gray mustache twisted upward in another smile. "There'll be almost a half-hour intermission after the first act. Time for everybody to get a drink and a sandwich—and what's the name of that heart stimulant?"

As the first reporter able to face him with a notebook in several years, I noted all this greedily.

"After that," O'Neill went on, there'll be "three short intermissions, not long enough for people to get out of their seats."

"Not long enough to get out of their seats!" I said.

"Well, they'll know if they go for a drink they're going to miss part of the play."

And remembering he was a great bottle man once, he said, "That wouldn't have stopped me at one time from getting a drink—knowing I was going to miss part of an act."

(He hasn't had a drop in 15 years.)

I was struck by the fact that this native of Times Square who may be remembered by the ages is different than the public thinks.

He writes in no dungeon; actually in a pleasant 4-windowed bedroom at a modern desk. Swims well. Goes to fights to watch Rocky Graziano slug. A juke box company recently learned he wanted a juke box. He didn't get the juke box, poor man. And as he sat there yesterday, he fibbed that his devoted and beautiful wife, Carlotta Monterey, the former actress, couldn't join us, as she was terribly busy killing cockroaches in the kitchen.

She phoned later, upon hearing of his yarn, and didn't like the joke at all. She maintained she was busy cataloguing his books. They do NOT have cockroaches, she said, pretty severely.

"Is it true," I inquired of the genial genius, "that you won't go to your opening—and never do go?"

"Yes," he said. "By the time the dress rehearsal is over, I'm sorry I ever wrote the thing and never do see it again—usually for about 15 years. Some I haven't read for 20 years."

I asked about the plot of *The Iceman Cometh*. "It's laid in 1912; the places are accurate; they are three places I actually lived in," he said.

He mentioned the old Jimmy the Priest's Saloon down on Fulton Street, since erased by the years.

"Do you mean you lived there?"

"Sure. When I was a sailor. Away back in 1911. It was a hangout for broken-down telegraphers. I was always learning the international code from them. But it was always too late in the evening for me to be very receptive. So I never remembered it the next day."

"And this play is about what?" I asked.

"It has no propaganda, except the propaganda that every man—."
His voice trailed off here into a chuckle. "I don't want to tell you too
much about the play."

O'Neill said he felt nobody should write a play particularly for a
certain star or around a star. "My plays are about life as I've known
it," he said. Only a handful, including the Gish sisters, have seen this
play, but then Ibsen didn't even let his own wife read his plays.

Very, very briefly then he spoke of *Long Day's Journey Into Night,*
the play which he has written to be published as a book, but never to
be produced as a play, 25 years after his death.

"It is a real story," he said, "also laid in 1912. There's one person in
it who is still alive."

Puzzled and intrigued, I wanted to ask, "Do you mean it's you—
it's your autobiography?"

But before I could ask it, he said: "I won't tell you a word about
it."

Nor did he.

Eugene O'Neill Discourses on Dramatic Art

George Jean Nathan/1946

Reprinted from the *New York Journal-American*, 26 August 1946, 13, by permission of Associated University Presses.

The re-emergence of Eugene O'Neill with three new plays after 12 years' silence is the most important and welcome news of the theatrical season which shortly gets under way. Under the circumstances, it seemed only fitting that I should engage him in conversation after his long period of retirement and on the public's behalf learn his views on things. Since I have known him well for more than a quarter-century, I knew he would feel that he could let himself go.

"What do you consider the greatest present need of the American stage?" I asked him.

"What it needs more than anything else," he replied, firmly, "is another Lotta Faust. There, my boy, was a love-apple, and who said anything about acting? You could get an effect just looking at her that you can't get from looking at and listening to any dozen current actresses full of the virtuoso stuff: When Lotta sang 'Sammy,' all the great Shakespearean actresses of the day felt like going into hiding, or, anyway, should have, compulsorily."

He recollectively hummed a bit of "Sammy," lit a cigaret, and blissfully went on.

"Then there was Lulu Glaser, another slice off the top of the pot-roast. Remember the show in which she came on carrying a live duck? I'll never forget it, because the duck quacked exactly like a famous road actress I saw while I was touring with my old man in *Monte Cristo*. But to get back to Lulu. A Lulu on the stage today would help it enormously. And a whiff of the golden days might return if, in addition to Lulu, they brought back the duck.

"Yes," he continued, "I've given it a lot of thought. It all came upon me again the other day when I bought a stack of copies of the old *Theatre Magazine* and then looked at the pictures in the Sunday newspapers. I'm not saying anything the one way or the other about repertory companies, national theatre foundations, library theatres, chicken dinners celebrating Bernard Shaw's birthday though he is white, or anything else like that that's supposed to be for the good of the theatre, and don't get me wrong. But if you don't agree that some fruit-jellies like Irene Bentley, Bonnie Maginn, Marie Doro and Edna May would contribute a heap to that good, I won't eat my hat because the very idea would give me indigestion.

"Incidentally," he concluded, "we've got a new little colored maid here in the apartment who wouldn't be such a hindrance to the stage either. Her name, in case you are interested, is Daisy Wilson and her parents christened her correctly. I'm sorry, but it's her night off."

He went out, considerately fetched me a bottle of beer, lit another cigaret, and inquired, "Where do we go from here?"

"What about your plays, if you'll pardon me for bringing up any such out-of-the-way subject?" I asked.

"I've tried to cut The Iceman Cometh about three-quarters of an hour, but all I feel justified in doing is cutting it about 15 minutes. It will have to run from 8 o'clock to whenever it now goldarned pleases—maybe quarter to 12. If there are repetitions, they'll have to remain in, because I feel they are absolutely necessary to what I am trying to get over. As for A Moon For The Misbegotten, which will go into rehearsal immediately after The Iceman opens, it is standard length and needs no cutting, and now that I've at last found the required hefty, 6-foot high actress for the lead I don't have to worry about it, which gives me just that much extra time to eat spaghetti and lie in the sun and worry about the third play, A Touch Of The Poet.

"What that one needs is an actor like Maurice Barrymore or James O'Neill, my old man. One of those big-chested, chiseled-mug, romantic old boys who could walk onto a stage with all the aplomb and regal splendor with which they walked into the old Hoffman House bar, drunk or sober. It's tough trying to locate such a one today. Most actors in these times lack an air. If a playwright doesn't work up entrances 15 minutes long for them and have all the other characters describe them in advance as something pretty elegant, noble, chivalrous and handsome, the audiences wouldn't be able to accept them for much more than third assistant barkeeps, if that."

Another cigaret, and he continued. "Speaking of barkeeps, you and I have gone through fire and water together—or shall we regard the 'and' as a polite concession to the melancholy circumstance that I am presently on the waterwagon? My ambition since boyhood, as you well know, has been to own a saloon. When these three plays of mine are on, why don't we open up one together? Not in town, but somewhere out on Long Island near the ocean, because I still don't want to miss my swimming. You once said you had a good name for such a dump, 'High Dive.' It wouldn't cost us much to start it, and I'll throw in my old barroom piano that you drop nickels into and that then promptly lights up in front like an Egyptian drugstore and begins booming out 'The Mississippi Rag.' It's in storage now and I'm getting lonesome for it. We might not make any money, considering that most of our friends would open charge accounts and lovably forget them, but it would be a great sensation again to eat up the free lunch."

Having subtly hinted that the conversational atmosphere was far from unconducive to another bottle of beer, at least, and having been appropriately commoded with it, I bade my friend proceed.

"Being a playwright with shows going on gets a fellow into some peculiar things," he observed, snitching a cigaret from my hip pocket. "The other day, one of the magazines came up here to take a photograph of me and I said O.K. shoot. 'What, without due preparation!' they exclaimed, highly offended. Well, I'll be doggoned if after two hours of this due preparation they didn't take me surrounded by Hindu and Indian masks, jungle drums, spears, swords, tomahawks, and Chinese hatchets. Why, I wanted to know. 'Primitive passion,' they said. 'Primitive passion, me?' I beamed. 'Naw, your plays,' they said. Daisy almost died laughing.

"Then there's this butler you see moseying around here. Carlotta had an awful time trying to get hold of one and you could have knocked her over with a feather when this one jumped at the job pronto. She couldn't understand it and asked him the reason. 'You see,' he explained, 'I'm a playwright too and we playwrights should work together.' He's a good butler, but there's only one trouble with him—he absolutely refuses to wear a coat on the job. I told him it was all right with me, however, as long as he was willing to wear pants."

"One final question," I said. "What do you think of the future of the American stage?"

"I believe," he answered, after considerable deliberation, "that Rocky Graziano is a much better man than most people believe and that it will be well to keep an eye on the kid."

O'Neill on the World and *The Iceman*
John S. Wilson/1946

Reprinted from *PM*, 3 September 1946, 18.

The press was assembled in a large room of the Theatre Guild's offices to meet Eugene O'Neill. They sat around a long table, picking up odds and ends of information from a press agent about *The Iceman Cometh*, the first O'Neill play since 1934, which will open at the Martin Beck on Oct. 9. When O'Neill came in, gaunt but tanned, his gray hair turning white at the temples, everyone stood up. As he sat down and the reporters settled back in their chairs, he apologized for the fact that he spoke very indistinctly.

"Even my own family complains about it," he said.

Then he waited for questions. His hands shook nervously, the aftermath of a recent illness. No one said anything.

"It seems a long time to be out on the Northwest coast where they never hear of the theater," O'Neill said. "They very seldom see any legitimate plays, or at least I didn't see any."

Still no questions. O'Neill rambled slowly on until Rosamond Gilder of *Theatre Arts Monthly* said it was wonderful to have O'Neill back, everybody was glad that he was back. O'Neill said that was very nice.

"While I was away they tore down the old Cadillac Hotel where I was born," he complained. "That was a dirty trick."

The reporters shuffled their note paper nervously. Finally someone asked about the intent of his cycle of nine plays, of which *The Iceman* is the fifth [*sic*]. All of the plays have not yet been written.

"I'm going on the theory that the United States, instead of being the most successful country in the world, is the greatest failure," O'Neill said, seemingly grateful to have something to talk about. "It's the greatest failure because it was given everything, more than any other country. Through moving as rapidly as it has, it hasn't acquired any real roots. Its main idea is that everlasting game of trying to possess your own soul by the possession of something outside of it, thereby losing your own soul and the thing outside of it, too. America is the prime example of this because it happened so quickly and with such immense resources. This was really said in the Bible much better. We are the greatest example of 'For what shall it profit a man if he shall gain the whole world, and lose his own soul?' We had so much and could have gone either way."

This attitude of O'Neill's is not confined simply to the United States. It spreads to all humanity.

"If the human race is so damned stupid," he said, "that in 2000 years it hasn't had brains enough to appreciate that the secret of happiness is contained in one simple sentence which you'd think any grammar school kid could understand and apply, then it's time we dumped it down the nearest drain and let the ants have a chance. That simple sentence is: 'What shall it profit a man?'

"I had a French friend, one of the delegates at the San Francisco Conference, who came to see me. I asked him, 'If it's not betraying any great secrets, what's really happening at the Conference?' He shrugged his shoulders and said, 'It's the League of Nations, only not so good.' And I believe it. Of course, I may be wrong. I nearly always am."

"I've heard," a reporter (female) said, "that the cast of *The Iceman* consists of 14 men and four tarts."

"Well," O'Neill replied, "there are 14 men and four-uh-ladies."

A press agent pointed out that there were only three-uh-ladies, unless O'Neill had added one lately. O'Neill agreed that there were only three.

The iceman in the title, he said, had a twofold meaning. The chief character is a salesman. There is the salesman's old story that when he is stewed he would go sobbing around from table to table in bars, handing out a picture of his wife and blubbering about "my poor wife." "But she's safe," the salesman would say. "I left her in bed with the iceman."

"That is a superficial meaning of the title," O'Neill said. "It also has a deeper meaning connected with death."

O'Neill hasn't been represented on Broadway for 12 years because he went out to the Coast with the intention of writing the cycle of nine plays and keeping at it until he did the whole thing. Eventually he went stale and put it on the shelf. Then he saw the war coming and the invasion of France.

"I had lived in France for three years," he said, "and when the Germans got to the Loire I felt as though they were in the place right next to my ranch. I had been very happy in France."

He hasn't done any writing since 1943 when he finished *Moon for the Misbegotten* which will be produced in December.

"I hope to resume writing as soon as I can," he said, "but the war has thrown me completely off base and I have to get back to it again. I have to get back to a sense of writing being worthwhile. In fact, I'd have to pretend."

He was asked which of his plays he liked best.

"That is really two questions," he parried. "It should be which play I like best and which play I *think* is best. I like *The Hairy Ape*. As for which one I think is best—well, *Iceman* is just coming on, so—." He spread his hands and smiled. "But really," he added, "I love *The Iceman*."

When the interview broke up, a press agent indicated a table laden with liquor and ice and suggested that everybody have a drink. Nobody did.

"I was going to ask some questions," a little blonde said as she gathered up her notes, "but I was too scared."

Eugene O'Neill Returns after Twelve Years

S. J. Woolf/1946

After a lapse of twelve years a new play by Eugene O'Neill will soon be seen on Broadway. And after an even longer absence the man whom many Americans consider the most distinguished dramatist this country ever produced has come back to New York from California as a permanent resident. Even the locale of the new play suggests that the production is in every sense a homecoming. The setting of *The Iceman Cometh* is New York—specifically, the lower West Side of 1912.

Begun before the war, *The Iceman Cometh* has been the subject of intense curiosity along Broadway for several seasons. Now that the author has settled into a Manhattan penthouse and has been regularly attending rehearsals, word of its theme and contents has got around quite generally. It ignores the coming not only of automatic refrigeration but of the atomic age as well, but its subject is as much a matter of pity and terror in 1946 as in 1912. His iceman, O'Neill explains, is death, and his use of the archaic verb "cometh" is a deliberate reference to biblical language and universality.

It would seem from this that, like some of O'Neill's earlier plays, *The Iceman Cometh* is not without religious overtones, for all that the scene of the action is a bar—Jimmy the Priest's—and that the author cheerfully admits the title also has a second, a superficial and ribald, meaning. (It seems that there is a character who goes about telling people that he has left his wife safe at home with the iceman.)

The length of the play has attracted almost as much attention as the title and the theme. It is a long work, requiring for its unfolding four acts, a cast of nineteen and a running time of more than four hours. The curtain will rise at 5:30 and, except for a dinner intermission from 6:30 to 7:45, will not finally fall until around 11. At that, *The Iceman Cometh* is half an hour shorter than either *Strange*

Interlude or *Mourning Becomes Electra*—generally regarded as two of O'Neill's best plays.

Posing for me in his Manhattan apartment, O'Neill made it clear that length is one theatrical problem that does not interest him. When I asked him how long a play should be he said: "As long as necessary to tell the story. No play is too long that holds the interest of its audience. If a short play is tiresome it is too long and if a long play is absorbing until the fall of the last curtain no one will pull out his watch to look at the time."

The Iceman Cometh, along with two other unproduced plays, *A Moon for the Misbegotten* and *A Touch of the Poet*, was written on the West Coast, where the author and his wife lived from 1931 until this year. O'Neill remarked that while he settled in turn in Seattle, Oakland and San Francisco, he never at any time lived near Hollywood. Before moving to New York the O'Neills disposed of much of the furniture in their California home, but they brought with them their vast collection of books and phonograph records, some favorite Chinese antiques and a large drum (made from a tree trunk) such as plagued the Emperor Jones as he slunk through that tropical forest.

Even among his prized possessions O'Neill seems a curiously detached person. He is tall and thin with a repressed manner that is almost shy. Greenwich Village, where his plays first attracted attention, has left no apparent impress on him. He dresses immaculately, his hair is neatly brushed and when he smokes, as he does almost continuously, he is careful to have an ash tray by his side.

His voice is low, and as he speaks he knits his eyebrows and his large, dark eyes become more than ordinarily intense. From time to time a quiet, repressed note of humor comes into his talk and an alarmingly sudden smile breaks over his face. In repose his face is sad. In retrospect one forgets his haggard cheeks, his thin gray mustache above a soft mouth and his slightly bulbous nose. What one remembers best is his mournful eyes that look oddly like those in portraits of Poe. Like Poe, too, he looks as if he were surrounded by an aura of mysterious sorrow.

Most of O'Neill's talk, while I was sketching, was of the theatre, and much of it was reminiscent. Several times he mentioned his father, the celebrated James O'Neill. As a child, the playwright traveled widely with the elder O'Neill's troupe. "Almost the first words of my

father I remember," he said, "are, 'The theatre is dying.' And those
words seem to me as true today as when he said them. But the
theatre must be a hardy wench, for although she is still ailing, she will
never die as long as she offers an escape.

"It was when he was starring in *The Count of Monte Cristo* that
my father decided the theatre was dying. I can still see him in that
play with outstretched arms, rising from a canvas sea shouting, 'The
world is mine.' It was a time when artificiality was as prevalent on the
stage as it was in everyday life. The simplest lines had to be
declaimed. Virtue always triumphed and vice always got its just
deserts. A man was either a hero or a villain and a woman was either
virtuous or vile.

"It was a prudish age which has left its impress in the form of
present-day censorship. This to me is one of the biggest obstacles to
the artistic development of the theatre. Now, before a play can be
safely produced, somebody has to say that it will not corrupt the
morals of 6-year-olds. But, to tell you the truth, I think some of the 6-
year-olds could give pointers to many of us oldsters.

"I remember when the censors got after one of my plays. The
result was a sudden increased demand for tickets, but the tickets were
bought by the wrong kind of people who laughed at the wrong places
and went away disappointed because they had not seen a smutty
show."

O'Neill regards the refusal of many producers to experiment as
another theatrical curse. "Many theatrical managers," he said, "fear
to keep abreast of the times. They know that a certain type of play
made money ten years ago and they keep to the same formula. It
was the little experimental theatre which opened the eyes of the
commercial producers to the fact that the taste of the public was
better than they thought."

It was no surprise that a dramatist who has consistently written
"experimental" plays should talk at length about theatre technique.
New techniques, O'Neill pointed out, often amount to no more than
fads. He mentioned expressionism as one fad that had waxed and
waned in the modern theatre, and while he poked fun at that
movement's excesses, he was quick to add that it had had "some
good influence in playwriting. The trouble with a fad—and this holds
true for any form of art—is that it affords an opportunity for people

who do not know the technique to pose as artists. There are as well-established rules for the theatre as there are for painting and music. The only ones who can successfully break the rules are the people who know them. A knowledge of rules is necessary, even if adhering to tradition is not."

It is in comments like these that one catches a glimpse of O'Neill's profound interest in craftsmanship. He gets around to craftsmanship even when speaking of what he considers the bad influence of motion pictures on the stage.

"The motion picture," he asserted, "has hurt the stage. In the first place, as soon as young actors and actresses make good, Hollywood grabs them. In the old days there were many more good actors and actresses available for stage productions than there are now. In addition, many plays today are written with Hollywood acceptance in mind. Artistic concessions are made in them with the hope that they will be bought by some movie company.

"This does not mean that I am opposed to moving pictures. I enjoy many of them. I recently saw a new picture based on the life of Nurse Kenny that I liked tremendously. It was written for the screen and it shows the opposition against which she has had to contend—the fate, after all, of all innovators. Some adaptations from stage plays are good. Several of mine have been extremely well done. But the entire technique of moving pictures is different. The only way a good stage play can be written is for the author to forget all about the screen. If eventually it is to be turned into a movie, it should be done by somebody who knows how to write for the screen."

Radio, too, O'Neill insists, has its own technique. He put himself on record as being opposed to the condensing of full-length plays into broadcasts that run an hour or even less.

"It is possible to write well for the radio," he added. "Norman Corwin has shown that to be true. But I feel that radio should stick to its own medium and not try to act as a substitute for the theatre. It has a field all its own. When television becomes more prevalent, still another method will be used. But no matter what happens, neither films nor other waves will ever take the place of reality."

He sat still for some minutes, saying nothing and staring out into space. In one of his thin hands was the everpresent cigarette—a mild brand with a cork tip and cotton filter. His thoughts seemed far away and I hesitated to break the silence. Suddenly he looked up and a smile spread over his face. He said that he had been thinking of the past.

Eugene O'Neill was born 58 years ago on the third floor of a hotel that stood on the corner of Broadway and Forty-third Street. After he had grown up and made a name for himself, he often stood across the street and looked up at the room. "But New York had changed," he said. "The old hotel had had several stories added to it. The green horse cars we used to take when we went to see friends who lived at Seventy-seventh Street had vanished, and above Fifty-ninth Street the Boulevard had become Broadway."

At the time of his birth Forty-second Street was uptown and the theatrical district was down around Union Square. The only electric sign on Broadway was at Twenty-second Street and it advertised the breezes that swept Manhattan Beach.

When he was 7, young Eugene was sent to school and eventually entered Princeton, where at 19 he was expelled for what he says was "general hell-raising." His first job was as a clerk in a mail-order house, but wanderlust was strong in him and he left for Honduras in search of gold. He failed to find it, and when he returned he became an assistant manager in his father's company. But a painted ocean did not satisfy him and he signed up for a trip to Buenos Aires.

In Argentina he clerked, sold sewing machines and worked in a packing house. He was a failure at everything and he spent months hanging about the waterfront with stokers and beachcombers. Still longing for travel, he sailed for Africa, but because he had no funds he was not permitted to leave the cattle steamer on which he had arrived. Finally, he got back to New York.

It was then that he made his only stage appearance. "Vaudeville had become popular," he recalls, "and my father gave me a part in a tabloid version of *The Count of Monte Cristo*. For an entire season we traveled about the country, appearing twice a day between a trained-horse act and a troupe of acrobats. When the season ended, we went to our summer home in Connecticut and I got a job as a reporter in New London."

Then, his health failing, O'Neill was sent to a sanitarium where, for want of something better to do, he began writing plays. At last he had found something that held his interest. When he recovered, he attended Prof. George Baker's famous class in playwriting at Harvard.

About this time—some thirty years ago—a theatre run by that

erratic genius, George Cram Cook, was operating in a crude building on a Provincetown wharf. The little theatre was then looked upon with amusement but Cook, undiscouraged and less interested in the box-office than in the stage itself, hired a barn on MacDougall Street in order to bring his group to New York. In the MacDougall Street place many of O'Neill's early plays had their first showings and began to attract attention. The Washington Square Players, forerunners of the Theatre Guild, also produced his work. Finally, a commercial producer ventured to put *Beyond the Horizon* on Broadway.

When I asked O'Neill which was his favorite among his plays he said he thought it was *The Great God Brown*, in which the actors wore masks. He also revealed that he had intended to use masks in *Mourning Becomes Electra* but gave up the idea when he couldn't obtain the kind he wanted.

"I hesitate to re-read my own plays," he said. "Few people realize the shock a playwright gets when he sees his work acted. Alice Brady and Alla Nasimova gave wonderful performances in *Mourning Becomes Electra* but they did not carry out my conception at all. I saw a different play from the one I thought I had written. As I look back now on all my work, I can honestly say there was only one actor who carried out every notion of a character I had in mind. That actor was Charles Gilpin as the Pullman porter in *The Emperor Jones.*"

He added: "I am not saying that some of the actors and actresses who interpreted my plays did not add something to them. But, after all, even an owl thinks her owlets are the most beautiful babies in the world and that's the way an author feels about his stage children. It is for this reason that I always attend the rehearsals of my plays. While I do not want to change the personalities of the artists acting in them, I want to make it clear to them what was in my mind when I wrote the play.

"I confess, though, that I have never been completely satisfied with anything that I have done and I constantly rewrite my plays until they are produced and even then I always see things which I could improve and I regret that it is too late to make more changes.

"For, after all, anyone who creates anything must feel deeply. Like Shaw, he may cover up his sincerity with humor, he may make light of his efforts, but those efforts are nevertheless heart-breaking."

The production of *The Iceman Cometh* ends a long silence, but in that silence O'Neill has not been idle. The war, he says, made it difficult for him to concentrate on work that seemed "trivial" compared to what was going on in the world. Yet there were times when he managed to forget the outer turmoil and to draft a new drama cycle about which he is loath to speak. At all times, he indicates, he works slowly. He is not adept at typewriting and he finds dictating to a secretary difficult. Accordingly, all his plays have been written in longhand.

Whatever reception *The Iceman Cometh* may receive, it is undoubtedly the work of a man who takes both the theatre and life seriously. The setting may be a bar, but it will not be the most unlikely place in which O'Neill has staged a tragic drama. In the past he has found drama of stature in the jungle, the New England village, the Midwestern farm and the forecastle. And the emotions of his characters invariably transcended the specific time and place.

Eugene O'Neill after Twelve Years

George Jean Nathan/1946

Reprinted from American Mercury, 63 (October 1946), 462–66, by permission of Associated University Presses.

Two weeks after this number of *The American Mercury* appears on the newsstands, what to my mind is one of the most impressive plays ever written by an American dramatist will be presented in the theatre. Its title is *The Iceman Cometh* and, as is not altogether surprising, its author is Eugene O'Neill.

It is now just twelve years and nine months since O'Neill's last play, called *Days Without End*, saw production, and in the long intervening spell the public has had small news of him. Now and then came vague and contradictory reports that he was working on a cycle of eight or nine plays to be named by the general and somewhat turgid title, *A Tale of Possessors Self-Dispossessed;* that he was very ill and no longer able to do any work; and that he had successively retired from the theatre to Sea Island, Georgia, and the Valley of the Moon in California, there to devote the rest of his life to nursing his health, raising Dalmatian dogs, and laughing at English dramatic criticism. But from the man himself there issued not so much as a peep. What, really, was he up to?

It happens that we have been close friends for going on thirty years now, and that I am in a position to tell. That in the period of his absence he completed the mentioned *The Iceman Cometh,* along with the subsequently to be produced *A Moon for the Misbegotten* and the still later to be produced *A Touch of the Poet,* the public has been apprised. These three plays, however, were by no means all. During the twelve-odd years, he not only outlined in minute detail not eight or nine but all of eleven plays of the cycle referred to—the eleven were to be played, however, as eight with three combined into duplex units and presented, like *Strange Interlude,* on the same afternoons, evenings and nights—but further definitely completed seven of them, including the three double-length ones, and got pretty well into the eighth.

174

In addition, he finished a separate and independent play of full length called *Long Day's Journey into Night,* production of which he will not allow, for reasons which I may not yet specify, for some years. Nor, yet again, was that all. Besides *Long Day's Journey into Night,* he also completed the first play of a much shorter and entirely different cycle of which no word has until now reached anyone. Its title, like that of the contemplated briefer series in its entirety, is *By Way of Obit.* It runs for forty-five or so minutes and involves, very successfully I think, an imaginative technical departure from O'Neill's previous work. It contains but two characters and is laid in New York in approximately the same period as *The Iceman Cometh,* of which more anon.

All of which, one will agree, is not such bad going for a sick man.

The plays, *The Iceman Cometh* and *A Moon for the Misbegotten,* as well as the two last named, are distinct and wholly apart from the cycle of eleven plays. *A Touch of the Poet,* however, was to be first play of that cycle. As to the cycle itself, O'Neill gradually convinced himself, after he had got as far as he had with it, that his drama-turgical plan was faulty. Without further ado, he destroyed two of the double-length, or four, of the plays he had written, preserving only *A Touch of the Poet,* the third double-header (*More Stately Mansions*) and one scene in another to be called *The Calms of Capricorn.* As for *A Touch of the Poet,* it seems to him to be a unit in itself and may well, he thinks, stand apart and alone. When and if he will return to work on the cycle as he has newly planned it, he does not know. In his head at the moment is an exciting idea for another play which bears no relation to the cycle. It will probably be his next effort after he has finished the production supervision of the three plays noted.

The reason he withheld these three plays for so long is that he has made up his mind never again to permit a play of his to be produced unless he can be present. His health was such that it did not allow him to come to New York earlier. There was also another reason. He did not believe that, while the war was on, the theatre was right for the plays, though none is in any way related to it. It was simply his feeling that wartime audiences would not be in a mood for such serious drama.

His determination to be on deck at all future productions of his plays stems from his experience with his play *Dynamo,* which was shown in 1929. He was unable to come to New York for the casting and rehearsals of that one and learned all too late that the Theatre Guild had cast in the leading female rôle the fair young cute one, Claudette Colbert, famous for the symmetry of her legs and not wholly unaware of the fact. Throughout the play, the young lady sought to augment her fame by placing the two reasons therefor on display whenever one of the other characters seemed to her to be diverting the attention of the audience, and the play as a consequence ran a bad second to her extremities.

"Henceforth," O'Neill averred, "I myself cast not only actresses but legs!"

In addition to the projected plays specified, the playwright has made copious notes on at least three or four others. Some of these notes were begun even before he went into retirement; others were made during that period. They include plans for, among the others, an heroic drama of ancient Chinese locale. This he has been mulling for fifteen years, though, if he does it at all, which is doubtful, it would not be put into experimental preliminary writing until he finishes the one—with an American locale—alluded to as likely his next.

The long cycle, when and if he returns to it, will concern a single Irish-American family over a span of approximately 130 years and will indicate broadly through its successive generations the changes in America and American life. Not the changes in the obvious theatrical sense, but the changes as they influence the members of the family. It will continue to be a study in character rather than a study in national progress. The latter will be held to a dramatic undertone. O'Neill's dissatisfaction with the work as far as it had gone proceeded from his conviction that it should deal with one family and not two, as it presently did. And also that, in the form he had written it, it began at the wrong point and over-told the story. Though he appreciated that he could rewrite what he had already done, he preferred to do away with much of it and to start afresh.

The cycle, as he now envisages it, will begin with the French-and-Indian Wars period and will present its first member of the family in the light of a deserter from the fighting forces.

O'Neill's attitude toward criticism of his work in particular and in general has not changed. However denunciatory and stinging it may be at times, he shows no indignation and maintains at least outwardly an appearance of smiling tolerance. Unlike a number of his playwriting contemporaries, he never makes public reply to it, though now and again to a close friend he will privately express his amusement over certain of its more wayward aspects.

An English critic (not Spender, who has been generally more clearsighted) recently, for example, had at O'Neill with the old, familiar contention that, though he may think of himself as a poet, he is far from one. In proof whereof, the critic delightedly quoted his speech by Marsden in *Strange Interlude:*

> We'll be married in the afternoon, decidedly. I've already picked out the church, Nina—a gray ivied chapel, full of restful shadow, symbolical of the peace we have found. The crimsons and purples in the windows will stain our faces with faded passion. It must be in the hour before sunset when the earth dreams in afterthoughts and mystic premonitions of life's beauty, etc.

"Didn't he realize," chuckled O'Neill, "that the attempt there certainly wasn't poetry, but poetic travesty? Marsden, as anyone must easily see, is a sentimental throwback, a kind of *Yellow Book* period reversion, and I was deliberately using that 'crimsons and purples in the windows,' 'staining our faces with faded passion' and so on stuff to indicate it."

The notion that O'Neill entertains a profound satisfaction with everything he has written and resents any opposite opinion—a notion that pops up between the lines in various critical treatises on his work, as, for example, Eric Bentley's recent *The Playwright as Thinker*—is nonsensical. I give you several instances out of my own personal critical experience. When his *The First Man* was produced, I wrote acidly of it, even indulging in some ridicule. Reading the criticism, O'Neill grinned. "You let it down too easy," he observed. "It's no good." When subsequently I wrote in the same vein about *Welded,* which he seemed to have faith in when he gave me the script to read, he allowed, "I know now I was 'way off; the play is all wrong; it's no good." When, on the other hand, I found certain things to my liking in *Gold,* he took me to task. "You're wrong. It's a bad play. I'm telling you."

He further believes that *The Fountain* is more defective than I found it to be, and that *Dynamo,* though granting its lapses, is considerably less so. Only in the case of *Days without End,* which I could not critically stomach, has he vigorously opposed my opinion, and even in this case he allows that he now feels he must rewrite the play's ending for the definitive edition of his works.

As originally conceived, this *Days without End* was laid back in the year 1857 or thereabout. Bringing it up to the 1930s seemed to me, among others, to render its double sex standard idea somewhat anachronistic and shopworn. O'Neill, however, was not to be persuaded.

What he has persuaded himself, nevertheless, is that his hero's final gesture calls for alteration, though the alteration consists simply in reverting to the dramatic scheme as he first conceived it.

He is a stickler for casting and direction. As to the latter, his constant concern is any sentimentalization of his work. "Where sentiment exists," he says, "there is sufficient of it in the characters, and any directorial emphasis would throw it out of all proportion and make it objectionable." As to casting, he is generally opposed to so-called name actors. "They distract attention from the play to themselves," he argues. "My plays are not for stars but for simply good actors.

"Besides, you can never count on the idiosyncrasies of stars; they may not stick to a play and may so damage its chances on the road. I'm afraid of them, as I've had some experience with them. Also, they sometimes want you to change certain things in your play. Not for me!"

To return to *The Iceman Cometh.* Laid in a low saloon in the New York of 1912, it may very roughly be described as a kind of American *Nachtasyl.* Like that play of Gorki's, though it in no other way resembles it, it treats of a group of degenerated social outcasts and the advent among them of a man with a philosophy of life new and disturbing to them. Since critical ethics here prevent me from going into the play in detail before production, I may not reveal too much more about it. I may record, however, that its language is realistic, at times violently so; that its cast of alcoholic down-and-outs includes gamblers, grafting cops, harlots, pimps, anarchist riff-raff, military failures, college-educated wastrels, stool-pigeons, *et al*; that it is written in four parts; and that it contains one of the longest and, I think, most moving soliloquies, only briefly interrupted, in modern drama, that placed in the mouth of its traveling salesman protagonist.

The play will again attest to the fact, lost upon certain of O'Neill's critics, that he is far from lacking a healthy sense of humor. Some of the comedy writing is irresistible. It will also demonstrate again the deepest appreciation of character known to any of his American playwriting contemporaries.

And it embraces, among many other things, the most pitifully affecting picture of a woman—the unseen wife of the protagonist—that I, for one, have encountered in years of playgoing.

The Ordeal of Eugene O'Neill

[James Agee]/1946

Reprinted from *Time*, 48 (21 October 1946), 71–72, 74, 75–76, 78. Copyright 1946 Time Inc. Reprinted by permission. [This essay was the issue's cover story.]

Twelve years ago, the most exalted playwright in the history of the U.S. theatre formally bowed off his worldwide stage. Eugene O'Neill intended to devote himself exclusively to one of the most ambitious dramatic projects ever undertaken: the writing of a cycle of nine plays. Purpose: to dramatize the fate of a U.S. family and of the U.S. itself during a period of some 180 years (1754 to 1932).

One afternoon last week, for reasons best known to himself, O'Neill was back on Broadway with a mysterious play, mysteriously titled *The Iceman Cometh,* which would run for four and a quarter hours, with a 75-minute break for supper.

Towards 4:30[1] on that "first night" afternoon, some 1,200 people made the Martin Beck Theater resonant with that exhilarating pre-curtain buzz, like leaves before a storm, which has been familiar to theatergoers for 2,500 years. There was plenty to buzz about. There was the exciting fact that *The Iceman Cometh* was the first new O'Neill play to be produced since *Days without End* (1934). There was its cryptic title, clumsily poetic, naively sardonic and intensely O'Neillian, which caused one foreboding wag to suggest that a better name would be *The Ice Tray Always Sticks Twice.* The play had been rehearsed under heavy wrappings of secrecy. Almost nobody in the audience was sure what it was about, though some had paid $25 a seat to find out. But some people were already buying seats for February. For, whether the play was good or bad, theatergoers knew that the return of Eugene O'Neill was a major event in the theater. Then, as the lights went faint, the buzz of excitement dissolved into silence. In the dimness, like the opening of a vast mouth, the curtain rose.

[1]Thenceforth the curtain would rise on *The Iceman* at 5:30. The purpose of the earlier curtain: to give reviewers more time to collect their dazed impressions.

180

It rose on something harshly picturesque, something that through four long acts was to keep its soiled color and fuddled humanity, but that did not seem really impressive when it was over.

The opening scene was pure George Bellows—a seedy Bowery-type bar in the year 1912, littered with slumped and sleeping drunken bums.[2] Soaks of all descriptions—a Harvard man, a British infantry captain, a Boer War correspondent, a Negro gambler, an unbadged police lieutenant, a disillusioned anarchist—they had been reduced by rotgut to creatures of one baggy shape. What kept them hanging by a claw to life was the kindness of the drunken-bum saloonkeeper (finely played by Dudley Digges), and their pipe dreams, their mumbling that tomorrow would turn up a winning card or bring forth a better man.

This morning, however—while tarts forked over to the barkeep pimp, and a young anarchist stool pigeon crawled in to hide away—the bums were waiting for a highflying drummer named Hickey, who once a year threw them a big party and got as drunk as they did. But when Hickey (James Barton) finally came, he was not the fellow they knew; the party was to go on, he said, but he was not drinking. Something had happened to him, he had found peace by facing "reality"; and he jabbed away at them to do likewise.

Sullenly, hostilely, they try; they swear off the bottle and go looking for jobs, only to be thrown back on themselves, knowing that they are done for and that Hickey has sown a despair that means death. For the Iceman (in the sense that the loss of illusion means the end for those who have nothing else to lose) is Death.

Then they learn Hickey's own story: he had murdered his wife because her constant forgiveness of his misdeeds had made him feel unbearably guilty. He had faced reality only because he had already resigned himself to death. As the cops snap their handcuffs on Hickey, the bums, reprieved to live a lie once more, go happily back to their drinking.

It was as a thick (though much too fatty) slice of life—a somber, sardonic, year-long comic strip with a comic strip's microscopic variations—that *The Iceman Cometh* was most telling. O'Neill's bums were presented flat, with a few mannerisms, a few memories;

[2]Outstanding in the Theatre Guild's generally good production were Robert Edmond Jones's sets.

they repeated their little specialty acts; they never grew more complex, they only grew incredibly familiar, like chickens seen turning over & over on a spit. But collectively they seemed more real and redolent, for O'Neill knew them from his younger days and really cared about them, mingling gusto with his compassion. In the bleary squalor of *The Iceman* there was none of the piped-in knowledge or condescension of the Ivory Sewer school of writers; in fellow-feeling, though never in intensity, O'Neill might be saying with Walt Whitman, *I am the man, I suffer'd, I was there.*

But this often static, enormously protracted play lacked the depth to match its length. That heavy dramatic undertow which often redeems long plays, and can count for much more than surface swell was not there. Hickey, who might be a powerfully dramatic figure, wound up a merely theatrical one, peeling off a human skin to serve as a symbol of blight, disgorging in an interminable final speech too much and too lucid self-knowledge. And all that O'Neill seemed to be saying in *The Iceman* was that men cannot go on living without illusions—a truism that never took on the ring of nascent truth. As theater, much of the play was first-rate O'Neill. But as drama, for all its honest brooding, *The Iceman* was scarcely deeper than a puddle.

But behind the drama on the stage was the greater drama of one of literature's great human ordeals.

Eugene O'Neill was born (1888) in a respectable Manhattan family hotel, but much of his early boyhood was spent in the wings of theaters all over the U.S. His father, James O'Neill, Sr., was famed for his role of Edmond Dantes in *The Count of Monte Cristo* (he sometimes earned $50,000 a year). Hence Eugene knew little of actors' boardinghouse hardships. But he came to hate the constant moving around, long, dirty train rides, hotels, living out of trunks, the general rootlessness. He longed for security and stability.

In 1907, he flunked out of Princeton (he now holds an honorary degree of Litt.D. from Yale). In a mood of youthful truculence, he prospected for gold in Honduras, married his first wife (whom he later divorced), repeatedly went to sea taking any job he could get, finally wound up as an able-bodied seaman. For O'Neill the discovery of the sea was almost a religious experience. Later in Manhattan, he bummed around at a saloon called Jimmy the Priest's

(Jimmy was the prototype of the saloon keeper in *The Iceman Cometh*). Later he acted in his father's stock company.

In 1912, O'Neill entered a tuberculosis sanatorium, spent his time there reading Ibsen and Strindberg. Cured, he took a course (paid for by O'Neill Sr.) at Professor George Pierce Baker's famed playwriting laboratory at Harvard. Next summer, the Provincetown Players, a little group of earnest amateurs, put on O'Neill's *Bound East for Cardiff.*

The O'Neill career had begun. Before *The Iceman Cometh*, it had yielded such theater milestones as *The Emperor Jones, The Hairy Ape, Desire Under the Elms, The Great God Brown, Strange Interlude, Mourning Becomes Electra* and *Ah, Wilderness!*

When, at the crest of his fame, Eugene O'Neill forsook profitable playwriting for the delights of uncommercial creation, he committed himself to a predicament that many writers eagerly dream of. The idea worked well for a while. Then it stopped working well. Then it stopped working at all.

O'Neill had no reason to worry about money. His plays had netted him $2,000,000; he could hope for a steadier income only if he had also written the Bible and a cookbook. His third marriage, with lovely Actress Carlotta Monterey, who had played opposite Louis Wolheim in O'Neill's *The Hairy Ape*, was an eminently happy one. After an all but mythically swift rise to fame, with 37 plays, he was still relatively young. In experience, he was a brilliant, confident professional, at the height of his hopes and powers. He was a hard, resourceful worker, who loved his work. He had a backlog of themes, better, in his opinion, than any he had ever dramatized before. They would keep him busy and happy for years to come. He was ready to get down to the most serious work of his life.

But there was no particular hurry. On a 160-acre tract of deep country near Oakland, Calif., O'Neill and his wife spent their first years of liberty designing and building a big house as beautiful as their prospects. They christened it Tao House.[3] In 1935, O'Neill began to block out his massive cycle of plays. Every day he worked from about 8 in the morning until about 1:30, writing as a rule quite freely and surely, in his elegant, complex, microscopic hand. Carlotta, often with the help of a magnifying glass, typed up each day's work as it came along.

[3]The Chinese character *Tao* symbolizes The Right Way of Life.

With six servants to care for their establishment, the O'Neills lived with the guarded, exquisite frugality possible to the rich: quietly idling, reading or playing records in the evenings, occasionally entertaining one or another of their few close friends, less often putting up people like Publisher Bennett Cerf, never giving parties. It was a fertile, happy life, for people who knew how to use it, and in their early middle age the O'Neills knew very well how to use it.

During those first years, according to O'Neill's great friend George Jean Nathan (in the October *American Mercury),* the playwright:

Outlined "in minute detail" the cycle of plays (which had grown to eleven) to be called (according to rumor) *A Tale of Possessors Self-Dispossessed.*

"Definitely completed seven of them, including the three double-length ones, and got pretty well into the eighth."

Completed three other plays: *A Moon for the Misbegotten* (which will be produced in December), *A Touch of the Poet* (which will be produced next year), *Long Day's Journey into Night,* which, for reasons unspecified, cannot be produced until 25 years after the author's death.

"Completed the first play of a much shorter and entirely different cycle. . . . "

"Gradually convinced himself . . . that his dramaturgical plan [for the cycle] was faulty"—the cycle should tell of one family, not two—and "without further ado . . . destroyed two of the double-length or four of the plays he had written. . . ." (In his time, O'Neill has ruthlessly scrapped several other plays.)

Conceived "an exciting idea for another play which bears no relation to the cycle."

"Made copious notes on at least three or four" other plays.

O'Neill's idyllic quiet, which was ultimately to be destroyed by illness, was first invaded by something more sinister. By 1938 the sickening geologic slipping and faulting of world affairs had so profoundly disturbed him that he had gone stale on his cycle. By 1939 he turned, for relief, to *The Iceman Cometh.* By 1940, his whole scheme of work began to fall apart. His financial and personal relationships were untouched; his leisure for work was still unlimited. But some subtle, insidious things (and some brutally simple ones) destroyed the apparent perfection of his life.

O'Neill loved and venerated France as holy ground; when the Germans moved in, O'Neill says, he felt as though they had moved on to the next ranch. Thenceforth he found it all but impossible to keep on writing at all. When their sevants left to do war work, the O'Neills in their big establishment were stranded as literally as a beached vessel. (Neither of them has ever learned to drive a car.)

So they sold their house, stored most of their belongings, and moved into a three-room apartment on San Francisco's California Street. There O'Neill suffered a paralytic stroke and for six months required constant nursing. The stroke was followed by an increasing (and incurable) palsy so severe that it made writing as physically impossible for O'Neill as it already was mentally. (To shave himself he still has to grip the razor with both hands and, even so, the act is nerve-racking. For five years the O'Neills lived in their little apartment. During those years, O'Neill had neither the heart nor the hand for creative work. But those years of silence and suffering may yet prove the most formative and productive years of his life. For there is no chemistry to equal that which works in the marriage of catastrophe with a courageous heart.

Why did O'Neill decide to return to Manhattan? Some people whisper about money difficulties, but that seems unlikely. Others suggest that after five years of infirmity, unproductiveness and cramped quarters the thought of having a new play produced might amount to a rebirth.

Whatever O'Neill's motives, he and his wife went to Manhattan last year, taking little except their toothbrushes and their big, indispensable collections of books and records (which jam two of the six rooms of their present apartment).

According to *Iceman's* Director Eddie Dowling, the actors, who at first were as shy as O'Neill, "warmed up to him after the first ten minutes; they knew he belongs in the theater." They "adored" him because his response was so keen, because he was so gentle and appreciative, and so quick to smile when anyone did something well. When he arrived late for a rehearsal, which rarely happened, they kept asking about him. Says Dowling: "They miss him when he's not there."

There is nothing upstage about O'Neill. The mass interview he gave the press, early last month, and his more intimate conversation after the conference, left an impression of the man which, in many respects, was much more affecting and revealing than the play with which he broke his long silence as an artist.

Newshawks had been warned that they were going to meet a man in poor health. They met a man as thin, brittle and white as a stick of chalk, who at the age of 58 looked 70. He shuddered with palsy. His face was shrunken tightly against his fine skull. His cheeks drooped wearily below his mouth. It was not until he had walked swiftly, but shakily, towards them and had taken his seat, that newsmen noticed much about him that was still youthful and perhaps more impressive than even before: the graceful, aquiline head; the quality of finality, of definitiveness—and his eyes, which one of O'Neill's friends calls "the crow's-nest of his soul."

His *paralysis agitans* involved his whole emaciated body in one miserable stammer. Sometimes he could scarcely project his palsied voice past his lips. Sometimes, uncontrollably, it filled the whole room with its blurting bass boom. What gave him great dignity was the complete purity of his manner in its courtesy, diffidence, simplicity, and the pungency of his expression. Since, to avoid the fatigue of unnecessary speech, he edits his thoughts, his conversation has some of the finish of literature.

O'Neill said that he regarded his illness with "enraged resignation. Outwardly, I might blame it on the war. . . . But inwardly . . . the war helped me realize that I was putting my faith in the old values, and they're gone. . . . It's very sad, but there are no values to live by today. . . . Anything is permissible if you know the angles.

"I feel in that sense, that America is the greatest failure in history. It was given everything, more than any other country in history, but we've squandered our soul by trying to possess something outside it, and we'll end as that game usually does, by losing our soul and the thing outside it too. But why go on—the Bible said it much better: 'For what shall it profit a man if he gain the whole world, and lose his own soul?'

"There is a feeling around, or I'm mistaken, of fate. Kismet, the negative fate; not in the Greek sense. . . . It's struck me as time goes on, how something funny, even farcical, can suddenly without any apparent reason, break up into something gloomy and tragic. . . . A sort of unfair *non sequitur,* as though events, as though life, were being manipulated just to confuse us. I think I'm aware of comedy more than I ever was before; a big kind of comedy that doesn't stay funny very long. I've made some use of it in *The Iceman.* The first act is hilarious comedy, *I think,* but then some people may not even laugh. At any rate, the comedy breaks up and the tragedy comes on. . . ."

Then he added: "I'm happier now than I've ever been—I couldn't ever be negative about life. On that score, you've got to decide YES or NO. And I'll always say YES. Yes, I'm happy."

Both his new play and his return raised an inevitable question: Is Eugene O'Neill the great dramatist many people have long considered him? The harder-minded critics generally agreed: a master craftsman of the theater—yes; a great dramatist—no.

O'Neill does not seem to be a man of great, searching or original intelligence. And however vivid his emotions and intuitions as a dramatic poet, he generally lacks the ability to stand aside from them and give them final hardness, clearness, earthiness, eloquence. Instead, he swims the crests of their waves; and sometimes, he drowns in them. He is a wonderful contriver of moods. But the moods are never reflected against a firm intelligence; they seem, rather, to move and expand for their own sakes, and characters and ideas, used as mere colorings for mood, shift for themselves as best they can.

That O'Neill is a poet is evident in almost any line he has written. That he lacks the ultimate (and primary) requirement of a great poet (to arrange words in eloquent and unimprovable order and beauty) is equally evident in the same lines. Lacking deep perception of real people, O'Neill constantly scores his points, and gets his effects, by external tricks.

But as a playwright, O'Neill remains the greatest master of theater the U.S. has ever produced. He is a marvelous craftsman, and one of the most high-minded who has ever worked. If he often undertakes too much, that is far better than undertaking too little. This habitual exorbitance goes far towards accounting for the compelling tone which resounds through all of O'Neill's work like the ringing of red iron on an anvil. This magnificent tone is the best and most constant quality in O'Neill's writing. It is the voice of the spirit of the man himself; nobody who hears that voice can question the ardent nobility of the spirit.

Mr. O'Neill and the Iceman

Kyle Crichton/1946

Reprinted from Kyle Crichton's *Total Recoil* (Garden City, N.Y.: Doubleday, 1960), pp. 113–31. [This interview is a revised and expanded version of Crichton's "Mr. O'Neill and the Iceman," *Collier's*, 118 (26 October 1946), 19, 39–40, 42.]

When Eugene O'Neill came to New York for the rehearsals of *The Iceman Cometh*, I arranged to interview him for *Collier's*. Since then I have learned how lucky I was: O'Neill had almost never been interviewed before, at least not for a lengthy magazine article. It has since come out that times were hard for the O'Neills at that moment, and he was placing great hopes on the new play. It had been years since he had done anything new, and royalties from his great earlier plays were barely keeping him going.

O'Neill was a thin, gray man who was already suffering from Parkinson's Disease, which was eventually to kill him. He smoked incessantly, and the task of lighting a cigarette or even starting a new one from the butt of the old one was almost more than he could pull off. When I offered to help him, he gave me an annoyed look and waved me away. His wife, the dark, handsome Carlotta Monterey, was in and out of the room while we talked, and she gave a laugh at one of my feeble efforts to help.

"He won't let you," she said merrily. "He'd stand on his head first."

O'Neill rather guiltily gave one of his small smiles, and I think it was then that I began to come awake about the man. I hadn't exactly expected to find him standing on the piano when I arrived, but neither was he wrapped in a robe like Euripides. He turned out to have a sense of humor that would make a monkey of you if you didn't keep your guard up. Nothing malicious or cruel, but a series of subtle little bursts given in a voice so hesitant you could hardly hear them and then suddenly—*bing!*—you knew you had been pinked.

After twelve years in the wilderness known as California, O'Neill had returned to civilization. He had disappeared so completely in

188

1933 that for all anybody knew he was dead or had retired into a cave. He had returned with two plays under his arm, both of which were to be produced that year by the Theatre Guild. *The Iceman Cometh* had a New York production, but the second (I think it was *A Moon for the Misbegotten*) closed in Cleveland after an unsatisfactory break-in tour. In any event, it might be said of O'Neill that he was a legend, but he was certainly not a ghost. He was turning up every day for *Iceman* rehearsals, making sure that the play got a fair break. He told me that he had missed the rehearsals for only one of his plays, *Dynamo*.

"You know what happened to that," he said darkly.

In a curious way, O'Neill was hard to interview. There was no difficulty in getting him to talk; the trouble was in knowing when he had stopped. I would launch him with a question, and he would start off in his quiet, hesitant way and gradually seem to disappear into a haze. Words would come out of the mist, to be followed by long periods of silence. If I broke in with another question, I invariably found that the silence was merely a pause and O'Neill had taken up the narrative again. There was also a muddied quality about his voice that made it difficult for a listener. It was rather nerve-racking, and I didn't win a single battle that day. If I *didn't* break in, that was the time O'Neill had definitely finished, and I found myself sitting there like a dummy. It finally got too much for me.

"Where'd you get a voice like that?" I blurted out bluntly.

I regretted the words as soon as they were out, and was relieved to find that O'Neill wasn't offended. He merely looked at me reflectively, as if wondering whether it was worth while setting me straight.

"You might talk funny yourself," he said, "if you had had a father who whacked you on the shoulder and cried 'Get that hump off your back; straighten up there; open your mouth and let the words come out.' "

This struck me at the time as interesting but not necessarily important. It was later, when I saw *Long Day's Journey into Night*, with the bitter and tortured story of O'Neill's family, that I realized what the reference to his father meant. It is even possible that the play had been written at that time; in any case, it would have been on his mind most of his life. O'Neill told me something about his father. I knew that he had played *The Count of Monte Cristo* all over America for years.

"He was a strong, cello-voiced man," said O'Neill, "who quoted Shakespeare like a deacon quotes the Bible."

I got the idea that O'Neill looked back on his relations with his father with amusement. There was no indication during our interview of the hatred for his father revealed in the play. It was plain that his father had great weight in shaping his life, but O'Neill rather made a joke of it with me. At one point O'Neill laughed and said:

"There's no secret about my father and me. Whatever he wanted, I wouldn't touch with a ten-foot pole."

O'Neill was born at the Cadillac Hotel, at the corner of 44th Street and Broadway in New York, and until the age of seven he traveled wherever his father went—which was plenty, because every town of 5000 in those days had a theatre and James O'Neill and *The Count of Monte Cristo* missed none of them. O'Neill said he remembered the hotels, which were often part of the depot in those days, and the thrilling sight of the switch engines and the fast freights going through.

O'Neill's great passion as a boy was for horses, baseball, and prize fights. The family had a farm in New Jersey during one of their temporary periods of suspended animation, and Gene picked up a lot of horse lore from their coachman, who owned a few nondescript trotting nags on the side. He raced them at little fairs,and Gene's ambition was to go along as stableboy, but his father always put his foot down. He had a firm conviction that youngsters should earn their spending money by hard work. Gene and his older brother mowed the lawn and trimmed the hedges, but the spending money was never enough to get them far from home.

"He didn't want to spoil us," O'Neill said, wryly.

That only piqued Gene's interest about horses. From the coach-man he picked up the habit of reading the racing forms, and now his ambition was far beyond the county fairs: he wanted to see the big New York tracks and the thoroughbreds. His experience with the racing forms turned out to be rather frightening. Not only could he memorize a complete racing form after only a glance or two at it, but he couldn't forget what he had learned.

"It was an intolerable memory," said O'Neill.

From pestering the coachman, he finally pressured the gentleman into taking him out to the Sheepshead Bay track to see the races. There they met an old friend of the coachman's, a famous trainer named Al Weston.

"They started to talk," said O'Neill, "and the minute they'd mention a horse I'd break in and say, 'Oh, yes; Laddie Z, by Buzzfuzz out of Guinevere; ran second at Morris Park, June 16th; fourth at Sheepshead, July 10th.' I knew them all; I couldn't help it. After half an hour of this, Weston gave me a hard look and said, 'Kid, either you'll be a jockey or you'll get yourself killed.' "

It was hard to pin O'Neill down about his schooling, because it seemed to have been a sketchy affair, conducted as a sort of running battle with his father. There had been an English governess and then assorted schools where the boys had spent a few months at a time, but the rest he seemed to have picked up from hearing his father spout Shakespeare. The boys would get an occasional break when they were left in private schools when their parents went on tour, but they knew they could be assured of a verbal smacking as soon as their father got home again.

"He always came through handsomely," O'Neill told me. "He'd ask us a few questions we couldn't answer, and then assure us of our general unworthiness and invariably end by saying, 'Well, I suppose you want a drink?' "

There was one benefit of being the son of an actor, and the boys took full advantage of it. This was the practice known as "professional courtesies." This meant, in the old days, that if you were connected with the theater, you went up to any box office and asked for "courtesies." If there were empty seats, the box-office man handed out a ticket and you were in. Others would be doing the same thing with James O'Neill and the *Monte Cristo* company. For years Gene saw every play in town.

"I don't know if it made me an expert on the drama," said O'Neill, "but it made me an awful lot of girl friends."

Gene never had an ambition to be an actor, and in this he was championed by his father, who didn't think he had enough gumption to come in out of the rain. But the great O'Neill once found Gene on his hands. It happened like this: Gene had gone into a gambling house in New York with five bucks, had tackled the faro bank and eventually come out with a thousand dollars. With that he had set out for New Orleans and had a fine two months drinking champagne and eating oysters. His money gave out just as his father arrived in town with a cut-down vaudeville version of *Monte Cristo.*

"I went around to put the bite on the old man for the fare back to New York," O'Neill said, "but he just waved a hand and said, 'Oh, no; you got here; you get yourself away.' Then he paused and said, 'I need a man in the act. Do you want it? Ten dollars.' Well, I was being overpaid, but it was experience and I went up with them around Ogden, Utah, and finally into Oregon. That cut-down version of the show was wonderful. Characters came on that didn't seem to belong there, and did things that made no sense, and said things that sounded insane. But the old man's part was there, and that's all anybody wanted to see."

Along about this time, Father conceived the idea of getting Gene an appointment to Annapolis. He was well acquainted with Irish politicians in Boston and New York, and had been assured that the matter could be arranged. But since Father suggested it, Gene didn't want it, and went off instead to Princeton. How he got into Princeton is still a mystery, for he had no academic credits whatever. When I asked O'Neill about it, he shrugged and said that things were different in those days and he was in on an arrangement to take specialized work. He lasted only one hell-raising year, and the authorities were glad to see him leave. O'Neill was eager to clear up one apocryphal story about that experience.

"They said I threw a beer bottle through President Wilson's window, but that wasn't true. I had great respect for Mr. Wilson; in fact he's the last politician I ever have had any respect for." He stopped and his vice trailed off. "It was the Division Superintendent of the Pennsylvania Railroad," he added. "That's whose window I threw the bottle through."

Knowing better than to go home after the Princeton fiasco, Gene took to the sea instead. He got a job on a Norwegian sailing vessel which was carrying lumber from Boston to Buenos Aires. The voyage took sixty-nine days, and later provided the material for some of his famous plays. At Buenos Aires he "sort of" left ship when it docked, and turned up next morning in a Swift packing house, which burned down soon after.

"I didn't do it," said Gene, "but it was a good idea."

He got away from Buenos Aires in the crew of a British tramp
(steam), which was headed for Baltimore. The British tramp wasn't
so jolly.

"British food isn't too good even when it's good," said O'Neill,
"and on that ship it wasn't even eaten by the British. They served
something called 'preserved' potatoes. Preserved how, for God's
sake; *I* never found out. The crew could do a lot of things, but it
couldn't eat preserved potatoes. We lived on hardtack and mar-
malade. I never felt better in my life; weighed a hundred and sixty-
five."

The family had bought a home at New London, Connecticut, and
Gene now got a job as a reporter on the New London *Telegraph*.
When he turned out to be a very bad reporter, they put him to work
providing fillers for the editorial page. Some of these were quips of
two and three lines, and O'Neill said he would prefer to forget about
them. The rest was poetry, most of it imitations of much better poetry.

"Kipling and people like that," said O'Neill. "Dante Gabriel
Rossetti would have a chance for a pretty good lawsuit if he could get
himself out of that grave and come back."

The work was easy enough, but the routine was hard. Gene got
through around four in the morning and rode a bicycle three miles
home. This was one thing, and his swimming was another. The thing
he liked best was swimming and the thing he hated most was not
swimming, so he swam every day of the year. In winter he broke the
ice to swim. There are people in New London to this day who don't
give a damn how famous O'Neill is; they still think he was crazy. The
combination of bicycle riding and swimming finally fixed Gene: he
busted up with pleurisy. When the pleurisy got so bad he couldn't
ride the bike, he went off to Gaylord's Sanitarium at Wallingford,
Connecticut, where he stayed five and a half months, came out
cured, and went right back to busting the ice for his dip.

In *Long Day's Journey into Night*, there is a tense scene between
the father and youngest son (Gene), in which the son accuses his
father of being so miserly that he is sending him to the cheapest
sanitarium he can find. Not knowing this at the time I interviewed
O'Neill, I had no chance to ask him why he had this opinion of
Gaylord's. Its reputation was good, and when I visited a friend there
some years later it struck me as being an excellent place. His stay was

short and the results were good, and it is hard to see what disturbed him. I think it was possibly his irritation at the whole episode. He was a little bitter when he talked to me about it.

"There's been a lot of romantic nonsense built up about that t.b. of mine," he said angrily. "Keats died of it and people like Stevenson had it, so if you want to do the right thing in a literary way, you get it."

As a matter of fact, O'Neill should have been grateful for the experience, for it seems to have changed his life. Using the illness as a pretext for getting out of the *Telegraph* job, he sat down in October 1913, and in a six-month period turned out ten one-act plays and two full-length plays.

"That's the year I thought I was God," said O'Neill. "I'd finish one and rush down to the post office to ship it off to Washington to be copyrighted before somebody stole it. I'd forgotten all about them until years later Archie MacLeish became Librarian of Congress and dug around and found them. He told me he didn't think there was much chance of anybody's wanting to steal them."

When the plays got nowhere, O'Neill decided he needed some practical instruction in playwriting, so he went up to Harvard to take Professor Baker's famous course. He came away with a high regard for Professor Baker and a corresponding disregard for Harvard.

"The course wasn't much good to me, for they spent the whole first year on fundamentals of the theater that I had learned in short pants. But that wasn't Baker's fault. He didn't have a thing to work with and no standing whatever with the English Department. They thought playwriting stopped with Congreve and barely nodded to Baker when they passed him on the campus. When we wanted to put on a play, we had to use the auditorium at Radcliffe."

But O'Neill didn't waste the year: he wrote a one-act play called *Bound East for Cardiff.* When he read it in class, they decided it wasn't a play. It had no plot, literally no beginning or ending; it was simply the story of a man dying and hating to die. That play became not only the beginning of O'Neill's career, but it established the modern theater in America. It was the first O'Neill production at the Provincetown Playhouse on Cape Cod, and overnight launched a new era on the American stage.

O'Neill left Harvard after a year because a friend offered him a job as dramatic editor of a new theatrical magazine that was being started in Chicago. He was to cover the New York plays. He came down to New York and took an apartment on the second floor of an old building facing Washington Square. For this he paid four dollars and a half a week, breakfast included.

"And none of your damned Continental breakfasts with a cruller and a cup of tea," growled O'Neill. "The real thing: eggs, buckwheat cakes, cereal, toast, and coffee."

The magazine never worked out, but O'Neill was paid for several months and spent the time reading foreign plays and working on his own. He read Ibsen, Shaw, Strindberg, Wedekind. He said that he had been most influenced by Ibsen and Strindberg. He also read American plays, and was shocked at what he found in them.

"The Great Divide is a fine play for two acts and then it falls to pieces because it has to end happily," said O'Neill. "It was that way with practically all of them."

From his steady attendance at Village dives and speakeasies, it was only a short time till he came into contact with the Provincetown group. Under the guidance of George Cram (Jig) Cook and his wife, Susan Glaspell, summer residents of Provincetown had taken advantage of a wharf owned by Mary Heaton Vorse and began doing plays. When they produced the first O'Neill play, they ceased being a social literary tea and became a theater, a great theater. It is difficult now to realize the stir caused in American intellectual life by the Provincetown experiment. A sudden explosion seemed to have struck the country. Greenwich Village was full of talented writers and a few great ones. Everybody talked, drank and produced. Plays literally flowed out of O'Neill—the great one-acters like *Bound East for Cardiff, Moon of the Caribbees, The Straw, Diff'rent* and *The Hairy Ape,* which was O'Neill's own favorite.

"Writing plays was the easiest thing in the world for me," said O'Neill. "I wasn't making anything up; I was writing about people I knew."

When the Cape Cod group finally broke up in jealousies and quarrels, O'Neill and Robert Edmond Jones reorganized the company in New York and established it at the Provincetown Playhouse in Macdougal Street. It was there that they put on O'Neill's *Emperor*

Jones and *All God's Chillun Got Wings.* The plays created an uproar among church groups and bluenoses.

They were declared blasphemous, immoral, and a danger to the good name of the city. The city authorities, always eager to appease the righteous, conducted a harassing campaign against the theater. Never had one small building held such a multitude of fire hazards. They were corrected, one by one, patiently; finally even the toughest of firemen had to admit that the structure was as safe as National City Bank vault. This merely stimulated the puritans to further effort.

"At six o'clock on the night of the opening of *God's Chillun,*" said O'Neill, still bitter from the memory, "the Gerry Society said we couldn't use the children in the first act. We had the stage manager come on and read the part."

By this time O'Neill was nationally known, but Broadway was as far away as ever. A few valiant members of the uptown theater mob had ventured into the wilds of Macdougal Street, and had returned to tell the tale, but the boys of Shubert Alley were not concerned. After two years of success at the downtown theater, John Williams, a Broadway producer of talent and courage, decided to take the plunge with an O'Neill play. But not a headlong plunge, just an initial dip: he presented *Beyond the Horizon* at special matinees. Was there an audience for it, and would the police leave it alone? The audience reaction was enough for Williams to establish the play for a modest regular run, and the police were strangely silent.

But matters were not so simple when *Desire Under the Elms* was produced. The heavy artillery of Arthur Brisbane, the most powerful editor in America, was unleashed. With the full weight of the Hearst newspaper empire behind him, he fulminated against this insult to American womanhood, manhood, and childhood. For a few days he forsook his favorite philosophical inquiry into the chances of a gorilla against Jack Dempsey in open combat. He was joined in his crusade against O'Neill's play by the ineffable Magistrate McAdoo and District Attorney Banton. Behind them loomed the awesome disapproval of the Powerhouse, the adjunct to Saint Patrick's Cathedral. But against them now appeared liberal forces quite indignant at seeing the theater made a football in municipal politics.

"We licked Brisbane, and I suppose that helped the play financially," said O'Neill, "but it ruined it otherwise. We got more people to the box office, but they were the wrong type of people for a show like mine. They came to find dirt and they found it in everything. The actors went to pieces, for they never knew how a line was going to be taken."

It was a paradoxical period for O'Neill. He had revolutionized the American theater and become a world figure, but he was making little money from his Broadway productions. *Anna Christie*, which was considered a smash hit, never grossed more than $7500 a week. *Desire Under the Elms* did even less, though it ended by making a small profit for John Williams. But the money wasn't bad for a man who had previously been starving, and he spent a good deal of it in a bar at Sixth Avenue and Fourth Street which was frequented by assorted remnants of the old Hudson Dusters gang. It was these characters who were later to be immortalized in *The Iceman Cometh*.

There was a second booze joint that was favored by the Provincetown company on opening nights. This was a little speakeasy in Third Street, where the proprietor locked the door and toasted the performers in his own brand of muscatel.

"It was extracted from an elephant with a syringe," said O'Neill.

But it was the Theatre Guild production of *Strange Interlude* that finally won over Broadway. It ran for two years to large grosses and the rabbit-warren inhabitants of Times Square were at last impressed. Since *Strange Interlude* took almost five hours to play, there was a struggle within the Theatre Guild on how it should be produced. Everybody agreed it was a great play, but there were grave doubts that the ordinary theater audience would take a play of that length. There were hints that perhaps the Guild couldn't do it at all, and there was a strong movement to split it into two parts.

"Lawrence Langner made them do it as a single play," said O'Neill. "He made such a pest of himself that they threw up their hands and let him have his way."

It was a financial risk for the Guild, since there could be no matinees and was played only six times a week, but it made a fortune for everybody concerned and set road records that stood for years.

O'Neill went to France after *Strange Interlude*, and stayed there for two and a half years. He liked Touraine best and while there wrote *Mourning Becomes Electra* and *Dynamo*. *Electra* is a monument of the American theater and a world classic. Its playing time was even longer than *Strange Interlude,* starting at five-thirty, allowing an hour's intermission for dinner after the first act, and running to the usual Broadway closing time of eleven o'clock. It was a great success and was followed by *Ah, Wilderness!,* a gentle, folksy play in an entirely different O'Neill mood, and then by *Days Without End,* which was a box-office failure. When I asked him about the latter disaster, he shrugged and said:

"The critics didn't understand it and it wasn't any good. Maybe that was it."

The casting of George M. Cohan for *Ah, Wilderness!* was an offbeat move that startled Broadway. When I questioned O'Neill about it, he evaded the issue, or at least spoke in that clotted style of his in an attempt to confuse me, but I got the impression that Cohan hadn't been his choice for the job. Under my pressing, he finally admitted it.

"George was a great fellow, but people thought of him only as a light comedian or a song-and-dance man, and that was my idea too. But an actor is an actor, and he did a good job on the play. The only trouble was that he overshadowed it. If you've seen anybody else in Cohan's part, you'll realize it's the boy's play."

O'Neill said he had few friends among playwrights, and regretted that he had never met George Bernard Shaw. Through acquaintances he had met Lenormand, the French playwright, in Paris, and they had hit it off immediately. O'Neill had an insensate desire to visit every boîte, sidewalk café, and dive in Paris, and Lenormand was just the man for him. One night Lenormand took him to see his play, *Simoon,* which was being acted at the Pigalle.

"Lenormand hadn't been there since the opening," said O'Neill, "and he was anxious to see how it was holding up. The big scene was a great storm on stage, and I thought Lenormand was going to have a fit when the winds started to roar. 'The dogs!' he howled, 'they're blowing the play right out of the theater.'"

Remembering what had happened to other theatrical people in the stock market crash of 1929, I asked if he had been one of the brave little boys dallying with shares on margin.

"I didn't have them on margin," said O'Neill sourly, "but I HAD them and went right on down with them."

After the failure of *Days Without End,* the O'Neills went out to

California on what they thought was to be a short vacation. O'Neill had never been able to work in the city and did most of his early plays in such places as New London and Ridgefield, Connecticut, but he had no intention of immuring himself on the West Coast. As we were discussing this, Carlotta Monterey came into the room, caught the gist of what we were saying, and cried gaily:

"I HATE California."

What really happened was that O'Neill's health began to fail so badly that they couldn't get away. He was in a hospital in Oakland when he was awarded the Nobel Prize for Literature in 1936, and was presented with the award by the Swedish Consul in San Francisco in 1937 while he was still in bed.

But it was during this period that he wrote the celebrated cycle of plays. There was great mystery about them. O'Neill was seeing nobody in his Coast hideout, but occasionally hints would drift back to New York that he was doing a series of plays that would not be produced until after his death. In the case of one, *Long Day's Journey into Night,* it was reported that it was not intended for production on the stage. It would be published twenty-five years after his death, and that would be all. I knew that O'Neill had finished four plays—*The Iceman Cometh, A Moon for the Misbegotten, Long Day's Journey into Night,* and *A Touch of the Poet*—but I got from him the impression that the cycle wasn't finished. When I pressed him about it, however, I got nowhere.

"Well, I . . . " he said hesitantly, as if afraid to hurt my feelings, and then moved his hands, grinned suddenly, and was solemn as an owl.

As a matter of fact, he was wrapped up in *The Iceman* and didn't want to talk about anything else. Our conversation took place in 1946 and I was surprised to learn that *Iceman* had been ready as long ago as 1939.

"I remembered the first war," he explained. "It's tough enough getting a serious play on when times are right; you don't have a chance when the guns start going off."

When I asked him what the theme of *The Iceman Cometh* was, he looked off into space for so long I thought I wasn't ever going to get him back.

"Well," he said finally, "it has two themes. The serious theme is that *The Iceman* is Death; the other one is that old traveling man's joke about the drummer who gets drunk in a bar and insists on showing everybody his wife's picture. 'She's safe at home in bed with the iceman,' he says proudly."

The Theatre Guild was having its usual fit about the length of *The Iceman*. From the length of the script, it looked as if it would run about three hours and a quarter. But it was decided to have a reading of the play and have it timed by four stop watches. When it was over, the confusion was worse than ever, for none of the watches agreed.

"It was like a horse race," said O'Neill sardonically, "in which four nags come tearing down the stretch and nobody can tell who won because they all jump over the grandstand."

When I suggested that he probably had the usual author's reluctance to cutting any of his precious lines, he looked at me with amusement.

"That's the way I write my plays," he said. "I put everything in but the sink, and then I start hacking away at it. I hardly ever do any rewriting; I just take things out. By the time we reach production, it would take an amputation to get anything else out."

He said that since 1944, when the palsy hit him, he hadn't been able to write in longhand (as he always had done) or on the typewriter. He said he was experimenting with something called the Soundscript, a sort of dictaphone business.

"All I have to do now," he said ironically, "is learn how to talk."

He was pleased with the way the Theatre Guild was handling *The Iceman Cometh,* and displayed by the brightness of his eyes and the lift of an eyebrow that the show had one of the most expensive casts in history. His only irritation came from an actor who had started in a small part in *Desire Under the Elms* and was now in Hollywood. He said he would gladly do *The Iceman* for his usual Hollywood salary: $750 a week.

"I told him to get the hell back to Hollywood," flared O'Neill. "When we start meeting those prices, we might as well close up."

O'Neill said he didn't write for Broadway, and he didn't write for money, and he most certainly didn't write with a star in mind. He had written one-act plays, and short plays like *Emperor Jones*, which ran only fifty-five minutes, and plays that ran for hours. He believed in opening "cold" in New York, without the customary out-of-town tryout period.

"We took *Ah, Wilderness!* out of town," said O'Neill, "but that was a comedy. With serious plays, it makes no sense to me. If you have a good director and good actors, they don't have to run all over the country practicing."

Although they had been in New York only a short time, their apartment had a permanent look. O'Neill's books were all there, many of them from his father's library, and he had thousands of phonograph records neatly catalogued. I was amazed at the number of old and new jazz records he had.

"Too many of these, maybe," he said lightly, running his hand over the jazz collection, but you could see he was crazy about them.

With show talk out of the way, O'Neill began wandering along nostalgically and a little sadly about the old days in New York. He said he hadn't been down to his old haunts in the Village because it would only make him feel bad. When he began talking about Louis Wolheim, he gave little reminiscent chuckles that showed Wolheim must have been one of the best friends he ever had. Wolheim was the great hulking, handsomely ugly man who had made his reputation in *The Hairy Ape* and had been a sensation in *What Price Glory.* O'Neill said they had hardly been out of each other's sight for years, and the picture of the burly Wolheim and the tiny O'Neill wandering in and out of speakeasies together must have been wonderful.

"We used to go to a place on Fifty-eighth Street after the show," said O'Neill, "but one night we were a little late, and they had closed up. We could see them through the glass, piling chairs on the tables. Wolheim rattled the door and bellowed to them to open up. They just shook their heads and went on with the chairs. Wolheim let out an awful roar and slammed his hand through the plate-glass window. There was a spurt of blood like Old Faithful geyser, and I thought he'd cut his damned fool arm off. Wolheim was yelling and everybody was yelling, and I had the devil's own time getting him away before the cops came."

He smiled in a fond, reminiscent way, and then went off into one of his hazes. What brought him back was my asking whether his great plays were still being produced around the world.

"Everywhere but here," he said, with dark anger. "You break your heart doing a play here, it has its run, and then it disappears forever. If they revive anything at all, it's some old chestnut they can have fun

with. After I'm gone, they'll probably do that with some of mine—
dress them up in phony period clothes, and play them for laughs."

This was obviously a very sore point with him, and I think even he
was relieved when I broke the tension by asking if he didn't ever have
the common fear of writers of drying up. He looked at me with mild
surprise.

"Oh, I always have plenty to write about," he said.

Our conversation tapered off after that, and I found myself looking
at the frail, palsied man with a constriction of the heart. The recital of
the Wolheim episode must have saddened him. The young, active
days were over; the writing days might also be at an end. I resolutely
held back from offering my help when he started again the tortured
task of lighting his cigarette.

As I left, I thanked him for one of the liveliest interviews I had ever
had, and added how happy I was that I had found him a down-to-
earth humorist rather than the solemn philosopher I had expected.

"Oh, yes; some days," he said with a sad smile. "Other days; other
moods."

The Black Irishman
Croswell Bowen/1946

Reprinted from *PM*, 3 November 1946, magazine section, 13–17; parts of the essay are included with revisions in Bowen's *The Curse of the Misbegotten* (New York: McGraw Hill, 1959), 309–17.

That just and merciful God in Whom Eugene O'Neill has struggled to believe ever since he was 13 and lost his Faith, certainly endowed him with a family, an environment and a temperament extraordinarily favorable to the making of a playwright.

The theatre was in his bones: His father was the celebrated James O'Neill, an actor of the old uninhibited school who played the lead in *The Count of Monte Cristo* some 6,000 times, and a substantial part of Eugene's childhood was spent in theatre wings.

Dramatic conflict was part of his earliest life: His mother, born Ella Quinlan, was a devout Catholic who, Eugene remembers, never approved of her husband's profession but, because she was an old-fashioned wife, followed him wherever he went. In addition that part of Eugene's boyhood that was spent away from the theatre centered around the waterfront in New London, Conn., where he could absorb the romance of the sea, and sense the dry rot of provincial New England.

But most important of all was the disposition through which Eugene has always viewed the world. Recently in New London, "Captain" Thomas Francis Dorsey, an intimate friend of James O'Neill and something of a fabulous Irishman himself, was discussing Eugene whom he had known well as a boy.

"Always the gloomy one," the Captain said, "always the tragedian, always thinkin'. My God, when he looked at you he seemed to be lookin' right through you, right into your soul. He never said much and then spoke softly when he did speak. Brilliant he was too, always readin' books. We're all Irish around here and knew the type. He was a real Black Irishman."

A Black Irishman, the Captain went on to explain, is an Irishman

who has lost his Faith and who spends his life searching for the
meaning of life, for a philosophy in which he can believe again as
fervently as he once believed in the simple answers of the Catholic
Catechism. A Black Irishman is a brooding, solitary man—and often
a drinking man too—with wild words on the tip of his tongue.
American letters are the richer for Black Irishmen. And of the lot of
them, and the list includes F. Scott Fitzgerald, James T. Farrell, and
John O'Hara among others, O'Neill is the blackest one of all.

O'Neill himself gives full weight to his Irish heritage. Talking to his
son, Eugene, Jr., a bearded professor of Greek, he said not long ago,
"One thing that explains more than anything about me is the fact that
I'm Irish. And, strangely enough, it is something that all the writers
who have attempted to explain me and my work have overlooked."

It is no accident that O'Neill's newest play, *The Iceman Cometh*,
certainly the biggest event of this season, is about "pipe dreams"—
which may be a Black Irishman's name for Faith. It is no accident that
its characters are lost men to whom the world and its ways are an
eternally insoluble enigma. It is no accident that Larry Slade, the one
character who at the end is left utterly without illusions, is a tired
Anarchist and an Irishman.

It has been said by a number of reviewers that, when the curtain
falls, nothing is left for Larry but to die. One observer has thought of
an alternative. "Larry," he said, "could write plays."

James O'Neill and Ella Quinlan O'Neill, his wife, both came from
substantial lace-curtain Irish Catholic families. James was born in the
town of Thomastown, County Kilkenny, Ireland, Nov. 15, 1846, and
was brought to America at the age of eight. His family settled in
Cincinnati, Ohio. His wife was a Cincinnati girl, and they were
married in 1875, after James O'Neill had established himself as an
actor.

James and Ella O'Neill had three children. The first, Edmund
Dantes, named after the hero in James's most successful play, *The
Count of Monte Cristo,* died soon after birth. A year later a second
son was born and was named James, Jr. The third son, Eugene
Gladstone, was born 10 years after James, Jr., on Oct. 16, 1888.

Two years after James, Jr., had been born, the O'Neills had moved
from Cincinnati to a small cottage in New London which was a
pleasant place to spend the Summer and not too far from New York.

The cottage was the closest the road-touring O'Neills ever came to a real home.

James O'Neill was a very worldly man according to the standards of his wife who is still remembered by New Londoners as an "unworldly, saintly woman." His friend Tom Dorsey, however, remembers him as "a soft-hearted man, always good for a touch. He was a great Irishman, a great Democrat and good Catholic." He was one of the leading figures in town. There was only one man to rival him: Richard Mansfield. The two were not boon companions.

When the time came for Gene to go to school, he was sent to a Catholic Convent run by the Ursuline Sisters. There he learned his Catechism thoroughly:

Who made the world?
God made the world.
Who is God?
God is the Creator of heaven and earth,
    and of all things.
What is man?
Man is a creature composed of body and soul,
    and made to the image and likeness of God.

When Eugene was 13 and ready for high school, his parents sent him to a non-Catholic military school in New York City. It was there that he lost his Faith. He does not know exactly at what moment or why.

When he was 14, Gene entered Betts Academy at Stamford, Conn., to prepare for college. In the Fall of 1906, when he was 17, he enrolled at Princeton. He spent as much time as he could with his older brother, James, Jr., in New York. It was about that time that the great drinking legend about O'Neill began. From reports of what went on, it would seem that O'Neill and his fellow hellers did not surpass the later exploits of another Princetonian, F. Scott Fitzgerald. Certainly such drinking today is run of the ginmill.

Gene had scarcely put on long pants before Jimmie, 10 years his senior, took him out on the town. Jimmie, in his middle 20s, was aspiring to be a New York newspaperman. Somehow, he never got around to doing much about his career because his drinking was more important to him. He thought it amusing to teach Gene to drink and be a heller with women. He even told his friends: "Gene learned sin more easily than other people. I made it easy for him."

But Jimmie did not make it easy for Gene to live with the feeling of guilt from which he never fully recovered. A Catholic who has lost his Faith travels a road on which there is no turning back and no destination. His conscience stays in his mind to plague him, but there is, for him, no Confession and no Absolution.

O'Neill pointed out recently that at an age when most young men were romantically in love with a "pure girl," he was "a Broadway wise-guy."

"At the time *Ah, Wilderness!* was on Broadway," he said, "many people said that I had written about my adolescence. The truth is that I had no youth. *Ah, Wilderness!* was a nostalgia for a youth I never had."

In the Spring of 1907, O'Neill was suspended from college. He and his undergraduate drinking companions had missed the milk train from New York to Princeton one Sunday night. This meant they had to get off a Trenton train at Princeton Junction. The drawbridge across Carnegie Lake was up and they had to swim across and walk several miles to college. En route, O'Neill threw a bottle through the window of the home of the division superintendent of the Pennsylvania Railroad. It was not, as the legend goes, President Wilson's house. Later that Spring O'Neill flunked all his final examinations and was dropped from the class.

His family were bitterly disappointed. Jimmie's drinking deeply had grieved both his mother and father, and now it looked as if Gene was going the way of Jimmie. O'Neill remembers his next four years as a period of "just drifting."

In the Summer of 1909, he drifted into a marriage with Kathleen Jenkins, a young girl he had met in New York. Both the O'Neill and Jenkins families objected to the marriage because Eugene was not making a living. A month or so after the wedding he sailed with a mining engineer for Spanish Honduras on a gold-mining expedition financed by his father. "At the end of six months I was invalided home, tropical malarial fever, no gold."

During his absence, his wife had borne a child who was named Eugene, Jr. When Gene came home, his wife continued to live with her family. Their marriage was terminated by divorce in 1912. O'Neill was not to see his firstborn until 1921 when the boy was 12.

Some months after his return, O'Neill went on a drinking spree in New York. One night he found himself with Jimmie on a train for New Orleans. When they arrived there, they found their father was in town acting in *The White Sister*. He refused to give the boys any money, but offered them work. Gene was made assistant manager. He toured with the show for three months before deciding he didn't like theatrical life. Finally, his father, disgusted with his son's drinking and apparent unwillingness to work, acted in his New London home one of the greatest scenes in his dramatic life, charging Eugene with filial ingratitude, and the wasting of precious opportunities.

"Go before the mast!" he told his son.

Eugene's first voyage was on a Norwegian freighter, 65 days to Buenos Aires. There he got a job with Westinghouse, then with Swift and Co., and later with the Singer Co. His father had cut him off from any family funds, and the jobs only served to keep him alive. His real interest was in bumming around the waterfronts and drinking with the men and women he met there.

At one point, he says, he was in complete destitution in Buenos Aires, and signed as a seaman on a British tramp steamer bound for New York. There, he lived at a lower West Side hotel and bar called Jimmy the Priest's "where you could sleep with your head on the table if you bought a schooner of beer." He was later to make Jimmie the Priest's the scene of *The Iceman Cometh*. From New York, he occasionally shipped out as a seaman, going to South Africa and England.

O'Neill expressed his revolt from his well-to-do, almost Victorian upbringing by this period of almost two years when he was completely at sea.

The return of the prodigal son, however, was not quite the joyous reunion the elder O'Neill might have hoped for. Eugene ended his wanderings by turning up at the stage door of a theatre in New Orleans where his father, as usual, was playing *Monte Cristo*. His father once again dreamed of Gene's accepting the heritage of his family and becoming a great actor. He was given the part of the jailor in *Monte Cristo*. He wasn't very good, he didn't like acting and he didn't like the play. As the tour wore on, his father complained about the quality of his son's performances.

"It is a wonder," his son said gravely, "that in a play like *Monte Cristo* I can do *anything* at all."

When the tour ended in the Spring, the O'Neills went home to New London. The publisher of the New London *Telegraph*, Frederick P. Latimer, a friend of the O'Neills, had a special fondness for Gene and a sympathy with his love of reading books and his intellectual and spiritual probings. He knew Gene liked to write sea poems, and he gave him a job as a reporter on the *Telegraph*. Part of the job was to write a piece of verse twice a week for a column on the editorial page called *Laconics*.

Latimer gave Gene a feeling of confidence he had never gotten from his family. "He's the first one," O'Neill wrote to Barrett H. Clark, one of his biographers, "who really thought I had something to say, and believed I could say it." Latimer later told Clark that when he and O'Neill "used to talk together and argue our different philosophies, I thought he was the most stubborn and irreconcilable social rebel that I had ever met."

All summer and fall, Gene worked as a reporter and rewrite man. He covered the waterfront, attended meetings, interviewed town leaders. In *Laconics* he wrote verse about "The sullen vessel straining at its chain" and "The bright green lawns that lean down to the bay" and he kidded his job:

> When my dreams come true all my comments wise and sage
> Will be featured double column on the editor's own page.
> Personals will be no object, I won't have to go and hunt
> The history of the tugboats that infest the waterfront.
> Fire alarms may go to blazes, suicides and murders too,
> I'll be editing Laconics when my dreams come true.

That Summer he also fell in love.

"That was a long time ago," he said recently, when he was asked if the love poems he wrote for *Laconics* were autobiographical. "She's married, I understand, to a highly placed person."

Her name was Beatrice and the legend of Gene O'Neill's great love for the tall beautiful choir singer with the voice of an angel still persists in New London.

In October, 1912, he wrote:

Is all off twixt I and you?
Will you go and wed some other gent?
The things I done, I'd fain undo,
Since thou hast went.

At the end of November, he composed a long poem for *Laconics*
called "The Lay of the Singer's Fall." He expressed his general
disillusionment with life and with love:

And the singer was sad and he turned to Love
And the arms of his ladye faire,
He sang of her eyes as the stars above
He sang of—and kissed—her hair;
Till the Devil whispered, "I fondly trust
This is folly and nought beside,
For the greatest of loves is merely lust!"
—And the soul of the singer died.

Three years later, O'Neill contributed to *The Conning Tower* in the
New York *Tribune* some verses entitled "Speaking, to the Shade of
Dante, of Beatrices."

"She doesn't class with mine at all," he wrote of Dante's Beatrice.
That ends the story of O'Neill and Beatrice. But we may learn more
some day. One of O'Neill's unproduced plays, *Long Day's Journey
into Night*, is locked up in a safe with instructions that it is not to be
produced until 25 years after his death. O'Neill, however, has
revealed a few details. It concerns the period of his life when he knew
Beatrice. One of the characters in the play is still living.

On Dec. 9, 1912, O'Neill wrote his last poem for the *Telegraph*,
"To Winter":

My eyes are red, my lips are blue
My ears frost bitt'n;
Thy numbing kiss doth e'en extend
Thro' my mitten.
. . . O Winter, greater bards have sung I loathe thee!

A few days later a doctor told him he had a touch of tuberculosis. On
Christmas Eve he entered Gaylord Farm Sanatorium on the top of a
windswept hill overlooking the Housatonic River at Wallingford, Conn.

What happened to him there, he was to describe later, in 1923, in
the *Journal of Outdoor Life*:

It was at Gaylord that my mind got the chance to establish itself, to
digest and evaluate the impressions of many past years [he was just

24] in which one experience had crowded on another with never a second's reflections. At Gaylord I really thought about my life for the first time, about past and future. Undoubtedly the inactivity forced upon me by life at a san [patient's slang for sanatorium] forced me to mental activity, especially as I had always been high-strung and nervous temperamentally.

It was in the sanatorium that O'Neill, who liked composing poetry and had considered writing fiction, decided to be a playwright.

At the end of May, 1913, O'Neill was told that his TB was arrested and he was discharged from the san.

Recently, O'Neill was asked what he thought had suddenly happened to him at this time to cause him to begin a period of sustained creative effort from which he has never since wavered:

I kept writing, he said, because I had such a love of it. I was highly introspective, intensely nervous and self-conscious. I was very tense, I drank to overcome my shyness.

When I was writing I was alive.

I could scarcely write, if at all, and live in the city. I would pick a place out of the ordinary run of places to do my writing.

One of the places he picked was a hut on the coast at Province-town, Mass.

The discovery of what writing did for him was perhaps a substitute for the Faith he'd lost at 13, O'Neill said recently. His life at the san, he thinks, was almost a religious experience in which he faced the possibility of death, looked for a new faith and found it in creative writing.

The elder James O'Neill, then 59, was glad that his younger son had finally found some reasonably respectable work. It wasn't acting, but writing plays was connected with the theatre.

"He did believe in me—in a way," O'Neill wrote later, explaining that his feeling of guilt because he had not become a great man in the eyes of his father was lessened. "But as I've said, he just thought I was crazy. He didn't see why I should write the kind of plays I did because there was no market for them, but he must have thought there was something to them. He believed I might some day amount to something—if I lived."

O'Neill destroyed the first 11 plays he wrote. Until a few years ago he thought they were gone forever. However, when Archibald MacLeish became head of the Library of Congress, he found that

O'Neill had filed the plays with the copyright office, and they had therefore come into the archives of the library. For most of O'Neill's early plays he drew on his experience at sea.

The Gorham Press in Boston offered to print *Thirst* and four other early Eugene O'Neill plays in their American Dramatists Series. Richard G. Badger, head of the publishing house, wanted costs of printing guaranteed by the author. James O'Neill provided the money and 1,000 copies of *Thirst* were printed. Very few were sold, and the actor didn't recover his investment. Today a copy of *Thirst* is worth about $75.

In the Fall of 1914, James O'Neill also paid his son's tuition at Harvard to take English 47, George P. Baker's famous playwriting course which was later moved to Yale and expanded to the 47 Workshop, the drama department of the School of Fine Arts.

O'Neill wrote two sea plays while at Harvard and both were undistinguished. Baker also read a third, *Bound East for Cardiff*, written before O'Neill entered the class. Baker's comment on it was that it was not a play at all, but it was the first O'Neill work to be produced. It was presented at the Wharf Theatre by the Provincetown Players in the Summer of 1916.

Two fellow students have written their impressions of him at Harvard:

". . . he was good-looking, very nervous, extremely impatient with 47, and anxious to get down to live in Greenwich Village. . . . He was friendly, though rather uneasy and inarticulate at times. . . . But when he delivered himself of a remark, it was impressive. . . ."

John V. A. Weaver, the poet, wrote: "Women were forever calling for Gene. There was something apparently irresistible in his strong combination of cruelty (around the mouth) and boyish charm. One girl told me she could not get his face out of her thoughts. He was hard boiled and whimsical. He was brutal and tender. From shopgirl to society queen they all seemed to develop certain tendencies in his presence."

After his Harvard course, O'Neill did go down to live in Greenwich Village. In the Summer he went to his hut in Provincetown. The drinking periods continued, followed by terrible remorse, and then by the days of seclusion.

"The legend that I wrote my plays when I was drunk," O'Neill has

said, "is absurd. It was when I was not writing that I drank. I'd drink
for a month and then go out and snap out of it by myself. It was
during these periods that I wrote."

For more than a year after leaving Harvard, O'Neill wrote
comparatively little, according to a date table of his plays which he
later drew up for the late Richard Dana Skinner, drama critic of the
Catholic *Commonweal*. Then, in the Winter of 1917, at his Provincetown hut, he wrote four sea plays: *In the Zone, Ile, The Long Voyage
Home* and *Moon of the Caribbees.*

O'Neill's poor health prevented his being drafted in the First World
War. How he felt about it he told his eldest son recently. Eugene, Jr.,
was rejected by the Army on physical grounds during the Second
World War. He remarked to his playwright father that although he
had escaped, he was sorry not to have taken part in so important an
experience.

"You have escaped now, but it will catch up with you in the end,"
the playwright said.

In 1918, O'Neill married a slender ash-blonde girl from New York
named Agnes Boulton. Author of a novel, *The Road Before Us,* and
very friendly and sociable, she attempted to make less of a recluse of
her husband.

Barrett Clark, who wrote an authorized biography of O'Neill, noted
as of 1926 that "the marriage has been happy and successful. . . . To
Mrs. O'Neill the dramatist owes a great deal more that can be
properly set down in these pages." Certainly during this marriage, he
produced some of his best work: *Beyond the Horizon* (Pulitzer Prize
winner), *Anna Christie* (Pulitzer Prize winner), *Emperor Jones, Desire
Under the Elms, The Great God Brown,* and *Strange Interlude*
(Pulitzer Prize winner).

Two children were born to this (his second) marriage, and to both
he gave traditional Irish names suggested by James Stephens: Shane,
born a year and a half after his marriage, and Oona, born five years
later.

Oona, in 1943, when she was 18, married Charlie Chaplin, then
54. Although Mrs. Agnes O'Neill said she was "very happy" about
the marriage, Eugene O'Neill told friends he did not approve. He
refuses now to discuss the matter.

Recently, O'Neill confirmed an apparently apochryphal story about his first Broadway play. He had been sitting one day on the beach at Provincetown looking out across the sea. A little boy sat beside him asking questions. O'Neill was gentle and patient:

"What's beyond the ocean?"

"Europe."

"What's beyond Europe?"

"The horizon."

"What's beyond the horizon?" the little boy persisted.

Beyond the Horizon opened at the Morosco Theatre in New York on Feb. 2, 1920. With his first Broadway production O'Neill won the Pulitzer Prize.

It was the story of two brothers, a materialist and a dreamer, in love with the same girl. The materialist, who was about to embark on a sea voyage, loses out. In the end, the rich materialist returns to find his brother dying. The girl falls in love with him, but it is too late. People live, O'Neill concluded, by dreaming about something beyond the horizon, something they can never attain.

Sixty-three-year-old James O'Neill attended the play's opening night. Although he couldn't figure out why, he knew the audience was receiving it favorably. Afterward, congratulating his son, he said: "Are you trying to send the audience home to commit suicide?" But there were tears of gladness in his eyes; his boy had made good in the theatre.

In the Winter of 1921–22, O'Neill began rehearsals for *The Hairy Ape*. For the part of Mildred Douglas, the girl in white who calls out "Oh, the filthy beast" and faints when she sees the hairy ape stoking the furnace in the ship's hold, he cast Carlotta Monterey. She was beautiful and an experienced actress. Her performance in *The Hairy Ape* was good.

A year later, Carlotta Monterey married Ralph Barton, caricaturist on *The New Yorker*. Seven years later she was to marry Eugene O'Neill.

In 1922, Eugene O'Neill, Jr., the playwright's son by his first wife, met his father for the first time. The first Mrs. O'Neill had remarried and was living in New York. O'Neill and his ex-wife discussed the boy's future, and O'Neill agreed to take on the responsibility for his son's education.

Father and son liked each other immediately. Eugene, Jr., had been brought up to feel very friendly toward the father he had never met. The more he heard about his father, the better he liked him.

In the Winter of 1920 the elder James O'Neill, then living in New York, had been struck by an automobile and knocked to the pavement. He had been taken to a hospital and, when he had recovered sufficiently, had had himself moved to New London to the Lawrence and Memorial Hospital. He had died there on Aug. 10, 1920.

"He came back to New London to die," Captain Dorsey said. There was a real Irish wake for the old actor. Gene and Jim came home for the funeral, and New Londoners remember that they mourned their father in the true Irish fashion—by drowning their sorrow.

By 1923, O'Neill had lost his mother and his brother. From then on his plays tended to become more and more preoccupied with death. In 1925, he wrote *The Great God Brown*. In one of the play's most moving passages, Dion speaks of his dead mother and father:

What aliens we were to each other! When he lay dead, his face looked so familiar that I wondered where I had met that man before. Only at the second of my conception. After that, we grew hostile with concealed shame. And my mother? I remember a sweet strange girl, with affectionate, bewildered eyes as if God had locked her in a dark closet without any explanation. I was the sole doll, our ogre, her husband, allowed her and she played mother and child with me for many years in that house until at last through two years I watched her die with the shy pride of one who has lengthened her dress and put up her hair.

While he was married to Agnes Boulton, his second wife, Eugene O'Neill bought and sold two large homes, one in Ridgefield, Conn., and one in Bermuda. "He never could stay in any one place very long," a friend said. "Each time he'd buy a place, he'd be sure that that was where he wanted to spend the rest of his life."

During the '20s, O'Neill was turning out, in some years, as much as two complete plays.

In the Summer of 1926 O'Neill met Carlotta Monterey again. Miss Monterey, who came from a wealthy California family and had been divorced from Ralph Barton the year before, was visiting at the

Belgrade Lakes in Maine where O'Neill and his family were spending the Summer.

O'Neill and Carlotta Monterey fell violently in love, their friends said. That Fall, O'Neill and his family returned to Bermuda, but two years later, on June 21, 1928, Agnes O'Neill announced that she would seek a divorce. On June 2, 1929, she obtained a decree in Reno.

Carlotta Monterey and O'Neill were seen together in 1928 and 1929 in various parts of the world—Shanghai, Manila, France. On July 22, 1929, they were married in Paris "at a quiet ceremony."

Today, Carlotta Monterey, said to be 56 but still beautiful and vivacious, has taken a capable and strong hold on the job of keeping O'Neill sufficiently isolated for the pursuit of his work.

After their wedding in 1929, the O'Neills went to live at the Chateau de Plessis at St. Antoine de Rocher, near Tours, France. *The New York Times* reported that O'Neill had signed a 13-year lease for the chateau, where he at once set to work on *Mourning Becomes Electra.*

O'Neill dedicated the manuscript of *Mourning Becomes Electra* to his wife. Mrs. O'Neill sent 50 copies of the inscription to friends with the following printed note:

> Fifty copies of Eugene O'Neill's inscription to the final longhand manuscript of *Mourning Becomes Electra* have been reproduced in facsimile. This copy is No. ____.
>
> CARLOTTA MONTEREY O'NEILL

To Carlotta,

In memory of the impenetrable days of pain in which you privately suffered in silence that this trilogy might be born. Days when I had my work and you had nothing but household tasks and a glimpse through the salon windows of a gray land of Le Plessis; with the black trees dripping and the Winter wraths outside; days when you had only selfforgetting love to sustain you—when lunchtime was spent discussing such preoccupations with a courageous, cleaving banter; days which for you were entirely lonely when I seemed far away and lost to you by a grim, savage, gloomy country of my own making; days which for you were like hateful living with unspeakable nagging at your nerves and spirit until an intolerable [ennui] in life silences and soothes the spirit. In short, days in which you collaborated as only a deep love can in the writing of this trilogy of the damned!

These scripts are like us and my presenting them is a gift which, already, is half yours. So, in hopes that what this trilogy may have in it may repay the travail we have gone through for its sake—I say I want them to remind you that I have known your love with my love even when I have seemed not to know; that I have seen it even when I have appeared most blind; that I have felt it warmly around me always (even in my study in the closing pages of my heart) sustaining and comforting, a warm, serene sanctuary for the man after the author's despairing solitude and inevitable deceits—a victory of love over life. Oh, mother and wife and mistress and friend!—And collaborator! I love you.

Since his marriage to Carlotta Monterey, O'Neill's life had taken on a new pattern. He had kept apart from the world. She had helped provide the seclusion necessary for his creative work. In 1931 they returned to the U. S. A. for the first time since their wedding because of the forthcoming production by the Theatre Guild of *Mourning Becomes Electra*.

They arrived in New York City on Sunday morning [May 17,] 1931, on the *Statendam* and secretly checked in at an uptown East Side hotel. The following Wednesday morning Ralph Barton was found dead in bed in his penthouse at 419 East 57th St. with a bullet in his brain and a .32-caliber pistol in his hand. On the bed with him were found a copy of Gray's *Anatomy* opened to the section on the heart, a copy of Carl Bateman's cartoon book, *Suburbia*, and a photograph of Carlotta Monterey. In the flyleaf of the book of cartoons was an inscription written to Barton by Carlotta while they were still married. It read: "To Ralph sometime on a certain Friday or was it Saturday?"

After some delays Homer Barton, brother of the dead man, released the suicide note. "I have always had excellent health," Ralph Barton had written, "but since my early youth I have suffered from a melancholia which in the last five years had begun to show definite symptoms of manic-depressive insanity.

". . . I have run from wife to wife, from house to house and from country to country in a ridiculous effort to escape from myself. . . .

"In particular, my remorse is bitter over my failure to appreciate my beautiful lost angel, Carlotta, the only woman I ever loved and whom I respect and admire above all the rest of the human race. . . . I do hope that she will understand what my malady was and forgive me a little. . . . I kiss my dear children—and Carlotta."

All the papers carried the suicide note, and the morning after the suicide, the New York *Journal* printed a story stating that Barton had had 92 girls in his life, but "not one came to mourn him today. . . . Of these, he loved one. She was not there [at the Campbell Funeral Home] for a final look at the man she once held tightly in her arms. . . ."

Homer Barton was quoted: "If Carlotta won't see him, nobody shall see him. It is the O'Neill influence that has kept Carlotta from this final farewell to Ralph."

O'Neill refused to discuss the suicide with reporters. His attorney, Harry Weinberger, later issued this statement: "Mr. and Mrs. O'Neill have asked me to state that contrary to newspaper reports of statements by Homer Barton, brother of Ralph Barton, they have not seen Mr. Ralph Barton since their return to the United States and Mrs. O'Neill, the former Carlotta Monterey, desires to state that she never saw or heard from Mr. Barton since her divorce more than five years ago."

After *Mourning Becomes Electra* was produced, O'Neill's restlessness was again asserting itself. Instead of returning to their French chateau, the O'Neills built a house at Sea Island Beach, Ga.

With O'Neill settled again in his own country, his old friends expected to see something of him. They looked forward to nightlong discussions in the old bars, to visiting the six-day bicycle races and ball games he liked so much.

They were disappointed. Gene O'Neill of the Greenwich Village days, the barroom days, the Broadway days, was gone.

At the O'Neill Sea Island retreat Mrs. O'Neill dressed for dinner every night in a long, flowing and gorgeous evening gown, but O'Neill, one visitor reported with satisfaction, wore dungarees and tennis shoes. His workroom there was built like a shipboard captain's cabin and faced the sea.

For the first year after the O'Neills' return to the U.S.A., the playwright accomplished little. In the Spring of 1932 he wrote the first draft of *Days Without End.* He was not satisfied with it and kept rewriting it for the next year and a half.

During September, 1932, he took two weeks out to write *Ah, Wilderness!* It was his first really conventional play, something everybody, even the drama critics, could understand, and it was a commercial success.

Richard Dana Skinner, author of a book on O'Neill called *A Poet's Quest,* said of *Ah, Wilderess!:* "This appealing and innocent and tender little comedy of adolescence is really much more important than it seems in the poet's unconscious scheme of things. It marked an end to that terrible fear which had made every symbol of youth appear like some hideous monster. It was unquestionably the beginning of a third and entirely new period in O'Neill's creative life, the period of full manhood of the soul."

Or perhaps Carlotta Monterey had become a mother to him, the "mother" he had hailed in the inscription to *Mourning Becomes Electra.* Perhaps she had shown him that things would be all right. Perhaps she brought a new youth to him, who was just 44.

His next play, *Days Without End,* about adultery, he found very difficult to write. Skinner, whose book O'Neill recently strongly recommended to an admirer who wanted a key to an understanding of his work, thinks it was because the playwright needed "to clear the path . . . to complete the play of deeper spiritual conflict."

Just how deeply the affair of the Barton suicide had affected O'Neill, one cannot say. He does not want to discuss it. Of the original *New Yorker* group, however, Harold Ross, the editor, Neysa McMein, the artist, and the others remember that Carlotta's marriage to Barton was violent and tempestuous. She bitterly resented Barton's interest in other women.

The heroine of *Days Without End* is a woman married to her second husband to whom infidelity is of the utmost importance. She considers marriage "a true sacrament." The hero had been unfaithful to her, and the conflict of the play is concerned with the hero's attempts to resolve the problem of telling her and thus perhaps destroying their love but achieving some kind of spiritual peace.

O'Neill solved the problem by introducing a Catholic priest who shows the hero the way. At the end of the play, the hero prostrates himself before the Cross to ask the help of the Son of Man—the One Whom, in all these years, he could never forgive for taking the love of his parents from him.

A light from the Crucifix illuminates the hero, and he cries: "I am forgiven! I can forgive, myself through Thee! O Lord of Love, forgive Thy poor blind fool!"

"Thou hast conquered, Lord," the hero's bad self calls out, "the damned soul—of John Loving!"

The play threw the critics into a tailspin and was not a success.

Then came a blow that hurt him very much. The Catholic Church refused to put the play on the White List. Only a few plays are placed on the White List. They must be plays that a committee of Catholic laymen decides it is safe to take young people to, plays that follow the principles of Catholic morality.

The committee said they would put *Days Without End* on the White List if O'Neill would insert a line in the play making it clear that the heroine's husband, whose infidelity had so upset her, was dead. The idea was abhorrent to O'Neill for two reasons. In the first place, such a charge involved his artistic integrity, something he had never compromised with. In the second place, it struck at his own life. Both he and his wife had been divorced.

Shortly after *Days Without End*, O'Neill started work on his most ambitious undertaking, a nine-play cycle of American Life from 1775 to 1932 to be called *A Tale of Possessors Self-dispossessed*.

In the '30s O'Neill's old restlessness reasserted itself, and in 1937 he and his wife sold their Georgia home and moved to California where they designed a country house which they had built near San Francisco. They called it Tao House after the liberal Chinese philosophy of The Right Way of Life.

While working on his American Life cycle, O'Neill completed three other plays, *A Moon for the Misbegotten,* which is to be produced in December, *A Touch of the Poet,* to be produced next year, and *Long Day's Journey Into Night,* the manuscript which is not to be published until 25 years after his death.

In 1938 O'Neill felt he had gone stale on his nine-play series, and the next year he turned back to his past for relief as he had when he had written *Ah, Wilderness!* This time he wrote *The Iceman Cometh* about a waterfront saloon in 1912.

O'Neill's life was upset by the war which forced him to close his house and move to a San Francisco apartment. The invasion of France so distressed him that he stopped writing. "The Germans invaded that part of France where I had lived," he said. "I felt as badly as if they had moved into Brooklyn when I was living in New York."

During the war he accomplished almost nothing. He had a stroke, from which he recovered except for a palsy, but from the shock of the world conflict he did not recover. A year before *The Iceman Cometh* opened he moved back to New York City.

John Mason Brown in *The Saturday Review of Literature* advanced an interesting theory about the play. He was discussing Hickey, the leading character, the hardware salesman who is shown reforming all the bums, until they discover the source of his newly found faith—he's murdered his wife. ". . . Whether he (and the whole story)," wrote Brown, "represents Mr. O'Neill's subconscious protest against those who have chaperoned and tidied-up his own recent living—is a matter for individual conjecture."

Whether Carlotta O'Neill influences O'Neill's views is also a matter of conjecture. This Fall she upbraided a reporter who, she thought, had been talking to her husband about politics. "A writer who talks about politics," she said, "is a fool. He should never talk about politics because politics change, art doesn't."

During the rehearsals of *The Iceman*, O'Neil sat most of the time next to Eddie Dowling, the director. Dowling tended to have the actors overplay some parts. O'Neill was for more subtle touches.

At one rehearsal a puzzled actress asked, "Was Hickey, the salesman, a good man?"

"Raw emotion," O'Neill said, "produces the best and worst in people. Remember, goodness can surmount anything. The people in that saloon were the best friends I've ever known. Their weakness was not an evil. It is a weakness found in all men.

"Revenge is the subconscious motive for the individual's behavior with the rest of society. Revulsion drives man to tell others of his sins. . . . It is the furies within us that seek to destroy us. In all my plays sin is punished and redemption takes place.

"Vice and virtue cannot live side by side. It's the humiliation of a loving kiss that destroys evil."

An eager, aggressive young actor stood up and asked O'Neill where he stood on "the movement." Two of the characters in the play are disillusioned radicals.

"I am a philosophical anarchist," O'Neill said, smiling faintly, "which means, 'Go to it, but leave me out of it.'"

O'Neill gives people the impression sometimes when he is talking to them that he is a cross between a Bowery bum and a Victorian gentleman. During a large press interview in September, a girl reporter came in late. "I've heard," the girl said, "that the cast of *The Iceman* consists of 14 men and four tarts."

"Fourteen men and four—ladies," O'Neill replied.

A reporter asked him what he was going to do on the opening night. "If I weren't in temperance," O'Neill said with a twinkle in his eye, "I'd get stinko."

My longest talk with Eugene O'Neill took place on the darkened stage of the Martin Beck Theatre where *The Iceman* was about to open. Around us were the sets by Robert Edmond Jones, O'Neill's old friend from the Provincetown days. We sat on a bench backstage, for a while, talking about his early life. He seemed old and sick, but I did not agree with *Time* that "his paralysis agitans involved his whole emaciated body in one miserable stammer."

He looked sharply at me as he talked and his face was still a face difficult to put out of your mind. He was well-groomed and expensively and quietly dressed in a double-breasted blue suit, but he gave the impression of a down-and-out man who had been completely outfitted the day before by some well-meaning friend.

He was still handsome. His hair was only slightly graying, a distinguished iron gray. He was thin and slightly bent over. His eyes were deep-set and sad and occasionally he cocked his head as he eyed me. His jaw was lean and forceful.

After talking a while, O'Neill got up and walked over to one end of a stage bar. He pulled up a stool, sat at the bar, and motioned for me to join him. He seemed to straighten up and come alive.

"Of course," he said, "America is due for a retribution. There ought to be a page in the history books of the United States of America of all the unprovoked, criminal, unjust crimes committed and sanctioned by our government since the beginning of our history—and before that, too. There is hardly one thing that our government has done that isn't some treachery—against the Indians, against the people of the Northwest, against the small farmers."

As he talked, he seemed in the tradition of all the great half-drunken Irishmen who sound off in bars all over the world. Their talk is always the same, extravagant, rambling, full of madness and violence, but studded with enough essential truth and insight to force you to listen with troubled fascination.

"This American Dream stuff gives me a pain," he went on. "Telling the world about our American Dream! I don't know what they mean. If it exists, as we tell the whole world, why don't we make it work in one small hamlet in the United States?

"If it's the Constitution that they mean, ugh, then it's a lot of words. If we taught history and told the truth, we'd teach school children that the United States has followed the same greedy rut as every other country. We would tell who's guilty. The list of the guilty ones responsible would include some of our great national heroes. Their portraits should be taken out and burned." He fondled a prop whiskey glass and a prop bottle with water and caramel syrup in it.

As his words took on more and more vigor, I got the feeling that O'Neill was, in a sense, the conscience of America asserting itself. I realized that one could say of him even today what his boss on the New London *Telegraph* had said of him in 1912: "He was the most stubborn and irreconcilable social rebel that I had ever met." He wrote about oppressed workers (*The Hairy Ape*) and about the tragedy of color discrimination (*All God's Chillun Got Wings*) long before they were fashionable subjects. I got the feeling that O'Neill's social views spring from the very pit of his soul, from a deep abiding love of humanity, from a deeply cherished dream of what the world could be.

"The great battle in American history," he went on, "was the Battle of Little Big Horn. The Indians wiped out the white men, scalped them. That was a victory in American history. It should be featured in all our school books as the greatest victory in American history."

O'Neill brought his fist down on the top of the bar. "The big business leaders in this country! Why do we produce such stupendous, colossal egomaniacs? They go on doing the most monstrous things, always using the excuse that if we don't the other person will. It's impossible to satirize them, if you wanted to."

The actors and stagehands began drifting back onto the stage. Two grips came to move the bar. We moved to the side. The conversation shifted to religion. Had he, I asked, returned to Catholicism, as one biography had implied he might?

A great look of sadness came into O'Neill's eyes. "Unfortunately, no," he said.

"*The Iceman* is a denial of any other experience of faith in my plays. In writing it, I felt I had locked myself in with my memories."

When he said that I thought of another remark he'd made: "Those people in the saloon were the best friends I ever had."

Profiles: The Tragic Sense

Hamilton Basso/1948

This essay is the third and final installment of a three-part *New Yorker* profile based on the last interview O'Neill gave prior to his death in 1953. Parts I (28 February 1948, 34–38, 40, 42, 44–45) and II (6 March 1948, 34–38, 40, 43–44, 46, 48–49) review O'Neill's life and plays, respectively, and contain little of the interview itself. Part III (13 March 1948, 37–40, 42, 44, 46–47) focuses on Basso's conversations with O'Neill, and is reprinted in its entirety by permission; © 1948, 1976 The New Yorker Magazine, Inc.

Because his thirty-eight plays stretch out in an almost unbroken sweep of disaster, including murder, disease, suicide, insanity, and incest, Eugene Gladstone O'Neill, not too surprisingly, has gained the reputation of being privately a rather morose fellow. His best friends are not so sure he is. They are not sure he isn't, however. Nor are they sure that the truth lies somewhere in between. He merely puzzles them. Russel Crouse, one of his closest friends, has said, "O'Neill is one of the most charming men I know, and I've known him for twenty-five years, but I can't say I understand him. His face is a mask. I don't know what goes on behind it, and I don't think anyone else does." Another friend says that whenever he sees O'Neill, he is reminded of the legend that the people of Ravenna always gave Dante a wide berth when they passed him on the street. The Ravennese, among whom Dante spent his last years, felt that the poet's burning, baleful eyes had actually looked upon the horrors of hell and that his dark complexion was the result of his being scorched in its sulphurous, overheated atmosphere. "That's the way I sometimes feel about O'Neill," this friend says. "We'll be talking, and he'll go into one of those long, staring silences of his, and I'll half expect him to turn to me and say, 'You're not a bad fellow, as far as I know, but if your eyes had seen what *these* eyes have seen, you'd go on home to your wife and children and not expect me to be nice.'" O'Neill's brown, deep-set eyes do have a look of brooding intensity, but, since his Irish lineage is absolutely unblemished, this is the only

resemblance to Dante it would seem possible for him to have. He is
what the Irish call a Black Irishman. Black Irishmen—William Butler
Yeats was one; George Bernard Shaw is not—are set apart from
other Irishmen, according to the Irish, by their black hair, dark eyes,
and mystic natures, which are supposed to put them in close touch
with the stuff that dreams, poetry, and tragedy are made on. O'Neill,
who was born in New York and is again living here after nearly forty
years of roaming about the world, has never marched in a St.
Patrick's Day parade or done anything else to call attention to his
Celtic descent, but he is one of the most distinguished Black Irishmen
of our time, even to the Irish of Ireland. In 1936, when O'Neill won
the Nobel Prize for literature, the Irish Minister to the United States
sent him a fine, proud letter saying what a lovely thing it was that had
happened and how pleased they all were over there. O'Neill, now
fifty-nine, isn't the Black Irishman he used to be, just as Shaw, who is
ninety-one, isn't the Red Irishman *he* used to be. O'Neill's hair,
eyebrows, and close-clipped mustache are all turning white, and he
looks about ten years older than he is. He is a little under six feet tall,
spare, and rangy, and carries himself with a sort of flexible erectness.
This accomplishment, according to a lady who has known him for
many years, is due to his bones. They are the kind of bones, she
says, that Gregory Peck has; clothes, in her opinion, hang especially
well on them. O'Neill's bones, now that he is making his headquarters in New York, are ordinarily draped with rather expensive, well-
tailored garments, which, in combination with his quiet, deep voice,
his unfailingly courteous manner, and his seafaring vocabulary, make
him seem an elegant, reserved, extremely shy gentleman who has
mysteriously acquired the outlook of a seaman on a tramp steamer.

O'Neill's nautical outlook is one effect of the somewhat famous two
years during which he made his living as a seaman when he was a
young man. The experiences he accumulated then have colored all
his subsequent thought and feeling. He tends to think of himself less
as a playwright than as a seaman who has taken up writing for the
stage. Of the twenty-nine plays in the most recent collection of his
works, ten are laid wholly or partly aboard ship. Nearly all the others
contain many references to the sea, and several have seafaring
people in their cast of characters. His conversation is salted with
phrases picked up at sea. "On the beach" turns up with particular

frequency. O'Neill's vocabulary is unseamanlike in one important respect; it is rarely stained with profanity. "Damn" is for him an explosive word. He doesn't like profanity in print, either. Having written everything he has wanted to write without using the rougher four-letter words—and having had as much trouble with Boston as anybody else—he is inclined to think that their value has been exaggerated. He also believes that some writers are too intent on calling a spade a spade when what they really mean is a trowel.

O'Neill has always felt drawn to the sea, but he can hardly remember a time in the last thirty-five years when he wasn't also attracted to the theatre. He thinks he could easily have drifted into some other career, however. "I remember when I was on the beach in Buenos Aires," he said in a recent conversation, in the course of which he glanced backward over his mature life. "I was then twenty-two years old and a real down-and-outer—sleeping on park benches, hanging around waterfront dives, and absolutely alone. I knew a fellow who used to work on a railroad down there and who had given up his job. One day, he suggested that we hold up one of those places where foreign money is exchanged. Well, I have to admit I gave the matter serious consideration. I finally decided not to do it, but since you aren't given to taking a very moral view of things when you are sleeping on park benches and haven't a dime to your name, I decided what I did because I felt that we were almost certain to be caught. A few nights later, the fellow who had propositioned me stuck the place up with somebody he'd got to take my place, and he *was* caught. He was sent to prison and, for all I know, he died there.

"Nearly everybody's life is determined to a large extent by just such accidents as these. You take my father, for example. Before he became an actor, he was a machinist. He worked in Buffalo, ten hours a day, for fifty cents a day. One night he was in a poolroom shooting pool. A man came in looking for extras to carry spears and play bit parts in a Shakespearean repertory company that Edwin Forrest had brought to town. If it hadn't been for that—if my father hadn't been shooting pool instead of being in church or at home reading a book, as perhaps he should have been—he would probably never have become an actor. Up to then, he hadn't given it a serious thought. In a way, the same thing happened to me. If I hadn't had an attack of tuberculosis, if I hadn't been forced to look at myself, while I was in the sanatorium, harder than I had ever done before, I might never have become a playwright. There are times now when I feel sure I would have been, no matter what happened, but when I remember Buenos Aires, and the fellow down there who wanted me to be a bandit, I'm not so sure."

O'Neill's rise to fame, once he decided to be a dramatist, was more rapid than even he had hoped it would be. In 1920, only four years after the Provincetown Players gave *Bound East for Cardiff,* one of his earliest one-acters, its first New York showing, he was awarded the first of his three Pulitzer Prizes, for *Beyond the Horizon,* and had established himself, with *The Emperor Jones,* as America's foremost dramatist. His position has never been challenged. Unlike many successful writers for the stage, however, such as Shaw and Barrie, in England, and Robert Sherwood and George S. Kaufman, in this country, he has not made a great deal of money. Of his total lifetime earnings of three-quarters of a million dollars, only about a third remains in his hands. O'Neill has had nine hit shows—*The Emperor Jones,* in 1920; *Anna Christie,* his second Pulitzer Prize winner, in 1922; *The Hairy Ape,* in 1922; *Desire Under the Elms,* in 1924; *The Great God Brown,* in 1926; *Strange Interlude,* which won the third Pulitzer Prize, in 1928; *Mourning Becomes Electra,* in 1931; *Ah, Wilderness!,* in 1933; and *The Iceman Cometh,* in 1946. Nearly all these successes, up to the time *Strange Interlude* was produced by the Theatre Guild, were housed in small theatres. The weekly gross for *The Emperor Jones* and *Anna Christie* sometimes fell as low as $2,500 (a weekly gross of less than $12,000 a week is considered peanuts on Broadway today), and O'Neill had accepted a low royalty rate. He didn't hit the jackpot until *Strange Interlude* came to town. Even then, it wasn't so swollen a jackpot as is generally believed. It has often been said that O'Neill made a million dollars from *Strange Interlude.* He actually took in $275,000. This was still, by almost any standards, a considerable sum, especially since incomes taxes were hardly what they are today. O'Neill used some of this money to make a few expensive improvements on a house he had bought in Bermuda, but a large part of it was added to his careful investments in the stock market. Because of his caution, he lost only fifty per cent of that money in the 1929 crash. His three last successes—*Mourning Becomes Electra, Ah, Wilderness!,* and *The Iceman Cometh*—were only modestly profitable, because a substantial part of his earnings had to be turned over to the tax collector. O'Neill isn't unhappy because he has not made more money. He has never written with money in mind—he once turned down an offer of a hundred thousand dollars to do one film for the movies—and he is surprised that he has made out as well as he has. He does wish, nevertheless, that people would understand that he is not, and hasn't ever been, a millionaire. "Not that I'd particularly mind being one," he says. "I just like to get the matter straight."

Even if he were a millionaire, O'Neill, since becoming a playwright, could hardly have lived more pleasantly, or in pleasanter places. In 1918, after marrying for the second time, he settled down in a former Cape Cod Coast Guard station on the dunes a few miles from Provincetown. O'Neill, who has always been a fine swimmer, spent almost as much time in or on the water as he did on shore, either swimming so far out that he could hardly be seen from land or paddling about in a kayak. After a swim and an eight-o'clock breakfast, he wrote until just before lunch, then took another dip. After lunch, he went back to work, usually to revise what he had written that morning, until late afternoon, when he knocked off and went swimming again.

O'Neill held to this watery way of life until 1925, when he and his wife bought a farm near Ridgefield, Connecticut, one of the quieter havens in the suburban artist-and-writer belt. He soon began to feel unbearably landlocked, however, and that same year he bought a house, called Spithead, on the water in Bermuda and started to practice total immersion again. The house was supposed to have been built by a pirate, an idea that appealed to O'Neill. In 1928, he went to France. He lived for a time in a village in the Basque country, moved on to Cap d'Ail, on the Riviera, and then, in 1929, after a second divorce and his marriage to the present Mrs. O'Neill, who is the former Carlotta Monterey, he took a two-year lease on a thirty-four room, two-tower château in Touraine. With time out for expeditions to Switzerland and the Canary Islands, and a voyage to Indo-China, the O'Neills lived there until their lease ran out, and it was there that *Mourning Becomes Electra* was written. Returning to the United States in 1931, they spent a short time in Northport, Long Island, and then went to Sea Island, Georgia, where they built a

house. It was largely designed by Mrs. O'Neill, who, devising an
Italianate contraction of their first names, christened it Casa Genotta.
O'Neill liked Sea Island. The ocean was just outside his door for him
to swim in, the beach was a fine place for him to soak up the sun,
and there was enough peace and quiet for him to get a satisfactory
amount of work done. On Sea Island, he wrote two more plays—
Days Without End and *Ah, Wilderness!*—and started to prepare for a
huge third project. But then Sea Island, to which O'Neill had been
attracted by its isolated tranquillity, started to boom. More and more
visitors came, and more and more houses were built. Reluctantly,
O'Neill sold his house, in the spring of 1936, and he and his wife
went to Seattle, where they stayed in a rented house until just before
Christmas, and then migrated to California. There, in 1937, they
acquired a hundred and sixty acres near Oakland, built another
residence, which Mrs. O'Neill also largely designed, and called it Tao
House, *tao* being the Chinese word for "the right way of life."
O'Neill, then forty-nine, and full of confidence in himself and his
future, settled down to what he hoped would be the major accomplishment of his life.

Considering that his first dramatic efforts were fifteen-minute, one-
act plays, O'Neill's ideas had become astonishingly expansive.
Strange Interlude, his saga of sex, sorrow, and soliloquies, took more
than four hours to unravel itself when it was produced in 1928, and
Mourning Becomes Electra, which put Aeschylus into Civil War dress,
ran even longer. The project to which O'Neill now gave his full
attention made these dramas seem mere curtain-raisers. This work, *A
Tale of Possessors Self-Dispossessed,* which he had begun to think
about on Sea Island, was originally planned as a cycle of six plays
dealing with the fortunes and misfortunes of an American family from
1828 to 1932. He had spent over a year making notes and blocking
out the plays, but when he settled down to the actual writing of them,
he decided that he hadn't gone back far enough in time. He blocked
out one more play, which took the action back to 1806, and commenced work on it. Before he had finished, it turned into two plays.
Then he decided that he should go back even further in time, and he
added a ninth play to the cycle. The series now began in 1775. Its
theme might be called the dominant theme of O'Neill's mature
philosophy—the corruption of character by materialistic greed. The

ninth play, which, chronologically, was to be the first of the cycle, deals with America during the French and Indian War. Its hero is an Irishman who has joined the British Army to escape the slavery of agricultural life in Ireland. It is his idea to desert as soon as he gets to America and to go into the wilderness, where, liberated from the economic and social bondage of the Old World, he can live as a truly free man. Once in this country, he strikes out for the wilderness. On his journey, wanting food and shelter, he stops at a frontier farm. It is only a clearing in a forest, but it is nonetheless the most fertile and promising soil he has ever seen. The farm is run by a young widow, who badly needs a man around the place, and who, as O'Neill saw it, also badly needs a man. The Irishman, caught between his dream of freedom and his hunger for land, and attracted by the woman's physical allure, finally abandons his dream and settles for the land. The bleak mood of the play was summed up in its title, *Give Me Liberty And—*. According to O'Neill's scheme, the seed of greed that had thus been planted was to grow and flower throughout the cycle.

The cycle, although primarily the story of an American family, was also intended to be the story of America. O'Neill thinks that we have not done very well as a country. Looking back upon the original promise of American life and pondering what he takes to be the present reality, he gets bitter and discouraged. "Someday," he says, "this country is going to get it—really get it. We had everything to start with—everything—but there's bound to be a retribution. We've followed the same selfish, greedy path as every other country in the world. We talk about the American Dream, and want to tell the world about the American Dream, but what is that dream, in most cases, but the dream of material things? I sometimes think that the United States, for this reason, is the greatest failure the world has ever seen. We've been able to get a very good price for our souls in this country—the greatest price perhaps that has ever been paid—but you'd think that after all these years, and all that man has been through, we'd have sense enough—*all* of us—to understand that the whole secret of human happiness is summed up in a sentence that even a child can understand. The sentence? 'For what shall it profit a man if he shall gain the whole world and lose his own soul?' "

Despite the burden of gloom with which his cycle was laden, the two years O'Neill spent in writing it were happy ones. He wrote for from five to seven hours every day, saw hardly anyone, and rarely went anywhere. He was content merely to fill page after page of manuscript with his careful, precise, minute handwriting. O'Neill, whose dislike of machinery extends to the typewriter, writes in pencil, and his script is so small that it can hardly be read. He manages to get over a thousand words on a sheet of paper eight by ten and a half inches; the average handwriting runs about two hundred. Mrs. O'Neill did his typewriting for him, using a magnifying glass.

O'Neill's work went well, and he took long walks and long drives in the California sunshine to break the routine of writing, and life in Tao House was serene and rewarding. Of all the places O'Neill has ever lived, he remembers his house in California as being the most agreeable. But by the middle of 1939, when he had finished the major part of his cycle, he felt that he had gone stale. He began to have doubts about what he had written and to wonder, in fact, whether the whole plan of his cycle wasn't faulty. He decided that it should deal with two families instead of one, and he put the project aside. Not wanting to be idle, he started writing The Iceman Cometh. He has not yet gone back to his cycle. All that he has to show for the years of thinking, planning, and writing that went into it is one play, A Touch of the Poet, the third of the sequence, which has not been produced. He has destroyed the manuscript of everything else in the cycle—three completed plays, three that were practically completed, and two on which he had done considerable work.

This act of destruction did not mean that O'Neill had abandoned his cycle. He was just clearing the decks in order to be able, some-day, to begin all over again. But the war intervened, and then came illness. One by one, his six servants went to work in the war plants that mushroomed on the Pacific Coast. The O'Neills would probably have stuck it out in their country house, but O'Neill, who had led an active and athletic life, was suffering from an illness that manifested itself in a severe, racking palsy. He has been examined by half a dozen specialists. Three of them have diagnosed his ailment as Parkinson's disease. The three others have said they don't know what it is. O'Neill believes that it is a violent aggravation of something he has had all his life. Even when he was a young man, his hands trembled slightly, and, since his mother's hands used to tremble in the same way, he thinks that the failing may have been inherited. "But

I'm sure I didn't help it any by drinking as much as I did," he said not long ago. Whatever the illness, O'Neill's hands now tremble so severely that he can no longer use a pen or a pencil, and he finds it impossible to dictate. "Imagine trying to dictate something like *Mourning Becomes Electra,*" he says. As a consequence, the thread on which everything else in his life for thirty-five years was hung, his work, has been brutally snapped in two.

Because of his illness, which naturally makes it impossible for O'Neill to drive—he was once an expert automobilist who tore about the French countryside in a Bugatti racer—and because Mrs. O'Neill does not drive, the O'Neills felt almost as marooned in Tao House, after their chauffeur left, as if they had been cast up on a desert island. They sold their house and moved into an apartment in San Francisco early in 1941. In 1945, they returned to New York, and they have been here ever since. O'Neill is considerably better, but he has not written anything since he left his house in California. He has, however, a stockpile of two plays in addition to *A Touch of the Poet.* One, *A Moon for the Misbegotten,* which is his most recent work, was tried out on the road by the Theatre Guild last year but was withdrawn because of casting difficulties. One of the troubles was the part of the heroine, which calls for a beautiful girl who is six feet tall and weighs two hundred pounds. The other play, *Long Day's Journey into Night,* which was written after *The Iceman Cometh,* will not be produced until twenty-five years after O'Neill's death. He refuses to talk about it and has shown the manuscript to only a few of his closest friends.

O'Neill is now living in a penthouse in the East Eighties, an apartment that, like his past residences, is in sharp contrast to his international reputation for gloom. It has six large and sunny rooms, and its walls and curtains are done in bright, cheerful colors. It is furnished with things that O'Neill has gathered all over the world. The dominant note is Chinese. A small, heavy, vaguely catlike stone animal, turned out by a Chinese sculptor a few centuries before Christ, greets visitors as they enter, and there are ancient Chinese prints on the walls of the living room. O'Neill keeps his desk in his bedroom in readiness for the day when he can begin work again. Some of his friends think that his bed, of the conventional box-spring-and-mattress variety, is a considerable improvement over the one he had in California. That one was a low-slung ebony affair, only a few inches off the floor, that had come from an opium den in San Francisco. It, and a black-glass mirror O'Neill used out there for shaving, are in storage. The mirror gave him a green, moldy appearance. A brisk, melodious canary named Jeremiah, a recent present from Mrs. O'Neill, shares his bedroom with him.

The canary helps compensate for the death of his dog, a handsome Dalmatian, registered as Silverdean Emblem but called Blemmy by his master. O'Neill, who misses Blemmy enough to keep a snapshot of him on his desk, also misses a player piano he called Rosie. It began its career in a New Orleans bagnio, and Mrs. O'Neill gave it to him for a birthday present. She unearthed the piano in New York, where the O'Neills were vacationing for a few weeks, and shipped it to California, along with a large box of old rolls, including "Alexander's Ragtime Band," "That Mysterious Rag," "All Alone," and "Waiting for the Robert E. Lee." It is in storage in California, but O'Neill plans to have it shipped East soon. In Rosie's absence, O'Neill depends for his musical entertainment, more conventionally, on a phonograph. He has a large collection of records, about evenly divided between jazz and serious music. The composers he admires most are Beethoven, Schubert, César Franck, and Irving Berlin. One of his happiest evenings in New York was spent at a small party a mutual friend gave for him and Berlin, whom he had never met before. Berlin played the piano and O'Neill sang, and the party lasted until three. Only an unusual occasion can keep O'Neill up late, and he generally gets to bed before eleven. He never goes to large parties, for he has always been excruciatingly shy, and, having been on the wagon for fifteen years, he no longer can depend on alcohol to help him relax. He enjoys seeing his old friends, however, and he goes to the movies now and then. He is also a sports fan. The six-day bicycle races and football, particularly the professional sort, are his favorite sports, and he was disgruntled last fall because his illness prevented his seeing any games.

O'Neill often listens to the radio. One of his favorite performers is Jack Benny, especially since an evening in May, 1937, when he heard a burlesque of Ah, Wilderness! that Benny did on the air. Benny felt he should have permission to do the burlesque, but none of the people in New York who look after O'Neill's business interests would give it to him, so he wired O'Neill, who was then at Sea Island. O'Neill replied immediately that it was one of the nicest compliments he had ever had. Another compliment was paid him more recently on the radio when the Theatre Guild on the Air put on one of his early plays, *The Straw.* It was a failure when it was produced on Broadway—most of its action takes place in a tuberculosis sana-torium—but it turned out to be one of the Guild's most successful broadcasts. O'Neill didn't hear it, however. He has never attended a performance of any of his plays. He stays with them through their final dress rehearsal, offering suggestions and advice on matters of acting, directing, lighting, costuming, and stage design, and then lets them go their own way.

   Late one afternoon, sitting with a companion in his living room, O'Neill, between long silences, spoke about this and other aspects of his work. "After you've finished a play and it goes into rehearsal," he said as the sky darkened outside, "it begins to go from you. No matter how good the production is, or how able the actors, some-thing is lost—your own vision of the play, the way you saw it in your imagination." He reached for a cigarette and struck a match. The small flame trembled in his hand. He drew on his cigarette and blew out the match. "I don't think acting is as good as it used to be. Type casting is a bad thing. You don't get actors and actresses by asking them to go out on the stage and play themselves. You just don't." He stopped to edit his thoughts. The sounds of the city were muffled and far away. "There have been only three actors in my plays who managed to realize the characters they played as I originally saw them. They were Charles Gilpin in *The Emperor Jones,* Louis Wolheim in *The Hairy Ape,* and Walter Huston in *Desire Under the Elms.* There have been other good actors and actresses in my plays, but only those three lived up to the conceptions I had as I wrote. There are too many actors and actresses who just go out there and play themselves. It's not a good thing, either for acting or for playwriting. The playwright comes to depend on the physical presence of the actors to fill out their characters for him, instead of writing his characters into the script. Whether my plays are good or bad—though I hope some of them are good—I've tried to do that, anyway. I've always tried to *write* my characters out. That's why I've sometimes been disappointed in the actors who played them—the characters were too real and alive in my own imagination. As for length—well, if you can't hold an audience for three minutes, three minutes is too long. If you can get them to listen to you for three hours, three hours may not be long enough."

Mrs. O'Neill, who had been out shopping, came in. She is still strikingly handsome, with dark hair, brown eyes, and a flawless profile. "My," she said, "isn't it *cold!* I nearly froze. But Gene! Why are you sitting here in the dark? Why don't you turn some of the lights on? It's so *gloomy."* She went about the room switching on the lamps, and O'Neill's face came out of the shadows.

"I'm supposed to be a gloomy fellow," he said. "Hadn't you heard?"

"You can be gloomy enough, sometimes," Mrs. O'Neill answered. "But why do they always have to exaggerate? Nearly everything that has been said about you is all wrong. Have you had coffee? Oh, Gene, you never think of anything! I'll get it for you."

She left the room, making a last remark about her husband's forgetfulness, and O'Neill sat for a time in silence again.

"What Carlotta just said is true," he said, crushing his cigarette into the ashtray. "Nearly everything that has been said about me *is* all wrong." Then he stopped again. To his right were several book-shelves. Among the books were sets of Zola, Victor Hugo, and Balzac. There were also big volumes of reproductions of paintings, books on exploration, books on the habits and customs of primitive peoples. Two shelves were given over to the English and American poets. "Richard Dana Skinner has written a book about me," O'Neill said after a while. "It's called *Eugene O'Neill, a Poet's Quest.* I don't agree with many things he says, but that just about sums it up. It *has* been a poet's quest. I began with a background of poetry. My father was reciting poetry all the time. Instead of singing in the bathtub, he'd break out into Shakespeare. I remember once, when we were all together in New London, he was telling my brother, James, and me about how hard he had to work as an actor. 'You call that work?' my brother said. My brother bet him ten dollars that he could learn the whole of Goldsmith's *The Deserted Village* in one week and I bet him the same amount that I could learn the part of Macbeth. My brother and I studied together. We were very close, my brother and I. We were a very close family—perhaps *too* close. Anyway, after our week was over, James and I stood before my father. My brother ran through *The Deserted Village,* collected his money, and then my father started to cue me my lines as Macbeth. I gave them back to him without a hitch. My father closed the book and looked at me. 'You certainly have a good memory,' he said, 'and I see you've worked hard, but never go on the stage.'"

O'Neill laughed. Then he became serious again. "It's too bad my father *ever* got started playing in *Monte Cristo,*" he said. "He was too successful. It ruined his life. If it hadn't been for *Monte Cristo,* he might have gone ahead and taken Booth's place, as everybody expected him to. One thing about him—he always urged me to go ahead. He didn't always get what I was trying to do, and perhaps he *couldn't* get it, but he never tried to make me turn aside."

There was a clatter of china from the kitchen and a warm smell of coffee filled the room. "It's very hard right now," O'Neill said. "Not being able to work. I want to get going again. Once I get over this thing—these shakes I have—I feel I can keep rolling right along."

Index

A

A. E. (George William Russell), 39
Abbey Players, 38, 39–40
Abbey Theatre, 38, 39, 113
Adams, Major, 130, 131
Adams, Maude, 50
Allen, Viola, 4, 28
American Spectator (magazine), 136
Anderson, Maxwell, 143; *What Price Glory*, 60, 62, 201
Article 47 (play), 117
Ashe, Beatrice, 208–9

B

Badger, Richard G., 211
Baker, George Pierce, 4, 10, 32, 41, 42, 77, 118, 171, 183, 194, 211
Baker, Phil, 128
Balzac, Honoré de, 235
Banton, Joab H., 196
Barrie, James, 227
Barrymore, John, 22, 72
Barrymore, Lionel, 72
Barrymore, Maurice, 117, 162
Barton, Homer, 216, 217
Barton, James, 181
Barton, Ralph, 213, 214, 216–17, 218
Beethoven, Ludwig van, 48, 233
Belasco, David, 78, 98, 117
Belgrade Lakes, Maine, 127, 215
Bellevue, Bermuda, 91, 92
Bellows, George, 181
Ben-Ami, Jacob, 22
Benny, Jack, 233–34
Bentley, Eric, *The Playwright as Thinker*, 177
Bentley, Irene, 162
Berlin, Irving, 233
Bermuda, 65, 70, 89, 91, 92, 93, 104, 127, 215. *See also* Bellevue, Bermuda; Spithead, Bermuda

Betts Academy, Stamford, Conn., 205
Boll, George, 141
Booth, Edwin, 154, 155, 236
Boyce, Neith, 95
Brady, Alice, 172
Brisbane, Arthur, 196
Brook Farm, Ridgefield, Conn., 44, 47, 50, 199, 214, 228
Brown, John Mason, 220
Buenos Aires, Argentina, 4, 7, 8, 30, 38, 41, 64, 65–67, 77, 118, 122, 171, 193, 207, 226, 227
Byth, James Findlater, 58, 68, 130, 131

C

Campbell, Jack, 137
Campbell, Mrs. Patrick, 47
Cap d'Ail, France, 228
Carlin, Terry, 95, 96
Casa Genotta, Sea Island, Ga., 128, 134, 136, 138–39, 143, 147, 149, 151, 152, 155, 156, 174, 217, 228–29, 234
Cerf, Bennett, 184
Chaliapin, Feodor, 86
Chaplin, Charles, 212
Chekhov, Anton, 61
Christopherson, Chris, 56, 68–69, 130
Clark, Barrett H., 129, 208, 212
Clark, Bill, 82
Cohan, George M., 134–35, 142, 198
Colbert, Claudette, 176
Coleridge, Samuel Taylor, *The Rime of the Ancient Mariner*, 51
Condon, James J., 68. *See also* Jimmy the Priest's
Congreve, William, 194
Conrad, Joseph, 7, 10, 28, 41; *The Nigger of the Narcissus*, 65
Continental Varieties (play), 138
Cook, Elisha, Jr., 135

237

Cook, George Cram, 95, 97, 99–100, 118,
    172, 195
Corrigan, Emmett, 3
Corwin, Norman, 170
The Count of Monte Cristo (adapted play), 4,
    9, 27, 31, 38, 41, 65, 71, 77, 95, 116–17,
    118, 154, 155, 161, 169, 171, 182, 190, 192,
    203, 204, 207, 208, 236
Craig, Gordon, 21, 22, 23
Croak, Jack, 82
Crouse, Russel, 224

D

Dante, 224–25
Davenport, Fanny, 117
Dempsey, Jack, 101
DePolo, Harold, 43
Deutsch, Kathe, 39
Digges, Dudley, 181
Doro, Marie, 162
Dorsey, Thomas Francis, 203, 205, 214
Dostoevsky, Feodor, 10
Dowling, Eddie, 185, 220
Downes, Olin, 6
Dreiser, Theodore, 146
Driscoll, Mr., 31, 67–68, 130
Dunning, Phil, 104
Duse, Eleonora, 50

E

Ell, Christine, 98
Escudero, Vicente, 138

F

Farnum, William, 71
Farrell, James T., 204
Faust, Lotta, 161
Faust (play), 80
Federal Theatre Project, 153–54, 155, 157
Fedora (play), 117
Finn McCool (dog), 40, 47
Fitch, Clyde, 120
Fitzgerald, F. Scott, 204, 205
Fontanne, Lynn, 106
Forrest, Edwin, 226
Francis, John, 96
Franck, Cesar, 233

G

Garbo, Greta, 115

Garden, Mary, 47
Gaylord Farm Sanatorium, Wallingford,
    Conn., 41, 42, 193–94, 209–10. See also
    O'Neill, Eugene Gladstone: illnesses of
Gilder, Rosamond, 164
Gilpin, Charles, 47, 58, 172, 234
Gish, Dorothy, 159
Gish, Lillian, 107, 160
Glaser, Lulu, 161
Glaspell, Susan, 95, 195
Goldsmith, Oliver, The Deserted Village,
    235–36
Gorky, Maxim, Nachtasyl, 178; A Night
    Lodging, 58, 61
Graziano, Rocky, 159, 163
The Great Divide (play), 195
Greenwich Village Players, 5
Greenwich Village Theatre, 56, 58, 60, 71
Gregory, Lady, 39
Guéthary, France, 127, 228

H

Haiti, 57
Hamilton, Clayton, 42
Hammond, Percy, 134
Hapgood, Hutchins, 95
Harvard University, 4, 10, 32, 41, 42, 57, 77,
    118, 171, 183, 194, 195, 211, 212
Hasenclever, Walter, 79
Hauptmann, Gerhart, 73
Helburn, Theresa, 107
Hell Hole, 77, 78, 97–98, 130
Hopkins, Arthur, 22, 100, 142
Hugo, Victor, 235
Huston, Walter, 106, 142, 234

I

Ibsen, Henrik, 10, 85, 160, 183, 195
Industrial Workers of the World, 47
Irving, Henry, 140

J

Jimmy the Priest's, 8, 30, 31, 36, 56, 57, 58,
    67, 68, 82, 128–29, 130–31, 159, 167,
    182–83, 207
John Golden Theatre, 81
Jones, Robert Edmond, 21, 22, 181, 195,
    221
Joyce, James, 39
Juarez and Maximilian (play), 82

K

Kamerny Theatre, 114
Kaufman, George S., 227
Keats, John, 194
Kemp, Harry, 99
Kenny, Sister Elizabeth, 170
Kipling, Rudyard, 193
Kropotkin, Peotr, 28

L

Langner, Lawrence, 82, 197
Latimer, Frederick P., 208
Lefty Louie, 77, 98
Lenormand, Henri-René, 124, 141, 143, 198;
    Simoon, 198
Le Plessis, Saint-Antoine du Rocher, Indre-et-
    Loire, France, 103–4, 106–7, 108–9, 113,
    121, 122, 130, 166, 197, 215, 228
Lewis, Sinclair, 128, 153
Lindbergh, Charles A., 148
London, Jack, 6, 7, 10, 41
London, England, 127
Long, Huey, 156

M

McAdoo, William, 196
McGeehan, W. O., 136
Macgowan, Kenneth, 71
MacKellar, Helen, 101
MacLane, Charles Agnew, 99
MacLeish, Archibald, 194, 210–11
McMein, Neysa, 218
Madison Square Theatre, 117
Maginn, Bonnie, 162
Mansfield, Richard, 205
Martin Beck Theatre, 164, 180, 221
Marx, Groucho, 140
Marx, Karl, 28
Mat Burke (dog), 47
Mather, Margaret, 117
Maugham, W. Somerset, 124, 143
May, Edna, 162
Mencken, H. L., 33
Moissi, Alexander, 86
Montague, Harry, 117
Morn to Midnight (play), 62
Morosco Theatre, 213
Moscow Art Players, 40, 59

N

Nantucket, Mass., 70

Nathan, George Jean, 33, 107, 111, 136, 184
Nazimova, Alla, 172
New London, Conn., 27, 31, 32, 77, 118,
    135, 171, 193, 199, 203, 204–5, 207, 208,
    214, 235
New London Telegraph, 4, 9, 31, 32, 41, 42,
    118, 171, 193, 194, 208, 222
New Orleans, La., 4, 31, 192, 207
New York City, 73, 76, 82, 117, 122, 128,
    139, 154, 158, 164, 167, 171, 175, 178,
    182, 185, 190, 195, 201, 216, 220, 225,
    232. See also Hell Hole; Jimmy the Priest's
Nietzsche, Friedrich, 22, 23, 28, 81

O

Oakland, Calif., 168, 183, 199, 229
O'Brien, Jack, 101
O'Casey, Sean, 113, 124, 139, 143
O'Hara, John, 204
O'Neill, Agnes Boulton (second wife), 7, 11,
    29, 40, 57, 100, 101, 108, 212, 214, 215,
    228; The Road Before Us, 212
O'Neill, Carlotta Monterey (third wife), 103,
    104, 105, 106–7, 108, 112, 128, 133, 138,
    140, 143, 144, 145, 146, 151, 159, 163,
    183, 184, 199, 213, 214–17, 218, 220, 228,
    230, 232, 233, 235
O'Neill, Edmund Burke (brother), 204
O'Neill, Ella Quinlan (mother), 203, 204, 214
O'Neill, Eugene Gladstone, as actor, 4, 9, 31,
    41, 42, 77, 118, 155, 171, 183, 207–8; on
    actors and acting, 71–72, 73–74, 85, 86,
    106, 142–43, 162, 178, 234–35; on African
    Americans, 46, 54; and alcohol, 56, 77,
    97–98, 99, 102, 128–29, 130–31, 159, 162,
    205, 207, 211–12, 214, 231, 233; arrested
    as German spy, 43; on art and artists, 22,
    23–24, 47–48, 129, 139–40, 172; on
    comedy, 186; and critics, 14, 19, 20, 42,
    45, 46, 47, 78, 83, 86, 93, 111, 122–23,
    132–33, 176–77, 218, 219; and divorce,
    215; education, 4, 7, 10, 27, 28, 32, 41,
    117–18, 171, 191, 192, 205, 206; on
    expressionism, 62, 79, 105, 169; and far
    east, 107, 108, 127, 215, 228; on foreign
    theatre and foreign productions of plays,
    38, 39, 47, 79, 113–14, 119, 124, 137, 138;
    and gold prospecting, 8–9, 28, 41, 58, 118,
    155, 157, 171, 182, 206; on human nature,
    33–35, 44, 52, 61, 140–41, 165; illnesses
    of, 3, 4, 9, 31–32, 42, 77, 99, 118, 171,
    183, 184, 185, 186, 193–94, 199, 209–10,
    226–27, 231–32, 236; and Irish heritage,

39, 203–4, 225; literary influences, 7, 10, 28, 41, 81, 143, 195; on masks, 111–12, 135, 143, 172; and motion pictures, 112, 115, 170, 228; on naturalism, 48–49, 83; and newspaper career, 4, 9, 13–14, 31, 32, 41, 42, 118, 171, 193, 194, 208; and Nobel Prize for Literature, 132, 145–46, 150, 152, 153, 155, 156, 157, 199, 225; philosophy of, 37, 44, 46, 52, 54, 61, 71, 139–40, 164–65, 186, 220–22, 229, 230; poetry of, 9, 32, 193, 208–9; politics of, 90, 155; and Pulitzer Prize, 11, 57, 75, 78, 212, 213, 227; on radio and television, 170; and sailing experience, 3–4, 7–8, 9, 28, 29–32, 33–35, 38, 41, 53, 64, 65, 77, 118, 155, 157, 182, 192, 193, 207, 225; suicide attempt, 131–32; on theatre, 21–25, 32, 42–43, 45–46, 47–49, 52–53, 59, 61–63, 71–72, 73–74, 81, 85, 109, 111, 113–14, 117, 118–19, 120, 136, 137–38, 153–54, 155, 161–62, 163, 169–70, 200–2; on tragedy, 15–16, 37, 53, 186; work experiences, 4, 8, 9, 28, 29, 41, 65, 118, 155, 171, 192, 207; work process, 29, 36, 43, 45, 57–58, 79–80, 91, 92–93, 104, 124–25, 127, 129, 149–50, 230–31; and writing, 4–5, 9–10, 16–20, 22, 42, 52, 72–73, 105, 124–25, 141, 166, 194, 200, 208–10, 219

Works: *Ah, Wilderness!* (play), 134–36, 148, 150–51, 183, 198, 201, 206, 218, 227–28, 229, 233–34; *All God's Chillun Got Wings* (play), 44, 45–46, 47, 50, 51, 53–54, 57, 74, 83, 114, 124, 125, 137, 196, 222; *The Ancient Mariner* (adapted play), 51; *Anna Christie* (play), 14, 15, 19, 26, 27, 30, 39, 47, 48, 50, 53, 56, 64, 65, 68, 69, 72, 74, 75, 79, 83, 105, 130, 142, 155, 197, 212, 227; *Anna Christie* (films), 72, 115, 136; *Beyond the Horizon* (play), 3, 5, 11, 26, 35–36, 50, 57, 75, 78–79, 120, 125, 142, 154, 172, 196, 212, 213, 227; *Bound East for Cardiff* (play), 11, 33, 42, 57, 66, 67, 96, 125, 130, 183, 194, 195, 211, 227; *By Way of Obit* (uncompleted play cycle), 175, 184; *The Calms of Capricorn* (uncompleted play), 175; *Chris Christopherson* (play), 3, 142; *Days Without End* (play), 135–36, 174, 177–78, 180, 198, 217, 218–19, 229; *Desire Under the Elms* (play), 56, 58, 60, 70, 74, 80, 83, 106, 114, 115, 125, 135, 183, 196–97, 200, 212, 227, 234; *Diff'rent* (play), 39, 57, 60, 195; *Dynamo* (play), 86, 105, 108, 111, 123, 126, 176, 177, 189, 197; *The Emperor Jones* (play), 14, 17, 19, 26,

27, 36, 39, 40, 44, 47, 57–58, 74, 75, 79, 83, 99–100, 106, 142, 155, 168, 172, 183, 195–96, 212, 227, 234; *The Emperor Jones* (film), 136; *The Emperor Jones* (opera), 136; *The First Man* (play), 74, 83, 105, 177; *The Fountain* (play), 17, 43, 72, 82, 105, 177; *Give Me Liberty And—* (uncompleted play), 230; *Gold* (play), 57, 105, 125, 142, 177; *The Great God Brown* (play), 58, 72, 80, 83, 89, 105–6, 108, 112, 120, 126, 143, 146, 172, 183, 212, 214, 227; *The Hairy Ape* (play), 26, 27, 31, 35, 39, 44, 47, 50, 57, 60, 61, 62, 64, 65, 68, 74, 75, 83, 101, 105, 106, 115, 146, 166, 183, 195, 213, 222, 227, 234; *The Iceman Cometh* (play), 158–60, 162, 164, 165, 166, 167–68, 173, 174, 175, 178–79, 180–82, 183, 184, 185, 188, 189, 197, 199–200, 204, 207, 219, 220, 221, 222, 227–28, 231; *Ile* (play), 33, 212; *In the Zone* (play), 11, 99, 130, 212; *Lazarus Laughed* (play), 83, 86–87, 89, 91, 92, 106, 115, 123, 126; *The Life of Bessie Bowen* (uncompleted play), 136; *Long Day's Journey into Night* (play), 160, 175, 184, 189, 193, 199, 209, 219, 232; *The Long Voyage Home* (play), 33, 125, 212; *Marco Millions* (play), 81, 82, 83, 125–26, 134, 148; *A Moon for the Misbegotten* (play), 162, 166, 168, 174, 175, 184, 189, 199, 219, 232; *The Moon of the Caribbees* (play), 11, 33, 74, 78, 79, 83, 91, 106, 125, 130, 195, 212; *The Moon of the Caribbees and Six Other Plays of the Sea* (collection), 5; *More Stately Mansions* (play), 175; *Mourning Becomes Electra* (play trilogy), 105, 108, 109–11, 112, 125, 126, 134, 146, 168, 172, 183, 197–98, 215–16, 217, 218, 227–28, 229, 232; *S. S. Glencairn* (play cycle), 56–57, 60, 61, 64–65, 66; *Strange Interlude* (play), 72, 81, 82, 83, 84–86, 89, 91, 93, 104, 105, 106, 108, 109, 119, 120, 123, 134, 136, 158, 167–68, 174, 177, 183, 197, 198, 212, 227, 229; *The Straw* (play), 3, 14, 74, 77, 83, 125, 142, 195, 234; *A Tale of Possessors, Self-dispossessed* (uncompleted play cycle), 146, 147, 150–51, 152, 164, 174, 175, 176, 180, 183, 199, 219, 229–31; *Thirst* (play), 11; *Thirst and Other One Act Plays* (collection), 96, 211; "Tomorrow" (short story), 58, 68; *A Touch of the Poet* (play), 162, 168, 174, 184, 199, 219, 231, 232; *Welded* (play), 43, 49, 105, 123, 177; *Where the Cross Is Made* (play), 125

O'Neill, Eugene, Jr. (son), 40, 104, 204, 206, 207, 212, 213–14
O'Neill, James, Sr. (father), 3, 4, 6, 9, 27, 28, 31, 38, 39, 41, 65, 71, 77, 81, 85, 95, 97, 116–17, 118, 122, 132, 154, 155, 161, 162, 168–69, 182, 183, 189–90, 191, 192, 203, 204, 205, 207, 208, 210, 211, 213, 214, 226, 235–36
O'Neill, James, Jr. (brother), 122, 204, 205–6, 207, 214, 235–36
O'Neill, Kathleen Jenkins (first wife), 182, 206–7, 213
O'Neill, Oona (daughter), 70, 88, 212
O'Neill, Shane (son), 3, 7, 29, 40, 41, 44, 47, 88, 212

P

Paris, France, 106–7, 132, 137, 215
Pasadena Community Theatre, 86
Paul Kauvar (play), 117
Peaked Hill Bar, 6, 7, 14, 29, 38, 40–41, 44, 70, 100, 104, 228
Peck, Gregory, 225
Pittsburgh, Pa., 150
Poe, Edgar Allan, 95, 116, 168
Princeton University, 4, 7, 27, 33, 41, 117–18, 121, 157, 171, 182, 192, 205, 206
Provincetown, Mass., 3, 6–7, 10, 11, 33, 38, 39, 42, 43, 44, 58, 70, 77, 95, 96–97, 98, 100, 118, 127, 194, 195, 210, 211, 212, 213, 228
Provincetown Players, 5, 11, 26, 33, 42, 46, 59, 77, 78, 95–96, 97–100, 118, 141, 142, 154, 171–72, 183, 195, 211, 227
Provincetown Playhouse (MacDougal Street Theatre), 45, 50, 54, 57, 59, 60, 61, 65, 72, 97, 118, 172, 195

R

Radcliffe College, 194
Reed, John, 42, 96
Reinhardt, Max, 86
Renner, Mrs. Theresa, 107
Ridgefield, Conn. *See* Brook Farm, Ridgefield, Conn.
Rippin, James, family of, 32
Robertson, Sparrow, 124, 136
Robeson, Paul, 45, 47, 58, 106, 114
Robinson, Lennox, 39
Rockefeller, John D., 56
Roosevelt, Franklin D., 155
Rosedale (play), 117

Ross, Harold, 218
Rossetti, Dante Gabriel, 193
Rothchild, Baron, 137
Rubaiyat of Omar Kayyam (poem), 135

S

San Francisco, Calif., 112, 168, 185, 199, 219, 232
Schnitzler, Arthur, *Anatol*, 61
Schubert, Franz, 233
Sea Island, Ga. *See* Casa Genotta, Sea Island, Ga.
Seattle, Wash., 145, 153, 155–56, 229
Selwyn, Edgar, 142
Shakespeare, William, 10, 155, 190, 191, 226, 235; *Hamlet*, 22; *Othello*, 47; *Macbeth*, 235–36
Shaw, George Bernard, 120, 162, 172, 195, 198, 225, 227; *Candida*, 7, 44
Shay, Frank, 101
Sherwood, Robert E., 227
Silverdene Emblem (dog), 128, 233
Singer Sewing Machine Company, 4, 9, 30, 65, 118, 171, 207
Skene, Don, 136
Skinner, Richard Dana, 212; *Eugene O'Neill: A Poet's Quest*, 218, 235
The Smart Set (magazine), 33
Smith, Joe, 130
South Africa, 4, 9, 30, 38, 41, 118, 171, 207
Spain, 127–28
Spanish Honduras, 8, 28, 41, 58, 118, 155, 157, 171, 182, 206
Spender, Stephen, 177
Spithead, Bermuda, 93, 94, 214, 227, 228
Stephens, James, 212
Stevenson, Robert Louis, 44, 194
Strindberg, August, 23, 73, 85, 123, 143, 183, 195
Sweet, Blanche, 115
Swift Packing Company, 4, 9, 30, 118, 171, 192, 207
Synge, John Millington, 12, 39, 113

T

Tairov, Alexander, 124, 137
Tao House, Danville, Calif., 168, 174, 183, 184, 185, 219, 229, 231, 232, 233
Theatre Guild, 81, 104–5, 108, 134, 135, 153, 158, 164, 172, 176, 181, 197, 200, 216, 227, 232
Theatre Guild on the Air, 234

Theatre Magazine, 161
Théâtre Pigalle, 137, 198
Tolstoy, Leo, *War and Peace*, 10
Tucker, Benjamin R., 28
The Two Orphans (play), 117
Tyler, George C., 3, 4, 33, 142

V

Voodoo (play), 47
Vorse, Mary Heaton, 95, 195

W

Wallack, Lester, 117
Washington Square Players, 5, 11, 154, 172
Washington Square Theatre, 118
Weaver, John V. A., 211
Wedekind, Frank, 195
Weinberger, Harry, 217
Werfel, Franz, 79
Westinghouse Electric Company, 4, 9, 30, 118, 171, 207

Westley, Helen, 107
Weston, Al, 191
Wharf Theatre, 11, 33, 42, 118, 194, 195, 211
The White Sister (play), 4, 28, 207
Whitman, Walt, 182
Wilde, Oscar, *The Picture of Dorian Gray*, 10
Willard, Jess, 57
Williams, John D., 4, 142, 196, 197
Wilson, Daisy, 162, 163
Wilson, Woodrow, 121, 192, 206
Winther, Sophus Keith, 145
Wolheim, Louis, 142, 183, 201, 202, 234

Y

Yale University, 121–22, 182, 211
Yeats, William Butler, 12, 39, 113, 115, 224
Youmans, Vincent, 141

Z

Zola, Émile, 235